# COMMANDOS & RANGERS D DAY OPERATIONS

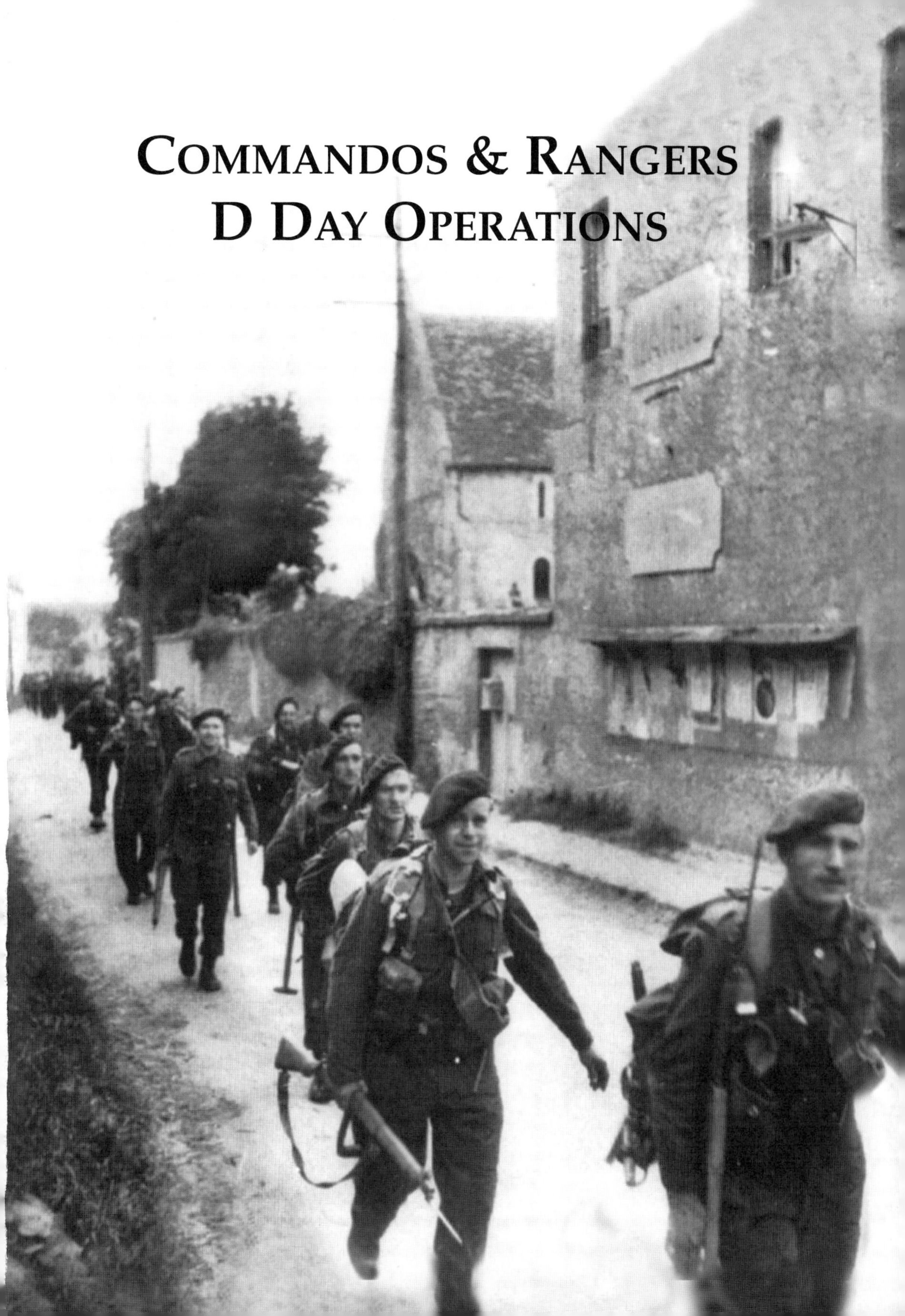

# Commandos & Rangers
# D Day Operations

Tim Saunders

Pen & Sword
MILITARY

First published in Great Britain in 2012 by
Pen & Sword Military
an imprint of
Pen & Sword Books Ltd
47 Church Street
Barnsley
South Yorkshire
S70 2AS



**ISBN 9781844158683**



A CIP catalogue record for this book is available from the British Library.


Typeset in Palatino 10pt

Printed and bound by CPI Group (UK) Ltd, Croydon, CR0 4YY

Pen & Sword Books Ltd incorporates the Imprints of Pen & Sword Aviation, Pen & Sword Maritime, Pen & Sword Military, Wharncliffe Local History, Pen & Sword Select, Pen & Sword Military Classics and Leo Cooper.
For a complete list of Pen & Sword titles please contact
PEN & SWORD BOOKS LIMITED
47 Church Street, Barnsley, South Yorkshire, S70 2AS, England
E-mail: enquiries@pen-and-sword.co.uk
Website: www.pen-and-sword.co.uk

# Contents

This book is dedicated to the Commando Trained officers and soldiers of 1st Battalion The Rifles who are bringing the Army back to the front rank of 3 Commando Brigade.

# Introduction

IN COMPARISON to the three Allied airborne divisions dropped as the opening act of the D Day invasion of Normandy, the British and French Commandos along with the US Rangers who landed with the amphibious assault force, have had relatively little written about them in any detail. This book seeks to bring together under one cover comprehensive accounts of all the action by these elite troops on D Day and, where appropriate, the following days.

There are a number of reasons for this lack of books. Other than, of course, Point du Hoc and Lord Lovat's brief walk on part at Pegasus Bridge, there are few real focuses of attention for their actions, as they were usually operating to the flanks under the temporary command of the various assault formations. Naturally, when these formations wrote their accounts, attached units, especially if they are regarded as 'elite', they tended to ignore the Commandos and Rangers in favour of their own units.

The dispersed nature of the Commando and Ranger records has also made life difficult for historians and authors. Even being aware of this at the outset, tracking down the orders, operational records and reports that I found in various archives, museums and institutions, took far more time and effort than anticipated. The work involved was worthwhile and provided a sound framework around which veterans' memoirs could be woven. Particular thanks must go to the numerous help desk officers at the National Archive at Kew for their unfailing good humour and charm.

I am also extremely grateful to veteran authors, their heirs and executors and, of course, publishers for their generous permission to quote freely from a range of documents from personal diaries through to published accounts.

The Commando and Rangers' battles almost exclusively fall into the category of Small Unit Actions. This is especially so following the heavy losses suffered by virtually all Commandos and Ranger units during their run in to the beach, the landing and the assembly phases. These casualties invariably caused plans to be recast or otherwise adapted but what is still very obvious is the exceptional quality of the Commando and Ranger leaders and the soldiers; they were absolute determination to see their mission through to its successful conclusion, while many more 'ordinary units' that were landing around them, were stunned into inertia by the shock of combat.

Once ashore, the Commandos and Rangers were invariably on their own, off on a flank. More often than not, however, they ended-up in enemy held territory with a degree of protracted isolation and opposition that had not been foreseen by the Combined Operations or divisional planning staffs. In these circumstances their performance was exceptional.

As a final note, while writing this book, I could not help seeing parallels with the isolated and independent nature of the battles being fought during what history may record as the height of the current Afghan Campaign. Chief amongst those very special members of the Army fighting in Afghanistan are 1st Battalion, The Rifles, who now in a leading role, serve alongside the Royal Marines of 3 Commando Brigade. I have no hesitation in dedicating this book to them in memory of the Army's Commandos past and present.

*Tim Saunders*
WARMINSTER, 2012

Chapter One

# Commando Origins

The Boer *kommandos* of the 1899–1902 War in South Africa made a great impression on the young Winston Churchill and did much to foster his appreciation of irregular guerrilla warfare and unconventional soldiers. Following the losses suffered by the British forces in the west during May and June 1940, the new Prime Minister Churchill, against the grain of military wisdom, diverted resources into a force that could, in a small way, take the battle to the enemy and 'break the bonds of the intolerable defensive'.

Churchill gave direction for the formation of 'Commando' companies and Special Service Battalions, consisting of 'troops of the hunter class, who could create a reign of terror on the butcher and bolt policy'. The War Office called for soldiers to volunteer from the various UK commands, for 'mobile operations'. Southern, Western, Northern Ireland and Scottish Commands were each to provide two battalions, while Eastern Command, London District and the Household Division one each. These units, while raised regionally, were made up of troops from ordinary units serving in the Command at the time. The policy of the day, of moving units

*The new Commando force practice a beach assault.*

away from their home area, meant that with the exception of the Household Division and Scotland the resulting Commandos were of a mixed regimental and regional origin.

The initial Commando units were numbered 2 to 11, with No. 1 Commando being formed from independent companies and No. 10 having insufficient volunteers to form. The Royal Marines raised a unit in due course, which subsequently became A Commando and later 40 (RM) Commando. Nos 12 and 14 Commandos were formed later in 1940, and the following year the vacant No. 10 Commando was filled by Commando troops made up of foreign nationals from the occupied countries of Europe.

Lieutenant Peter Young of the Bedfordshire and Hertfordshire Regiment, based in Yeovil, remembered the call for volunteers in the aftermath of Dunkirk:

> *Commanding Officers were to ensure that only the best were sent; they must be young, absolutely fit, able to drive motor vehicles, and unable to be seasick. It was a leap in the dark, for absolutely nothing was said as to what they were to do, and in any case most regular soldiers make a point of never volunteering for anything.*

With a more senior officer drafted in over his head, he volunteered for Special Service and for his pains, 'got a rocket' from his CO. Lieutenant Young was, however, summoned for interview by Southern Command, where he was interviewed by an officer with a 'superficial resemblance to Mr Pickwick' and asked if he was 'all for this sort of thing (whatever that was)'. An answer of 'yes' was followed by a question about his familiarity with small boats. With another affirmative answer, Lieutenant Young 'was in' and duly summoned to training with Lieutenant Colonel (freshly promoted straight from Captain!) John Durnford-Slater's newly formed No. 3 Commando. With the officers selected, they were sent out to find suitable Other Rank candidates. Amongst them was Private Jackman, who had served with 2nd Dorset in France and once back in barracks in Yorkshire had soon fallen out with his Company Sergeant Major.

> *I was always in trouble; fatigues and jankers were a regular part of my miserable military existence. I was really browned-off by the dull routine of coastal defence hundreds of miles away*

*Commando training invariably involved marching long distances over rough terrain. The Highlands of Scotland were ideal.*

*from my home town on the south coast, which was being bombed, while I was out of it.*

*When the call for volunteers came, I put my name forward and the company commander signed it straight off; they were pleased to see the back of me!*

By the end of June, the Commando units were assembling in various places on the coast of Scotland, Wales and the West Country: anywhere where there was demanding terrain and a rough coastline. Colonel Durnford-Slater recalled that he had thirty-five officers and five hundred men.

*Instead of putting troops into barracks the Commando system was to give each man a subsistence allowance of 6s. 8d a day; the man was then required to find his own accommodation and food. This was in every way a splendid arrangement, it increased a man's self-reliance and self-respect, developed his initiative and made him available for training at any time of the day or night … or left in barracks for administration.*

Those who were unsuitable, failed to perform and/or exploited the unusual administrative and disciplinary system, officers included, were Returned To Unit (RTU). Then, as now, RTU was the ultimate sanction of senior Commando officers and was freely used. A set of Commando standards developed very quickly, which were to be the foundation of their enduring success.

Eventually organised into a Special Service Brigade under the Director of Combined Operations, Admiral of the Fleet Sir Roger Keyes, himself a coastal raider during the Great War, the Commandos prepared for operations. From bases in towns on the coast they continued to train and conducted 'some rather amateurish, pin-prick raids on the French coast'.

*Sir Roger Keyes.*

## Operation COLLAR

Commando-type raids had been launched against Norway in May 1940, but what is acknowledged to be the first raid by British Commandos was launched during the night of 23/24 June 1940 on the French coast south of Boulogne-sur-Mer and le Touquet by one hundred and twenty men of No. 11 Independent Company who 'brassed up a few likely targets'. This 'Boy's Own adventure' yielded few militarily worthwhile results but did provide Churchill with news that Britain was hitting back!

## The Guernsey Raid

It was, however, H Troop of No. 3 Commando and again No. 11 Independent Company who were to launch the first significant raid in July 1940, about which Colonel Durnford-Slater commented:

> *Looking back, I can see that under such rushed conditions, with no experience, no proper landing craft and inadequate training, this first operation was foredoomed to failure.*

Operation AMBASSADOR's objective was Guernsey airport, which had been newly occupied by five hundred Germans. The Directorate of Raiding Operations was only twelve days old when the raid was mounted from Dartmouth; such was the Prime Ministerial pressure for action.

Conveyed across the Channel in 1918-vintage destroyers,

*Colonel Durnford-Slater in Royal Artillery uniform*

HMS *Scimitar* and *Saladin*, the force was to land from RAF Search and Rescue boats. Almost 'swamped by a wave' Lieutenant Peter Young recalled:

> *As I struggled ashore (through chest deep waves) water poured from every part of my equipment; we wore full battledress, steel helmets, canvas shoes and gaiters. With clothing and equipment heavy with water.*
>
> *We plodded up the steps with a dreadful squelching noise, half expecting to be ambushed any minute-and that in a place where it was impossible to deploy. Our worst fears seemed to be realised when as we neared the top there came a sudden burst of fire. Everyone froze.*

It, however, turned out to be a negligent discharge of a Thompson sub-machine gun and H Troop withdrew without making contact with the enemy. An enemy machine gun did eventually open fire causing 'some consternation'.

No. 11 Independent Company's operations fared no better; boats broke down, another landed its Commandos on the island of Sark rather than Guernsey and the last boat ran into a rock. Suffice it to say, this raid, 'a ridiculous, almost a comic failure', provided many lessons for the newly raised Commandos.

## Commando Training

Churchill's reaction to the Guernsey Raid was stinging. 'Let there be no more silly fiascos like those perpetrated at Guernsey. The idea of waking all these coasts against us by pinprick raids is one to be strictly avoided'. He directed that more worthwhile raids be prepared but the Commandos were regarded by the War Office as Winston's private army and officialdom 'wanted to abolish us'.

Initially Commando units selected and trained their own men but as units and the Directorate of Raiding Operations became more established there were two developments. Firstly individual training that led to the award of the Commandos' distinctive green beret was concentrated at Achnacarry House, in Westen Scotland. Achnacarry subsequently became the Commando depot, overseen by the

*Lieutenant Colonel Charles Vaughan*

formidable former Guards Sergeant Major, Lieutenant Colonel Charles Vaughan.

In the second development, Admiral Keyes concentrated Commando units' raiding and amphibious training at Inveraray in Western Scotland. Here new doctrine and techniques to support raiding were being developed and courses run for both units and individuals who would return to their own Commando to pass on the latest tactics to enable them to train more thoroughly and prepare for those 'significant raids' that the Prime Minister demanded.

*Boat training was a key element of the Achnacary training package.*

It was at Inveraray that according to Lieutenant Colonel Durnford-Slater, the Commandos first made their acquaintance with purpose-built landing craft.

> *...I had a message... to the effect that two such craft were on their way to me for No. 3 Commando. With my officers and NCOs, I rushed to the beach. We were just in time to see them coming in*

*A naval officer still aboad the Landing Craft Assault, observes an early amphibious exercise in Scotland.*

*at about six knots, a big wave forming at each square bow. They rode very low in the water and had no superstructure. I felt a glow of excitement as they came right up to the steep beach and lowered their ramps. … They do look like the real thing, I said.*

Wherever Commando training was conducted, the aim was to produce both soldiers and Commando units that were thoroughly trained, enormously fit, resilient and independently minded.

## The US Rangers

In 1942 with the first US troops starting to arrive in the UK, Brigadier Lucien Truscott was well aware of the need for American servicemen to gain combat experience on which to base training and development of tactical doctrine. He believed that in the situation of the time, this experience would be most easily gained alongside British Commandos and applied for and received permission to raise such a unit. However, the name was too typically British for the Americans. The US Army looked back into their own military traditions and came up with the name Rangers: a name that had been used by irregular units during the War of Independence.

*Brigadier Lucien Truscott*

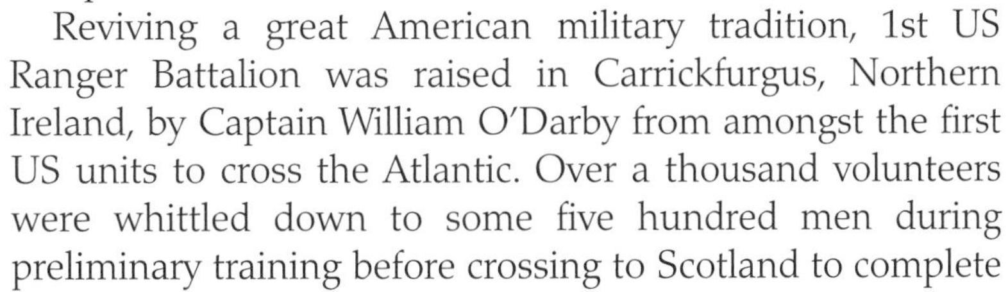

Reviving a great American military tradition, 1st US Ranger Battalion was raised in Carrickfurgus, Northern Ireland, by Captain William O'Darby from amongst the first US units to cross the Atlantic. Over a thousand volunteers were whittled down to some five hundred men during preliminary training before crossing to Scotland to complete their Ranger course alongside British Royal Marine and Army Commandos at Achnacarry House in the Highlands of Scotland. As

*American Ranger candidates training in Scotland.*

a result they were similarly organised and equipped and familiar with British methods. The Rangers serving in the European theatre only had the same limited, largely theoretical, parachute capability as their British counterparts.

**Commando Operations**

Stung by the abortive raid on Guernsey, in 1941 more substantial raids were planed. These included an attack on the island of Vaagso in the north of German-occupied Norway. In his briefing Admiral Keyes's staff officer told No. 3 and elements of other Commandos that they were to attack Vaagso and that,

> *The object is primarily to destroy all the oil installations; secondly, to destroy shipping; and thirdly, to bring back prisoners, and volunteers for the Norwegian navy.*

*Combined Operations cloth arm badge was worn from 1942 onwards.*

Operation ARCHERY took place on 26 December 1941, while a parallel raid, Operation ANKLET, was mounted by No. 11 Commando on another occupied island nearby, as a diversion. The raid by 570 Commandos was a great success and provided much needed good news at home during what was a very dark period of the war.

This raid was followed by one on the Lofoten island well to the north of Norway. Operation CLAYMORE was launched by Commandos from No. 3 and No. 4 Commando, and a troop from the Norwegian Independent Company. Their landing was unopposed and they met scant opposition, sinking 18,000 tons of shipping, destroying a cod liver oil plant and some 800,000 gallons of oil and glycerine, the latter being a component in explosives. In addition, the German armed trawler *Krebs* yielded a complete set of Enigma code books and rotor wheels for the cipher machine: all vital to reading German naval communications.

**Larger Scale Raids**

On the night of 28 March Operation CHARIOT was launched against the heavily defended St Nazaire port facilities. Mounted by HQ Combined Operations the objective was the destruction of the

*Landing Craft waiting to pick up the Commandos from the snow covered Vaagso.*

*An exhausted Lord Lovat and his Commandos back in the UK having conducted the only really successful element of the Dieppe Raid.*

*Captured Commandos at St Nazaire. Private McCormack, wounded in the action, receives medical attention from the Germans.*

*Some made it back.*

great dry dock that would be necessary to repair the battleship *Tirpitz* and thus force her to return to Germany for repairs.

The destroyer HMS *Campbeltown*, packed with explosives, rammed the Normandie Dock's gates and on detonating, rendered the facility unusable. Commandos landed in support and demolished other important dock facilities before unsuccessfully attempting to withdraw; only twenty-seven men got away. However, the result of the raid, despite the cost, was considered to be a considerable success.

Operation JUBILEE, the raid on the French north coast port of Dieppe was altogether of a different scale, involving two Commando units and the best part of 6,000 infantry from 2nd Canadian Infantry Division. Overall the operation was a costly failure but the Commandos' attack on the flanking coastal batteries was the only bright feature of the raid. In particular Lieutenant Colonel The Lord Lovat's attack with No. 4 Commando on the Hesse Battery was an almost textbook success and marked the Noble Lord for promotion within the Commando organisation.

The Dieppe Raid was the first operation for the US Rangers. Four officers and forty-six men were distributed amongst the JUBILEE Assault Force. The Official History 'Grand Strategy' series, records the meeting of 9 June 1942:

> *'Mr Roosevelt, he said, had stressed the great need for American soldiers to be given the opportunity of fighting* [in the west] *as soon as possible.'*

Consequently, a US Army Brigadier General attached to Combined Operations HQ readily agreed, and provided members of 1st US Rangers to the operation. They were distributed amongst British Commando and Canadian infantry units to gain as wider cross-section of experience as possible. During the fighting alongside the British and Canadians the US Rangers suffered their first casualties from enemy action; as in all Commando/Ranger training there had already been plenty of accidents and injuries.

In a reversion to smaller scale raids, Operation FRANKTON, made famous as the 'Cockleshell Heroes' raid, was launched by Royal Marine canoeists on enemy shipping in the port of Bordeaux during December 1942.

While Commandos were developing raiding techniques in the United Kingdom, other Commandos were of course active in the

*Canadian Prisoners march through the the streets of Dieppe.*

Mediterranean Theatre and in the Far East. It was the TORCH landings in North Africa in late 1942, that took Commandos and the US Rangers to North Africa, from the UK as a part of the invasion force. Here they performed well and the US Ranger Battalion provided cadres to expand the Rangers into Colonel Rudder's Force. They and British Commandos subsequently played significant roles in the landings in Sicily, Operation HUSKY. No. 3 Commando landed under command of 231 Malta Brigade on the toe of Italy during September 1943 before returning to the UK to prepare for the great assault on Hitler's vaunted Atlantic Wall scheduled for the following spring.

Meanwhile, additional Ranger units had been formed, still on British Commando lines but now leavened with Ranger experience and practice from the Mediterranean.

*Captain Pat Porteous the first Commando VC.*

## Chapter Two

# Invasion Plans

With the now battle-hardened Commandos and Rangers being returned to the UK in preparation for the D Day landings, planning was well under way for the invasion, which was appreciated as being a much sterner test than the assault landings in Sicily and Italy. As a result, an altogether heavier organisation of Commando units was being prepared. This reflected the change in role from a light raiding force into a body of élite amphibious assault infantry, capable of taking on a wider range of battlefield tasks. New scales of equipment included more and heavier mortars and medium machine guns. Commando units, however, maintained their capability for independent action, which was reflected both in the D Day plans and practice.

*Seated left to right: Admiral Ernest J. King, Winston Churchill, Franklin D. Roosevelt. Standing between Churchill and Roosevelt is Admiral Lord Louis Mountbatten who, as former chief of Combined Operations, was responsible for the development of techniques for amphibious landings.*

## Organisation

The Army and Royal Marine Commando's authorised organisation differed in detail but any attempt to be specific is further complicated by both the habit of adapting an individual Commando unit's Order of Battle (ORBAT) to specific tasks or simply reflecting the unit commander's experience and preference. Being an independently minded force, where results counted above all, they got away with it!

The ORBAT opposite, although that authorised for an Army Commando, should be regarded as an average, reflecting the increased firepower necessary for the D Day assault and their more conventional role in battle once ashore.

The D Day establishment totalled 458 all ranks comprising twenty-four officers and 461 Other Ranks (ORs) divided into a Commando HQ and six troops. 'Companies' did not at this time feature in Commando organisation. To make a comparison with conventional infantry, a Commando troop of 1944 can be considered to be a very large platoon or a very under strength rifle company.

*Eisenhower and his senior staff who took over planning for D Day in January 1944.*

**Commando Headquarters** – 7 Officers and 85 ORs – Commanded by a Lieutenant Colonel, with a Major as a second in command. The Commando HQ incorporated command and administrative functions but had a much slimmer organisation than a normal infantry battalion. Included were Transport and Intelligence Troops and an eighteen man Signal Section.
**Assault Troops** x 5 (normally A - E Troops) – each of three officers and 63 ORs.

**Troop HQ** of one officer (normally a Captain) and 9 ORs, including a Sergeant Major and the Officer Commanding's batman/runner. Medical cover was provided by a stretcher bearer and an attached Royal Army Medical Corps orderly. Two men manned the Troop's two 2-inch mortars, and two men crewed a single PIAT; a Commando troop's only anti-tank capability.

**Two Sections** each comprising of Section HQ – one officer (normally a Lieutenant) and one other rank.

**Two Sub-Sections** of thirteen men each commanded by a Sergeant armed with sub-machine gun. A Corporal commanded the six man rifle group. The Gun Group was also led by a rifle-armed Corporal, with a Bren gunner and two riflemen.

**Heavy Weapons Troop** (Normally F Troop) - two officers and 37 ORs.

**Troop HQ** of 2 officers and four ORs

**Mortar Section** of 17 men, with three 3-inch mortars.

**Medium Machine Gun Section** of 16 ORs manning Vickers K Guns.

## D Day Planning

Churchill had insisted that planning and developing techniques for a return to mainland Europe should begin long before there was ever a glimmer of hope of actually executing such a landing. This Anglo-American contingency work was eventually code named ROUNDUP but planning in earnest, however, was taken on by Lieutenant General Sir Fredrick Morgan who was the Chief of Staff to Supreme Allied Commander (Designate) or COSSAC. He had been appointed following the Casablanca conference in January 1943 to produce detailed proposals for the cross-channel attack. He and his staff were responsible for finally selecting the beaches of Normandy as the location for the invasion: Operation OVERLORD.

*General Morgan*

The scale of preparations and the depth of planning required to break Hitler's Atlantic Wall, even on the less well defended beaches of Normandy was unprecedented. General Morgan scoped the plan and produced its first detailed draft, which envisaged a landing on a three division frontage, supported of course by Commandos and Rangers, who would take on specific objectives such as coastal batteries and be responsible for clearing enemy coastal positions between the beaches.

In late December 1943, while still in the Mediterranean, Field Marshal Montgomery, nominated to take over command of the armies of 21st Army Group, was shown a copy of the plan by Churchill and he didn't like it. The frontage was too narrow, thus allowing the enemy to concentrate his force against him and he saw sundry administrative and control difficulties with Morgan's plan. A few weeks later Montgomery was back in London advocating, amongst other things, a significant enhancement to the size of the assault force.

The final version of the expanded plan was detailed and presented by General Montgomery, in April 1944, in the Hall of St Paul's School, London. He wanted the Allies to land with six-plus divisions in the initial assault wave across five beaches, spread along sixty miles of Normandy coastline. The amphibious landings were to be preceded by the insertion of no less than three airborne divisions on the flanks of the invasion area.

It was readilly appreciated that Montgomery's increase in the size of the invasion force would create a demand for extra shipping, troops and material of all types and would also delay the landing by about a month. Amongst the additions was a requirement for additional British Commando units to link up the additional Second Army beaches. The bill for this particular enhancement was to be met by the conversion of an additional Royal Marine battalion to the Commando role. This unit became 48 Commando.

## The Commando and Ranger D Day Role

As has already been intimated the main D Day role of the Commandos and Rangers was to link up the landing beaches, by clearing the Germans' coastal strong points between the five individual beachheads. This was the responsibility of 4 Special Service Brigade, which was made up of Royal Marine Commandos, who were to land behind the various assault infantry brigades.

*General Montgomery*

Brigadier Durnford-Slater, Second Army's Commando advisor, expanded on the role of 4 Special Service Brigade:

> *No. 4 Brigade were to be used for work which was equally hazardous but not so spectacular. They were to operate as individual Commandos against key points in Hitler's West* [sic - Atlantic] *Wall. Having captured these key points, they were to join up as a brigade and were to join No. 1 Brigade on the left flank. I thought this was exactly the right thing for them. They would get their battle experience in the initial assault, and then come up to support the 1st Brigade. I was happy and confident about the whole thing.*

With a similar role, Colonel Rudder's Provisional Ranger Group, landing at Pointe du Hoc and on the western extremity of OMAHA Beach, would clear the cliffs west towards Grandcamp-Maisy in order to help link up the two US lodgements astride the Vire estuary.

Lovat's 1 Special Service Brigade was also to land behind the assault troops and to strike across country to link up with 6th Airborne Division and then clear and take up positions on the very left flank of the Allied lodgement.

2nd US Rangers had an additional task before they could assist

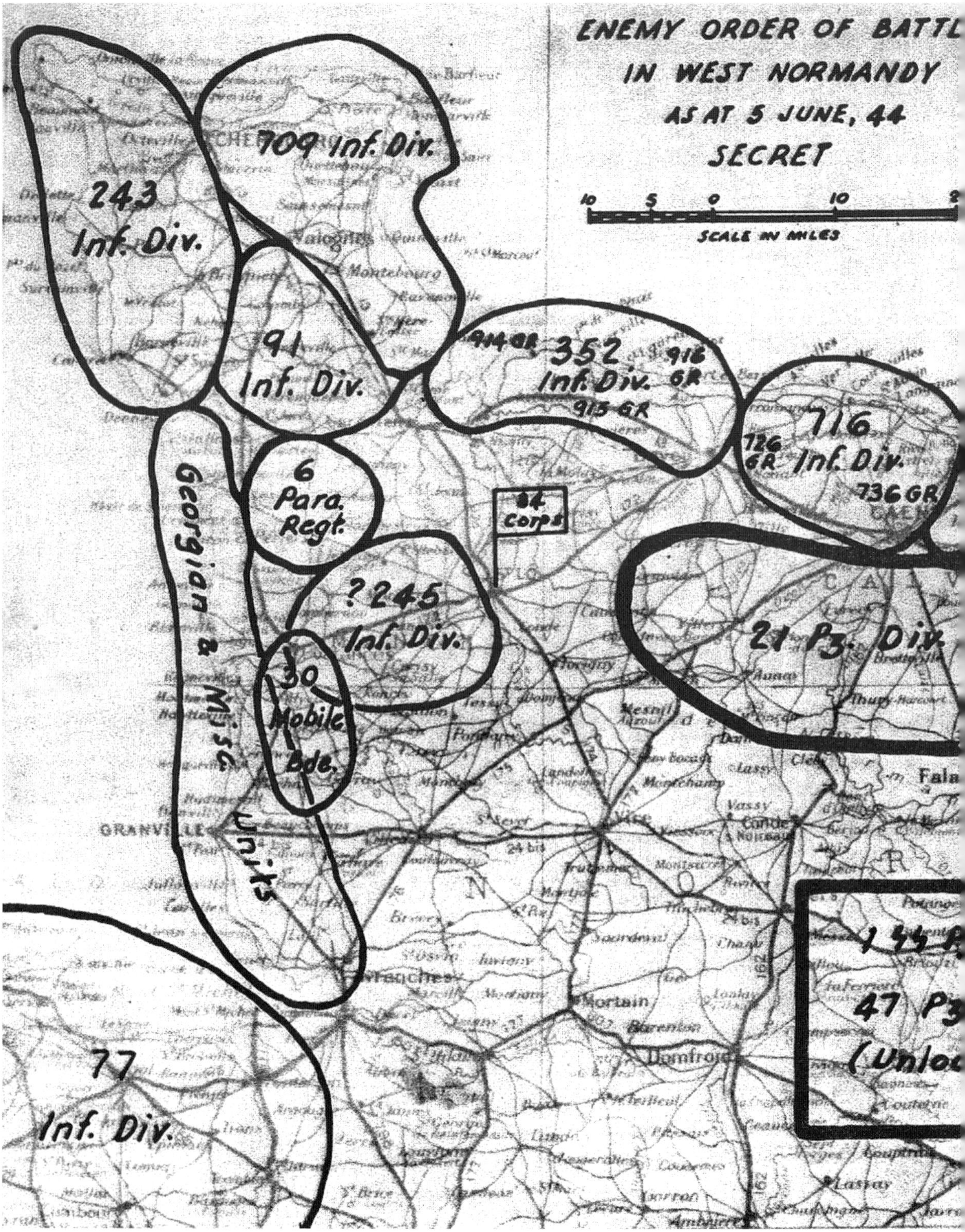

ENEMY ORDER OF BATTL
IN WEST NORMANDY
AS AT 5 JUNE, 44
SECRET
10 5 0 10
SCALE IN MILES
709 Inf. Div.
243 Inf. Div.
91 Inf. Div.
914 GR
352 Inf. Div.
916 GR
915 GR
726 GR
716 Inf. Div.
736 GR
6 Para. Regt.
84 Corps
Georgian & Misc. Units
?245 Inf. Div.
30 Mobile Bde.
21 Pz. Div.
47 Pz
(Unloc
77 Inf. Div.
GRANVILLE
Mortain
Avranches
Vassy

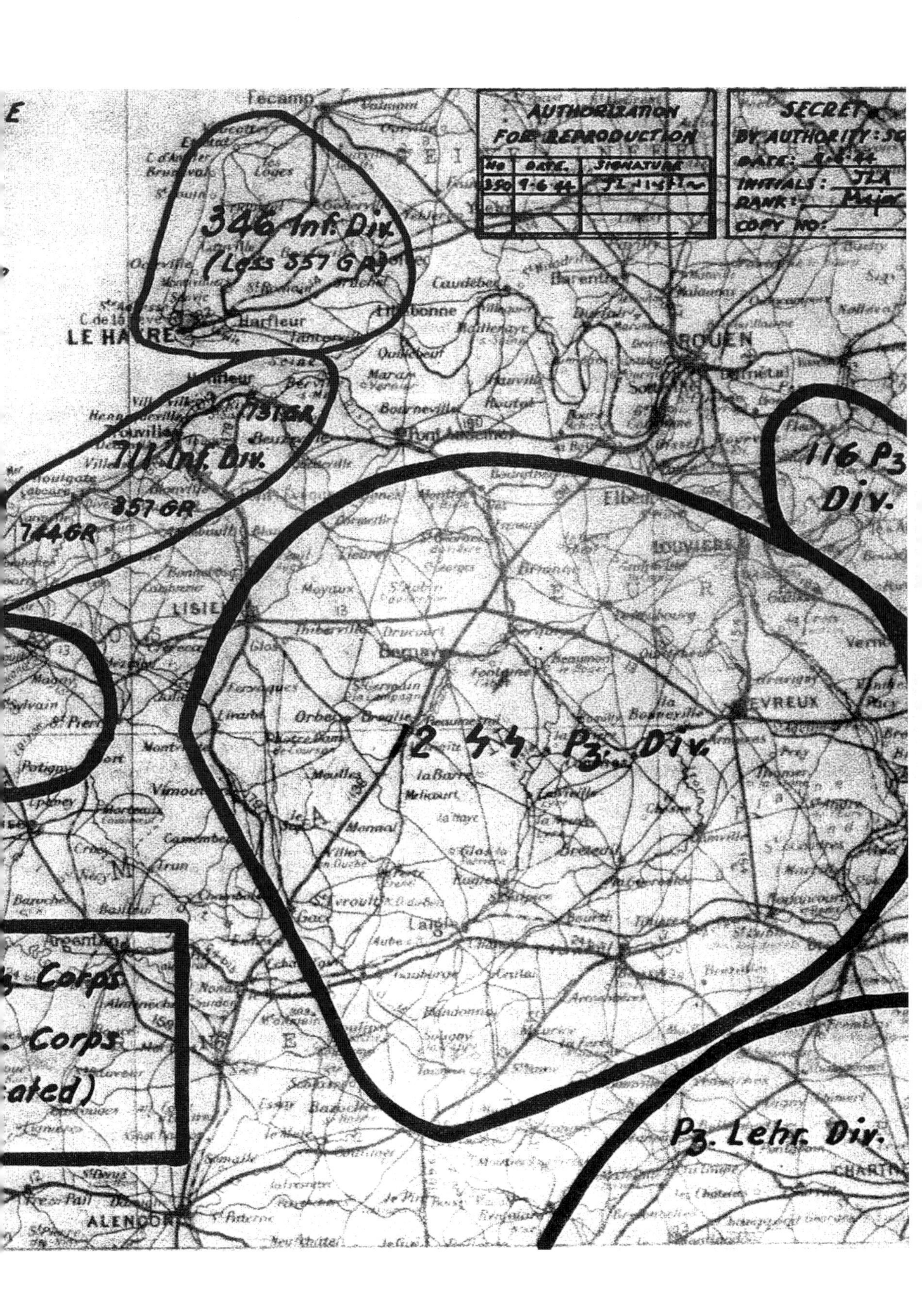

AUTHORIZATION FOR REPRODUCTION
SECRET
346 Inf. Div.
(Less 357 G.R.)
711 Inf. Div.
731 G.R.
357 G.R.
744 G.R.
116 Pz. Div.
12 SS Pz. Div.
Pz. Lehr. Div.
Corps
Corps
LE HAVRE
ROUEN
EVREUX
LISIEUX
ALENÇON

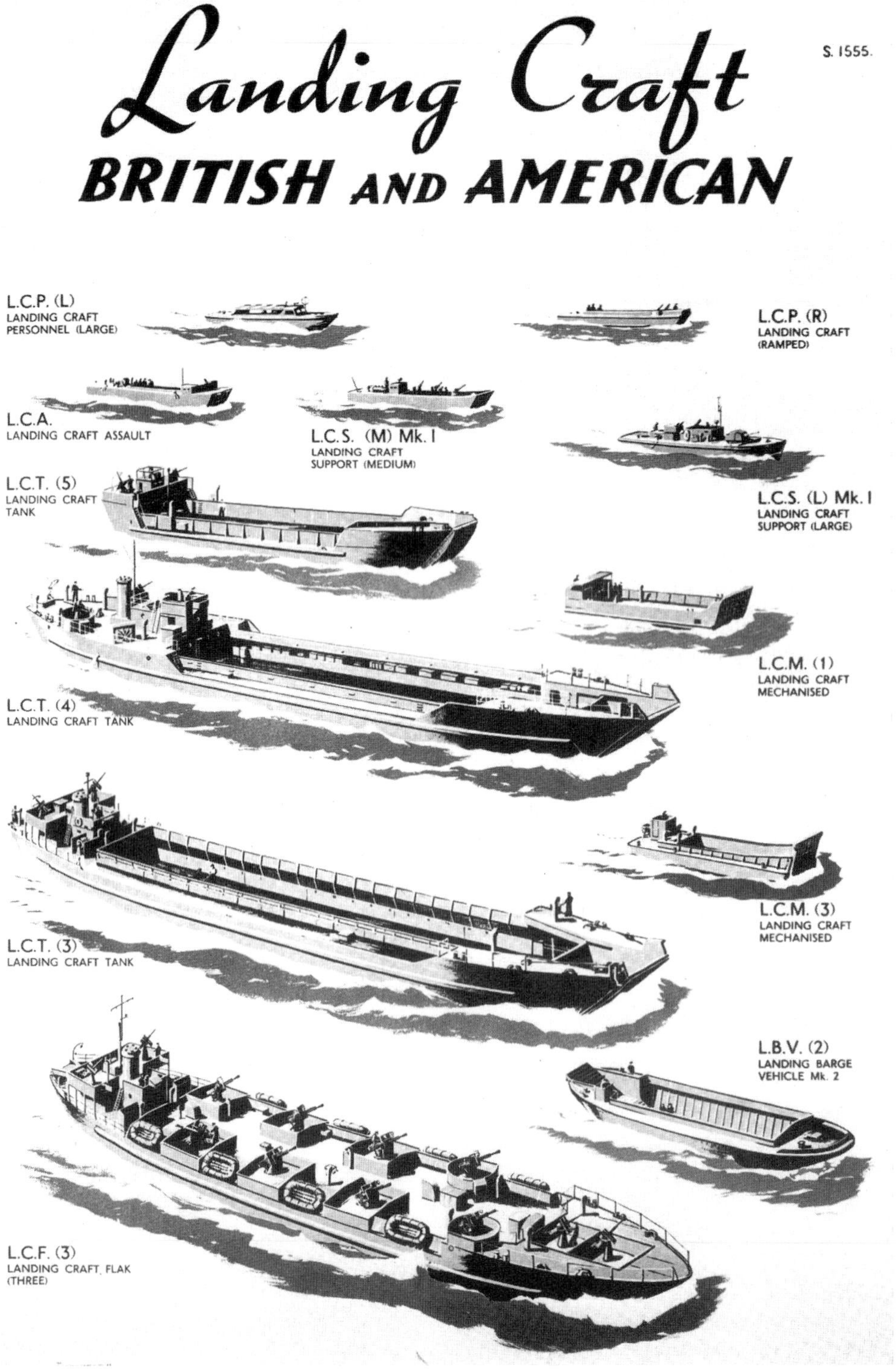

# Landing Craft
## BRITISH AND AMERICAN

S. 1555.

L.C.P. (L)
LANDING CRAFT PERSONNEL (LARGE)

L.C.P. (R)
LANDING CRAFT (RAMPED)

L.C.A.
LANDING CRAFT ASSAULT

L.C.S. (M) Mk. I
LANDING CRAFT SUPPORT (MEDIUM)

L.C.S. (L) Mk. I
LANDING CRAFT SUPPORT (LARGE)

L.C.T. (5)
LANDING CRAFT TANK

L.C.M. (1)
LANDING CRAFT MECHANISED

L.C.T. (4)
LANDING CRAFT TANK

L.C.M. (3)
LANDING CRAFT MECHANISED

L.C.T. (3)
LANDING CRAFT TANK

L.B.V. (2)
LANDING BARGE VEHICLE Mk. 2

L.C.F. (3)
LANDING CRAFT, FLAK (THREE)

the lateral clearance of enemy coastal positions. They were first to assault and clear the powerful German clifftop coastal battery at Pointe du Hoc. This direct attack on an enemy battery was an exception to this general pattern of D Day Commando and Ranger operations.

46 RM Commando was to be retained afloat during D Day as the Commando reserve under HQ 4 Special Service Brigade. As a

*US medics embarking during an amphibious training exercise in the spring of 1944.*
*Fine weather at Slapton Sands in Devon, DD tanks wade ashore followed by Landing Craft.*

proper reserve they were without a specific task but options included reinforcing other Commando or Ranger units and previously unidentified and seriously troublesome enemy positions along the coastline, were included. In particular they were to be prepared to attack the Houlgate battery well to the east of the Orne, which if not neutralised by Bomber Command or naval gunfire was to be attacked by 46 Commando.

Albeit planned to be fighting on D Day with their traditional isolated independence, the Commandos and Rangers were in many respects in new territory; for instance the landing would be in full daylight not during their preferred darkness. A daylight landing was the choice of the planners for navigational and organisational reasons following the lessons of the various chaotic night-time Mediterranean assault landings. Experience emerging from the various landings in the Pacific also indicated that where the Allies held air and naval firepower superiority, daylight was best to apply the crushing weight of fire on the enemy.

## Training

On their return to the UK (those who had been to the Mediterranean), the Commandos and Rangers conducted training in the wilder parts of the British Isles and took in numerous replacements from training at Achnacarry. As, however, the indications of their D Day tasks became more specific, training was focused on the details of the job; for example the Commandos were to be increasingly found using the blitzed parts of Southampton that had been turned over to urban warfare training.

Even though D Day was to be an amphibious assault, the Commandos and Rangers had little more to do than maintain their existing skills with assault craft, while the Amphibious Warfare Centre at Inveraray struggled to train the additional assault brigades required by Montgomery's expanded plan. As the number of troops in the south of England grew, pressure mounted on firing ranges and training areas, consequently the emphasis of training shifted to individual skills and fitness; speed marches were an almost daily event.

The Rangers, like the Commandos, had been carrying out general training suitable for a variety of tasks but with the objective of the clifftop battery at Pointe du Hoc being allocated to them, they

*Lord Lovat instructs Rangers in 'quick time' techniques of firing the Thompson sub-machine gun.*

were given detail of their mission sooner than their British counterparts. Scaling the 80 – 100 foot cliffs to assault the battery required the development and training in a variety of methods of scaling the cliff. The Rangers located similar loose limestone cliffs on the Isle of White and at West Bay near Bridport in Dorset

**The New Commandos**

At the time of Dieppe, there had only been a single all-volunteer Royal Marine Commando unit, 'A' Commando, which was by 1944 renumbered/named 40 Commando. With Major General Robert Sturges, Royal Marines, now commanding the Commando Group, his Corps took the brunt of the last phase of Commando expansion. Up to this point Commandos had been an all-volunteer service but with manpower at a premium and commanding officers increasingly reluctant to release quality men, 'pressed men' were to be found training at Achnacarry. Not all were in favour. Brigadier Durnford-Slater wrote:

> *Now other Marine Commandos, a mixture of volunteers and conscripts, were being formed. I was dead against the idea.*
>
> *Perhaps I was prejudiced. I was proud of the volunteer tradition of the Commandos. More important, I was convinced, in spite of Mountbatten, whose idea this was, that units of conscripted marines could not be expected to maintain the high Commando standards.*

*Men of 45 Commando's Cycle Troop during a kit inspection prior to D Day.*

With as many as twenty-five per cent of conscripted Marines being RTU during Commando training, Brigadier Durnford-Slater addressed the issue and even though 'offence was taken' by the Royal Marines, afterwards 'the officers and men sent to us were of a more suitable type'.

45 Commando Royal Marines served with 1 Special Service Brigade and, though only raised in August 1943 and qualifying as Commandos in December of that year, 'was coming good'. In 4 SS Brigade, only 41 Commando were well established and had returned from Italy with operational experience, which meant that 46, 47 and 48 Commandos lacked experience, being newly converted/formed from ordinary Royal Marines infantry battalions.

47 Commando had been formed by the conversion of 10th Battalion Royal Marines at the Dorset Regiment's barracks in Dorchester. Only those Marines who volunteered to remain with the new unit and had been selected by their officers remained to undertake Commando training. The medical officer Lieutenant John Forfar explained:

> *Minimum standards included height greater than 65 inches, weight greater than 120 lb, chest girth fully expanded at least 34 inches with a 2in. range of movement, normal vision without spectacles, normal hearing and no organic disease. Finally there was a wonderful let-out clause, namely, 'a deficiency in physique can be compensated for by an over-abundance of spirit'.*

Despite the reservations of the Commando establishment, the Royal Marine Commandos performed very well and once they had gained battle experience became as good as any other unit.

## The French Commando Troops

Colonel Dawson No. 4 Commando had been allocated the particularly difficult task of clearing Ouistreham and his brigade commander, Lord Lovat, believed that he needed reinforcement. These reinforcements were to come from No. 10 (Inter Allied) Commando. This unit was made up of troops from a variety of occupied nations; there were two troops of French Commandos available to help No. 4 Commando.

As Dawson was a Francophile and a fluent French speaker, relations with the new members of No. 4 Commando were off to a

*Leader of the Free French, General Charles de Gaulle, inspects* Fusiliers-Marins *in England.*

good start and remained so, in contravention of the general perception of intransigence that has grown up around General de Gaulle's Free French Forces. Lieutenant Colonel Dawson recounted:

> *If I wanted both French troops to do something then I'd ask Kieffer* [Commandant (Major) Philippe Kieffer, the senior French officer] *to get it done, but if it was just a matter of one of the troops then I could give the order to the troop commander concerned but always with Kieffer present. Kieffer was there to command the French troops* [administratively] *and act as my second in command of them* [in battle]. *He turned out to be a very able operations officer indeed.*

### Royal Navy Beach Commandos

Those members of the 'Senior Service' who would land on the beach early during the D Day landings were trained as Royal Navy Commandos or as they were sometimes known 'Beachhead Commandos'.

The first amphibious Commando raids proved need for control and co-ordination between craft and Commandos on the beaches and specialist 'beach parties' started to be formed and used during 1942 from general service, reservists and hostilities- only officers and ratings. They proved to be an immediate success, forming a vital link between the assault force and the Navy afloat. So much so that Royal Naval Commando units were formally raised. Each RN Commando consisted of ten officers and sixty-six other ranks divided into an HQ of a Principal Beach-Master (PBM), normally a Captain RN, and three sections. Each section or party was twenty-five strong including a beach-master, three assistant beach-masters and twenty-two ratings. Individual sections would be allocated a particular beach sector.

*The Beach Group flash.*

The Royal Navy established their own training depot at Ardentinny, again in Scotland, for between 500 and 600 men, with officers and ratings being mixed together for the preparatory training or 'beat-up'. Those sailors who survived the transformation into fit soldiers went on to complete Commando training and testing at Achnacarry. It is a testimony to the thoroughness of the beat-up that very few were RTU by Colonel Vaughan, who presented the successful men their coveted green berets and Commando knives.

Royal Navy Signalman Bernard Stone recalled a part of his training:

> *We went on schemes in civilian dress, with no money or papers, and with police and the Army trying to find us; teaching us to operate in enemy territory. Unarmed combat, weapon training and landings with live ammunition being used all became part of the days work until, without realising it, we had become a tightly knit fighting unit.*

Coming ashore amongst or immediately behind the first wave of landing craft, the Beach Commando's tasks included the visual marking of the beach with flags and lights to indicate sector and boundaries, they would also facilitate the move off the beach by vehicles and equipment through gaps created and marked by the assault engineers. After the craft of the assault waves had departed, the RN Commandos would control the landing of subsequent waves, calling craft in according to changing priorities when there was space on the beach.

The Canadians had their own Royal Canadian Navy W Commando who performed the Beach role on Juno.

## Royal Air Force Servicing Commandos

Admiral Lord Louis Mountbatten in his capacity as Chief of Combined Operations believed that as the scale of raiding and landing increased that there would be a need for the Royal Air Force to have its own Commando unit to carry out technical functions and facilitate the air support of landing operations. They were commonly referred to as RAF Servicing Commandos. Lesely Baker explained that:

> *This met with some opposition from the RAF but eventually in 1942, it was decided to form 15 separate units each comprising approximately 150 personnel. The requirement was basically for skilled technical personnel, mainly from fighter command, who would be willing to train at an appropriate Commando school for operating with squadrons who would be supporting invasion forces.*

The notice published in all RAF units' orders read 'Volunteers wanted in all trades for units to be formed to service aircraft under hazardous conditions'. Again, RAF Commando training for volunteers was located in Scotland, culminating in the Achnacarry Commando course.

Their task was to provide the technical skills to operate the emergency airfields established as a priority in the beachhead, to take damaged aircraft and where possible repair or cannibalise them for spares. Once the temporary airfields had been built by the Airfield Groups RE the RAF Servicing Commandos would be amongst the first to occupy them and bring them into service. These duties took them well into the battle area.

## The Enemy

Both Rangers and Commandos were to tackle Hitler's Atlantic Wall: the Rangers by direct escalade and the Commandos by landing behind the leading assault troops and either heading across country or rolling up the enemy's defences along the coast in link-up operations. In this they would be facing three divisions: two coastal, the *716th* and the *711th*, the latter east of the Orne; and a field-

*Above:* **Osttruppen** *former Soviet Prisoners of War are briefed by a junior German officer.*

*Right: Rommel (centre) in his role as inspector of the Atlantic Wall touring the Normandy beach defences.*

*A 50mm anti-tank gun in a concrete emplacement with all-round traverse positioned above the high-water mark and sited so as to bring down fire on landing craft or tanks on the beach.*

grade division; the *352nd* who held the ground from the western part of Gold Beach into the US Sector.

Commander of 1st Special Service Brigade, Brigadier The Lord Lovat, described the German's defensive scheme:

> *The immediate defences were laid out with German thoroughness: they were not … a continuous row of grouse butts, but rather a system of ingeniously interlocked defence works equipped with every weapon, from underwater obstacles and devices to set the sea on fire to wire and minefields at the water's edge, ranging back through strongpoints laced with machine-guns and anti-tank guns to distant artillery and self-propelled half-track cannon – all bearing on the beach. Beyond lay German infantry dug into weapon pits – again with interlocking fields of fire. The tanks and armour were held some distance to the rear. It was a question of how long they would stay there!*

These German defensive positions were grouped into *Stützpunkte* (strongpoints) and *Widerstandnester* (resistance-points), half to three-quarters of a mile apart, with in places intermediate positions to thicken up the defences, such as the stretch of coast that Lord Lovat described:

> *Each pill-box was a citadel of reinforced concrete, sunk hull-down and half-buried in the ridges of the dunes. Walls two feet thick stood six feet above ground level, their height made up by a very solid roof giving further feet of concrete head cover. They were*

*Brigadier The Lord Lovat*

*certainly bomb – if not blast – proof, and made equivalent precautions at home appear inadequate. Positions sited in depth, 100 to 150 yards apart, were surrounded with barbed wire, with minefields in between. No pill-box faced directly to the front, but each was at an angle to either side, sited to enfilade the wire and deal effectively with approach from the flanks. Each was manned by a crew of half-a-dozen men firing 75 mm cannon and light automatics. In support to the rear were heavy machine-guns set in less solid foundations but equipped with revolving tank turrets.*

## Final Briefing

In April 1944, Commando Group HQ moved near to Southampton where 1 and 4 Special Service Brigades were concentrating in camps for briefing and training before moving to secure camps in the Marshalling Area. Here they received their final briefing and left to board their ships or landing craft as appropriate to their D Day task.

*An obsolescent gun turret from a Panzer Mk III with an outdated short 75 mm gun set on top of a concrete bunker.*

Corporal Raymond Mitchell recalled 41 RM Commando's move west from Ramsgate to the Commando Concentration Area and the final briefings:

> *At 1730 hours on 24 May, those of the Commando who would be taking part in the D-Day assault reported to Troop Offices. Shore leave was granted until 2230 hours, after which all ranks bedded down on bare boards to pass a short night. By 0600 hrs on the morning of the 25th, the Commando had entrained for another of those amazingly extensive 'Concentration Camps' which was immediately dubbed 'Stalag C19'. Unlike the previous ones, however, which could be identified at the time only as 'somewhere in Hampshire', C19 was obviously very close to Southampton* **[on West Common]** *with frustrating views of civilian life proceeding normally beyond the perimeter fence.*
>
> *Next day the camp was sealed – no troops could leave except in official supervised parties. The fence was patrolled by armed guards throughout the twenty-four hours and it was forbidden even to speak to passing civilians.*
>
> *Briefing sessions began next day, Whit Monday, 29 May, in oppressively hot marquee Operation Rooms. The effect of hearing the details of Operation OVERLORD for the first time, with the knowledge of soon being personally involved, was mind boggling. Nevertheless, as the vast scope of the operation, details of the forces to be deployed along the fifty-mile invasion front; the naval and air support to be provided, and the steps being taken to mislead the enemy, were revealed, there were few who had any doubts about its success.*
>
> *Being 'put in the picture' was effected by the use of large scale plans of the actual invasion coast, but with all place names replaced by code words. The Second Army's first day objective, for example, was to be a city named 'Poland'* [Caen], *and the river on the extreme left flank of the invasion front was 'The Ganges'* [Orne]. *Nevertheless, it wasn't long before everyone was fully aware of the precise stretch of coast to be attacked.*

Armed with the vital BIGOT Top Secret information of where and when the invasion would take place the Commandos were confined to camp and forbidden to contact the outside world. The last few days of waiting saw the issue of a booklet on France and invasion money: French Francs.

## Embarkation

On 4 June the Commandos embarked on the larger Landing Ships Infantry (LSI), complete with their diminutive Landing Craft Assault (LCA) secure on davits, in Southampton docks, while those destined to cross in smaller craft were to do so from the shore station HMS *Tormentor* on the nearby River Hamble.

Lieutenant Forfar of 47 Commando, who were heading for the docks to embark on two landing ships, recalled that:

> *The home of Marine Scott of Q Troop was in Southampton and lay on the route from the marshalling area to the ship. From the back of a truck as he passed by he took a nostalgic last look at his home: it was his last … A few days later a telegram boy appeared there with the dreaded "We regret to inform you –" telegram.*

HMS *Tormentor* occupied the old Coast Guard House and RAF wireless station at Warsash, which had been originally set up by the Royal Navy for the purpose of training small-boat raiding parties and was consequently familiar with Commandos, particularly those who had taken part in the Exercise FABIUS D-Day rehearsal assaults on Hayling Island.

*Commandos laden with kit and bikes negotiate a narrow gangplank onto a waiting assault craft at Warsash.*

HMS *Tormentor* was the home base for three flotillas of Landing Craft Infantry (LCI). These very seaworthy but uncomfortable craft, of various sizes between 100 and 108 feet long with a top speed of 14.5 knots, were not intended for use in the first assault waves but were designed to convey approximately 100 troops who would be landed behind the leading brigades and therefore fitted the Commandos' needs. They did not have a bow ramp to facilitate an assault landing but a pair of gangways designed to discharge troops in an orderly fashion onto a reasonable secure and well-ordered beach. It took six LCIs to carry a whole Commando across the Channel.

Amongst those who boarded the two LCIs allocated to them (523 and 527) at HMS *Tormentor* was twenty year-old French Commando Leon Gautier who recalled:

> *At 5 pm on the night of 5 June 1944, 4 Commando left Warsash in Hampshire and waited near the Isle of Wight and began crossing the Channel at 10.30 pm. Our mood was apprehensive. We were thinking about what would happen in the morning but we knew we had a job to do and our British friends had a great spirit. We were proud to say we were with the British and they said the same.*

| Unit | Embarkation | Name/Number | Beach |
|---|---|---|---|
| 1st SS Brigade | | | Sword – 6th Airborne |
| No 3 Commando | Warsash | LCI(S) *289, 290, 291, 292* and *293.* | Sword – 6th Airborne |
| No 4 Commando | Southampton Warsash | *Prince Astrid* and *Maid of Orleans* | |
| | | LCI *523* and *527* (French Troop) | Sword – 6th Airborne |
| No. 6 Commando | Warsash | 5 x LCI | Sword – 6th Airborne |
| 45 RM Commando | Warsash | 5 x LCI (Small) | Sword – 6th Airborne |
| HQ 4 SS Brigade | Warsash | 5 x LCI (Small)Afloat | |
| 41 RM Commando | Warsash | 5 x LCI (Small) | Sword |
| 47 RM Commando | Southampton | HMS *Princess Josephine Charlotte* & SS *Victoria* | Gold |
| 48 RM Commando | | SS *Princes Margaret* & HMS *Prins Albert* | Juno |
| 46 RM Commando (Reserve) | Southampton | LSI Reserve – afloat until D+1 | |
| 2nd US Rangers | Weymouth | HMS *Prince Charles* (A, B & C Coys)<br>SS *Amsterdam* (D & E(-) Coys)<br>SS *Ben-my-Chree* (F, E(-) & HQ)<br>LCT *No. 46* (4 x DUKWs) | Pointe du Hoc/Omaha Beach |
| 5th US Rangers | Weymouth | HMS *Prince Badouin*/HMS *Prince Leopold* | Pointe du Hoc/Omaha Beach |

Having been loaded well after most of the assault infantry, to preserve their condition by not having to endure a long period confined in Landing Craft Infantry, the Commandos took their appointed places amid the waiting shipping of Assault Groups S, J and G. As darkness fell on the evening of 5 June 1944 at 2200 hours the craft bearing the Commandos started to weigh anchor and thirty minutes later steamed as a part of the largest invasion force ever assembled.

### Ranger Embarkation

Further west at Weymouth on 3 June, the Provisional US Ranger Group went through the similar American embarkation system having marched along the sea front to the quayside. Here the waiting LCAs ferried the Rangers out to the ships of Assault Group O-4; four Landing Ship Infantry (LSI) converted merchantmen or ferries at anchor in Weymouth Bay. Each ship had ten LCAs, which would begin their journey taking the Rangers to their beaches before dawn on D Day.

*2nd US Rangers making their way along the Seafront at Weymouth to the harbour heavily laden with assault equiptment.*

## Conditions aboard the HMS *Prince Charles*

By the afternoon of 4 June, the Rangers were fully briefed, maps issued with the real names on, along with French Francs but the four LSIs were tugging uncomfortably on their anchor ropes. Out on deck, the Rangers saw huge breakers hurling themselves against Chesil Bank and even the relatively sheltered waters of Portland Harbour and Weymouth Bay were being whipped up by the near gale force winds.

Back in Southwick House, Admiral Ramsey's Naval HQ near Portsmouth, Eisenhower and his senior commanders had met at 2100 on the evening of 3 June. Digesting the bad news given to

*Rangers crammed into a British LCA for transfer to the transport ships waiting in Weymouth Bay.*

*The D Day Assault Force assembling in the Solent on 4/5 June 1944.*

them by their chief meteorologist Group Captain John Stagg that a weather front would produce strong winds and thick cloud that would hamper if not preclude effective air and airborne operations and amphibious operations as well, consequently, D Day was postponed for twenty-four hours.

Waiting aboard their LSIs the 2nd Rangers had been laid low by food poisoning thanks to some badly canned hot dogs.

> *It was bad enough having to contend with one's nerves before battle, now the food which they had been served was rancid. The whole battalion was laid low, and many began to doubt if they could go ahead with their mission. Some even suspected their food had been tampered with.*

The bout of food poisoning, however, passed quickly and aboard the requisitioned Isle of Man steamer *Ben-my-Chree* in the early evening of 3 June, the officers were celebrating the promotion from captain to major of Cleveland Lytle, aided by Rudder's gift of a quart of gin. (British ships were not 'dry'.) Major Lytle, commander of Force A, became loud and agitated and volubly critical of the Pointe du Hoc task and plan. Lytle also allegedly told his embarrassed audience that according to the French Resistance the guns had been removed from the Pointe after one of the bombing raids some days earlier. The alcohol had given voice in Major Lytle to the concerns that many men in action for the first time shared. When restrained by the medical officer Lytle punched him. Eventually he was restrained and taken below, and Colonel Rudder was summoned as Lytle's behaviour and damaging criticisms meant that he could not lead Force A. Consequently, Rudder relieved him of his command and himself remained aboard *Ben-my-Chree* to lead the attack in person. Rudder had been specifically ordered not to lead the assault and to land with Force C, but in the circumstances leadership from the front and minimizing changes of commander at a very late stage was necessary. The downside was that he would be unable to execute his wider command and coordination function once he was embroiled in the battle.

*HMS* **Ben-my-Chree**
*(Manx for 'girl of my heart').*

At 2130 hours on 4 June, Eisenhower and his service commanders had assembled again in Southwick House for their next routine meeting. Outside, driving rain was lashing the windows; and the canvas of Montgomery's HQ in the nearby woods (code named SHARPENER) flapped noisily. Group Captain Stagg reported that his team had identified a ridge of high pressure developing behind the frontal system. Vital data had been reported by ships specially stationed in the Atlantic. His analysis was that this could provide a temporary window in the unsettled weather in the Channel and assault area in time for the assault on 6 June. Eisenhower asked how many hours he could count on for the attack. Stagg replied that 'The

*Colonel James Earl Rudder*

*To go or not to go – transports wait out the postponement in Portland Harbour.*

morning would be fair and good weather might last throughout the afternoon'. Asked for his opinion by Eisenhower, Field Marshal Montgomery said 'I would say Go!' and after a moments thought the Supreme Commander gave his decision:

**'OK let's go!'**

As dusk fell on the evening of 5 June the four ships bearing the Rangers were heading east with the remainder of Force O to point Zulu off the southern tip of the Isle of White, the cliffs of which were so familiar to the Rangers. Here the five massive convoys bearing the assault force

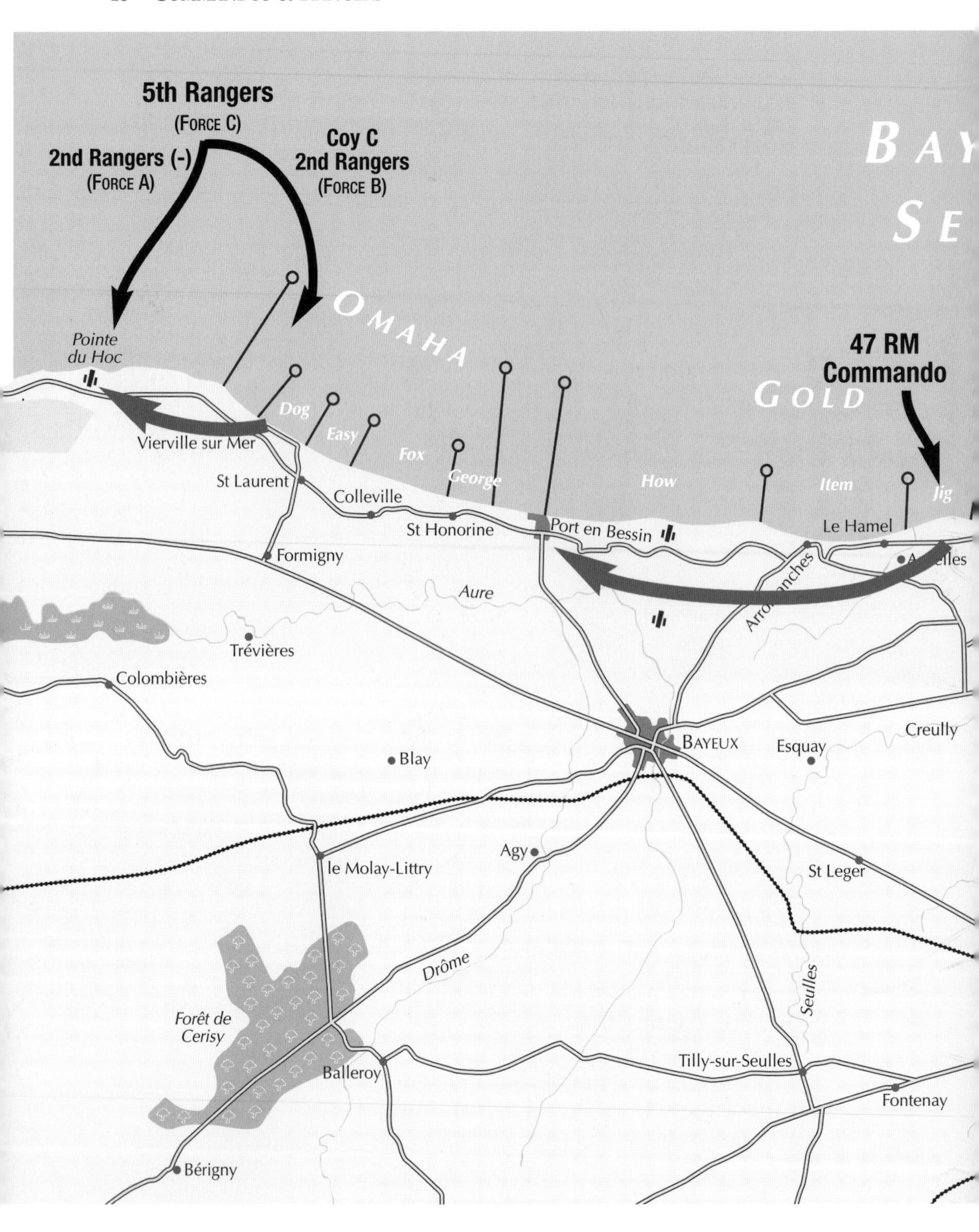
5th Rangers
(Force C)
2nd Rangers (-)
(Force A)
Coy C
2nd Rangers
(Force B)
47 RM
Commando
Omaha
Gold
Dog
Easy
Fox
George
How
Item
Jig
Pointe
du Hoc
Vierville sur Mer
St Laurent
Colleville
St Honorine
Port en Bessin
Le Hamel
Formigny
Aure
Trévières
Colombières
Bayeux
Esquay
Creully
Blay
Agy
le Molay-Littry
St Leger
Drôme
Seulles
Forêt de
Cerisy
Balleroy
Tilly-sur-Seulles
Fontenay
Bérigny

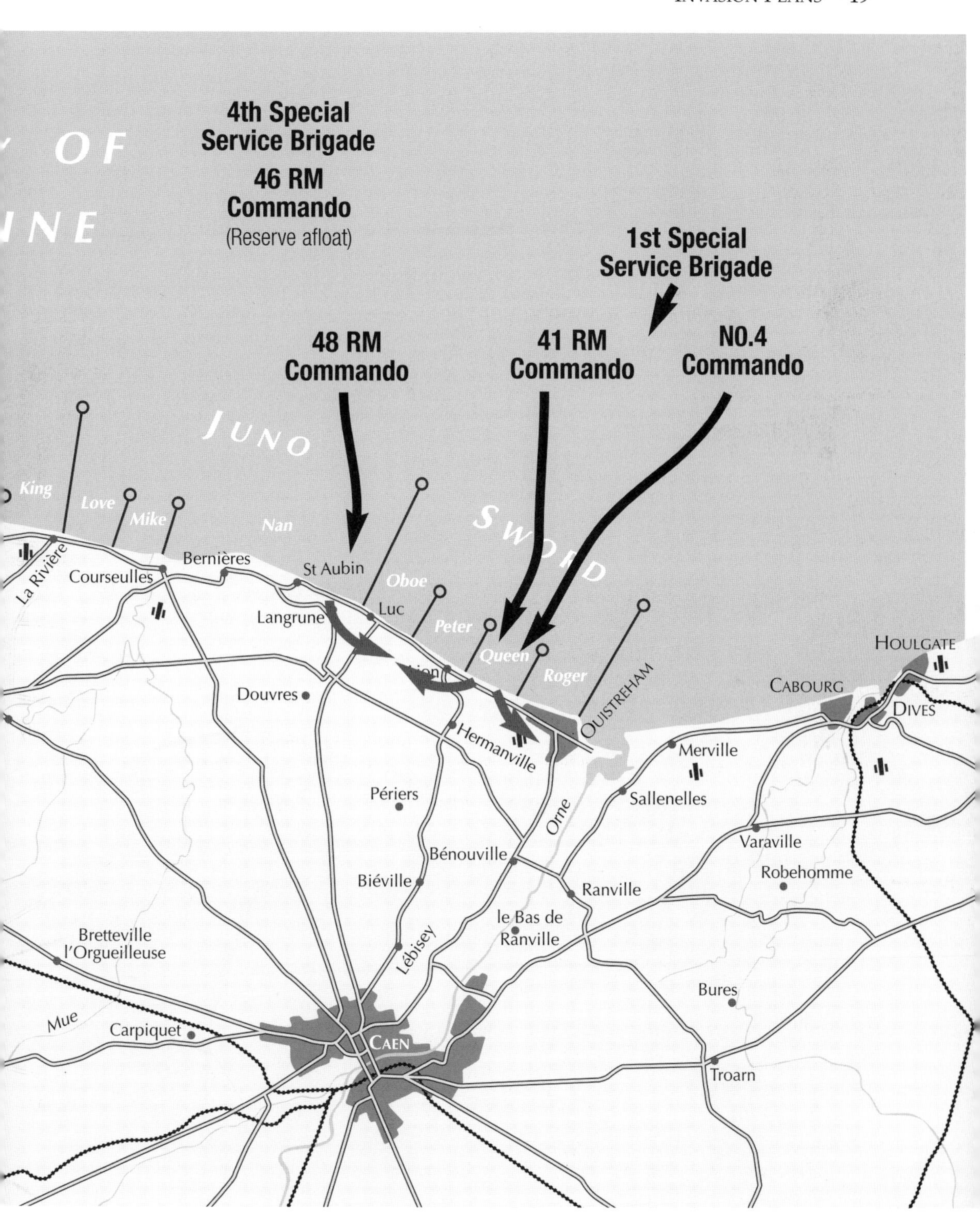
4th Special
Service Brigade
46 RM
Commando
(Reserve afloat)
1st Special
Service Brigade
48 RM
Commando
41 RM
Commando
NO.4
Commando
JUNO
SWORD
King
Love
Mike
Nan
Oboe
Peter
Queen
Roger
La Rivière
Courseulles
Bernières
St Aubin
Langrune
Luc
Douvres
Hermanville
Ouistreham
Houlgate
Cabourg
Dives
Merville
Sallenelles
Orne
Périers
Bénouville
Biéville
Varaville
Robehomme
Ranville
le Bas de
Ranville
Lébisey
Bretteville
l'Orgueilleuse
Bures
Mue
Carpiquet
Caen
Troarn

turned south into the 'Spout', five marked and mines swept lanes. Even for Commandos and Rangers who were more accustomed to the cramped quarters aboard the landing ships and craft it was an uncomfortable night as the sea was still rough with a brisk wind blowing.

A hundred miles south across the Channel the German defenders of Normandy were at a low state of alert: commanders were called to a command post exercise, Rommel was away to Germany and the soldiers of the Atlantic Wall relaxed as best they could. The German assessment was that the tides were wrong for their estimate of an Allied landing.

It was not high tide shortly after dawn and the weather forecast was too bad for the Allies to come; their U-boats in the Atlantic missed the forming ridge of high pressure.

*Wind and wave lash Hitler's Atlantic Wall.*

## CHAPTER THREE

# Rudder's Rangers at Pointe du Hoc

The Western Allied Naval Task Force was to land the First US Army over two beaches: V US Corps on Omaha, a five mile arc of beach backed by dunes and bluffs, perfect for amphibious operations, in an otherwise unbroken wall of 100 foot high cliffs; while VII US Corps was to land on the on the east coast of the much more low lying Cotentin Peninsula. Between the two beaches lay Pointe du Hoc, misspelt as 'Pointe du Hoe' by the Allied cartographer who copied the original French map. Here, up on the cliffs was sited a German coastal battery. The US official historian explained the considerable importance of the position:

> *At Pointe du Hoe, four miles west of Omaha Beach, the Germans had constructed a fortified position for a coastal battery of six 155-mm howitzers of French make; four guns were in open emplacements and two were casemated, with further construction work on casemates reported under way in April and May. This battery was one of the most dangerous elements in the German coastal defenses of the assault area. With a 25,000-yard range, the 155's could put fire on the approaches to Omaha Beach and on the transport area of V Corps; in addition they could reach the transport area from which VII Corps, to the west, would unload for assault at the base of the Cotentin Peninsula ("Utah" Beach).*

From early in the planning process the Pointe du Hoc battery was identified as being too important to be left to the uncertainty of neutralisation of Allied bombers or even naval gunfire. No matter how confident the Allied Naval and Air commanders were that they could do the job, the Army wanted 'boots on the ground' to ensure that the battery could not open fire and potentially play havoc with the landing. Involving either a long approach across enemy held territory from OMAHA or a direct cliff escalade this was from outset clearly a Ranger mission. Of the two Ranger battalions in the North-west European Theatre available for the cross-channel attack 2nd US Rangers were the

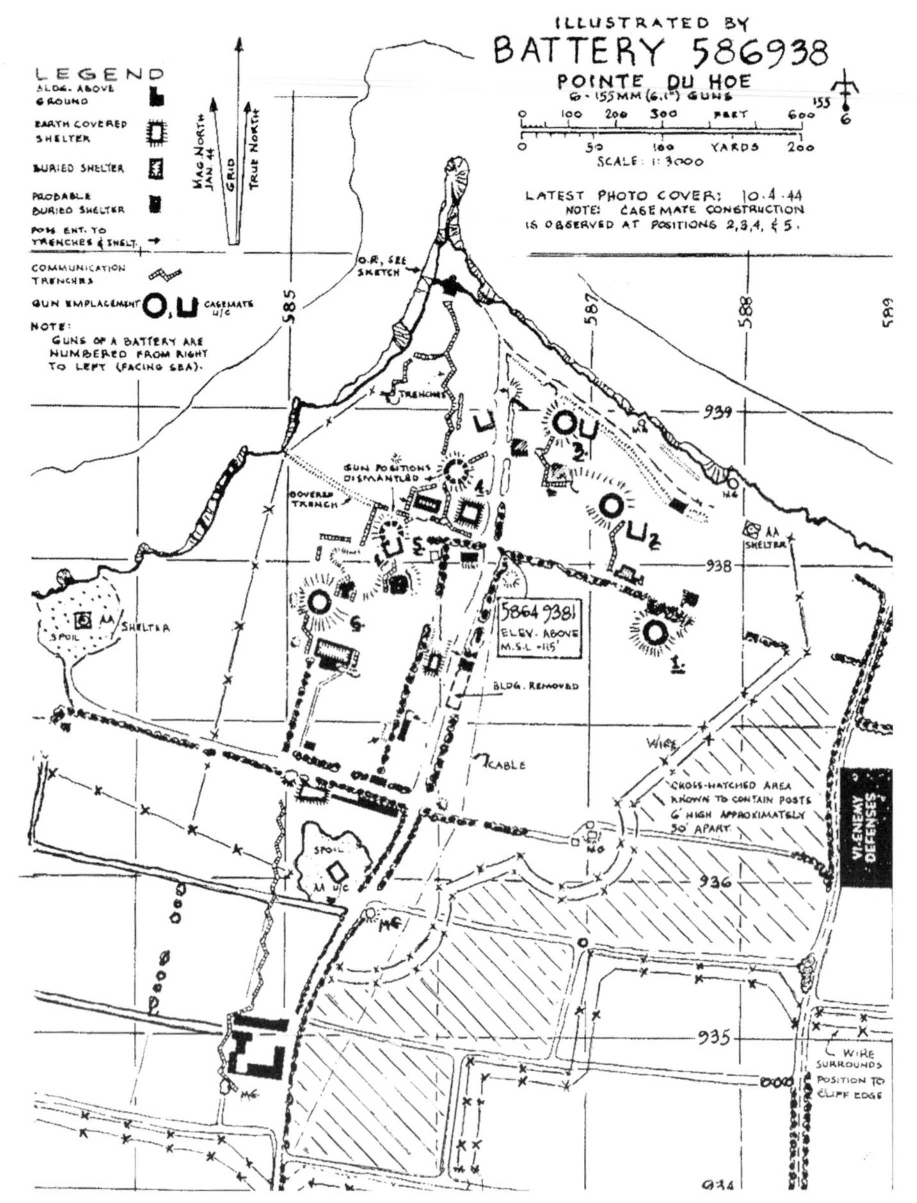

*Map from the Rangers' Operation Order showing the open gun pits and the casemates under construction.*

more experienced half of Colonel Rudder's Provisional Ranger Group and were therefore allocated the assault mission on Pointe du Hoc. The other half, 5th US Rangers, were to land behind the assault force and if all went well would then join 2nd Rangers in cutting the coast road inland from Pointe du Hoc. If, however, 2nd Rangers' escalade attack by three of its companies failed:

> *An alternate plan was ready if the support force of Rangers had not received word, by H+30, of success in the other three*

> *companies attack on the cliffs at Pointe du Hoe. In this event, the larger Ranger force would land on the western end of Omaha Beach (Vierville sector) behind the 116th Infantry and proceed overland toward the Point, avoiding all unnecessary action en route to its objective*

Having taken Pointe du Hoc from seaward or landward attack, the Ranger Group's mission would be completed by an advance westward to seize objectives, including the Grandcamp-Maisy battery that would facilitate the link-up of the OMAHA and UTAH beachheads. This would be in support of the 116th Infantry, who would be landing at OMAHA and under whose overall command the Ranger Group fell.

**The Pointe du Hoc Battery**

The position at Pointe du Hoc was naturally and strongly protected from attack by sea by the eighty-five to 100 foot high cliffs which were 'sheer to overhanging; below them is a narrow strip of beach, without the slightest cover for assaulting troops'. Close examination of air photographs led planners to believe that the defences were concentrated on the landward side, which was later confirmed by French sources. The US historian commented:

> *The battery was part of a self-contained fortress area, mined and wired on the landward side. Its flanks were protected by two supporting smaller positions mounting machine guns and ... anti-aircraft guns. These positions were sited to put enfilade fire on the beaches under the Point, and to aid its defence against any inland attack. Enemy troops at Pointe du Hoe were estimated at 125 infantry* [726 Infantrie Regiment] *and 85 artillerymen* [2 Battalion 1260 Artillerie Regiment], *included in the sector of enemy coastal defences, from the Vire to the Orne, held by the* 716 Infantriedivision.

The intelligence was incorrect in one important detail. The US sector between Port-en-Bessin and the River Vire had been reinforced by *Generalleutnant* Dietrich Kraiss's *352. Infantriedivision*, a relatively newly-raised field formation. As late as June it was thought still to be in *LXXXIV Korps* reserve around St-Lô, thirty kilometres from the coast. Parts of its *916.*

Generalleutnant *Dietrich Kraiss, Commander* 352. Infanteriedivision

*Regiment* were in fact located along the clifftops between St-Laurent-sur-Mer and Grandcamp-Maisy. Also in the area, and now falling under the command of Kraiss's command, were elements of *716. Infanteriedivision*, including the *439. Ost-Bataillon*. As the Germans regarded them as being 'of limited fighting value' they were deployed in widely spaced resistance points: *Widerstandnester* (WN) or strong points *Stützpunkte* (S) on the least dangerous sector of the divisional front. Those positions flanking Pointe du Hoc (S 75) were one mile to the west and two miles to the east. One Company of 125 infantrymen from *III/726 Grenadiers* manned the *Stützpunkt* defences around the Pointe du Hoc Battery.

The six 155mm guns of French origin (designated K420[f] in German service) belonging to *II/1260 Artillery Regiment* were in the process of being casemated in heavy steel reinforced concrete bunkers (type 679). It was obvious from the attentions of the Allied air forces that the Pointe du Hoc guns and their crews were extremely vulnerable in their open pits and evidence from Allied landings in the Mediterranean indicated that any landing here would be accompanied by a crushing bombardment, which would render unprotected guns useless. During April and May 1944, it was assessed by Allied intelligence that the cliff edge command bunker and two of the casemates were complete and occupied, which left four of the guns still in open gun-pits. This deployment was seemingly confirmed by air photography.

*Medium bombers on a pre-D Day raid on Pointe du Hoc.*

*One of the Pointe du Hoc guns mounted in the original open gunpits.*

## The Ranger Plan

As with all the components of the invasion, there was a wealth of information available on which to plan the operation, much of it pictorial and some of it based on intelligence from the French Resistance and the SOE. It all pointed to the necessity of a heavy preliminary bombardment:

> *Special attention was given the Pointe du Hoe battery in the preparatory air and naval bombardments. As early as 15 April, medium bombers of the Ninth Air Force had begun* [daylight] *attacks to soften up the position and to slow enemy efforts to construct further casemates. In order not to tip off the invasion plans, these early attacks could not be made too often and were combined with wide-ranging missions directed at other points on the French coast from Brittany to Belgium. On 22 May and 4 June, Ninth Air Force bombers struck again and on the night of 5/6 June RAF heavies included the Pointe in a major attack on batteries along the whole invasion coast. Naval bombardment of the Omaha sector and its flanks began at 0550 on 6 June; particular attention, especially by the main batteries of the battleship Texas (14-inch guns), was paid to Pointe du Hoe in this fire. At H-20 minutes (0610), 18 medium bombers of the Ninth Air Force made a last strike on the Point.*

The plan arrived at by Colonel James Rudder was for three companies (D, E and F) of his 2nd Rangers (Force A) to tranship from the SS *Ben-my-Chree* into the Landing Craft Assault (LCAs) land on the little beach at the foot of the cliffs at 0630 hours (H Hour in the US sector). From the beach, they would climb the cliff and destroy the guns clearing the numerous other concrete

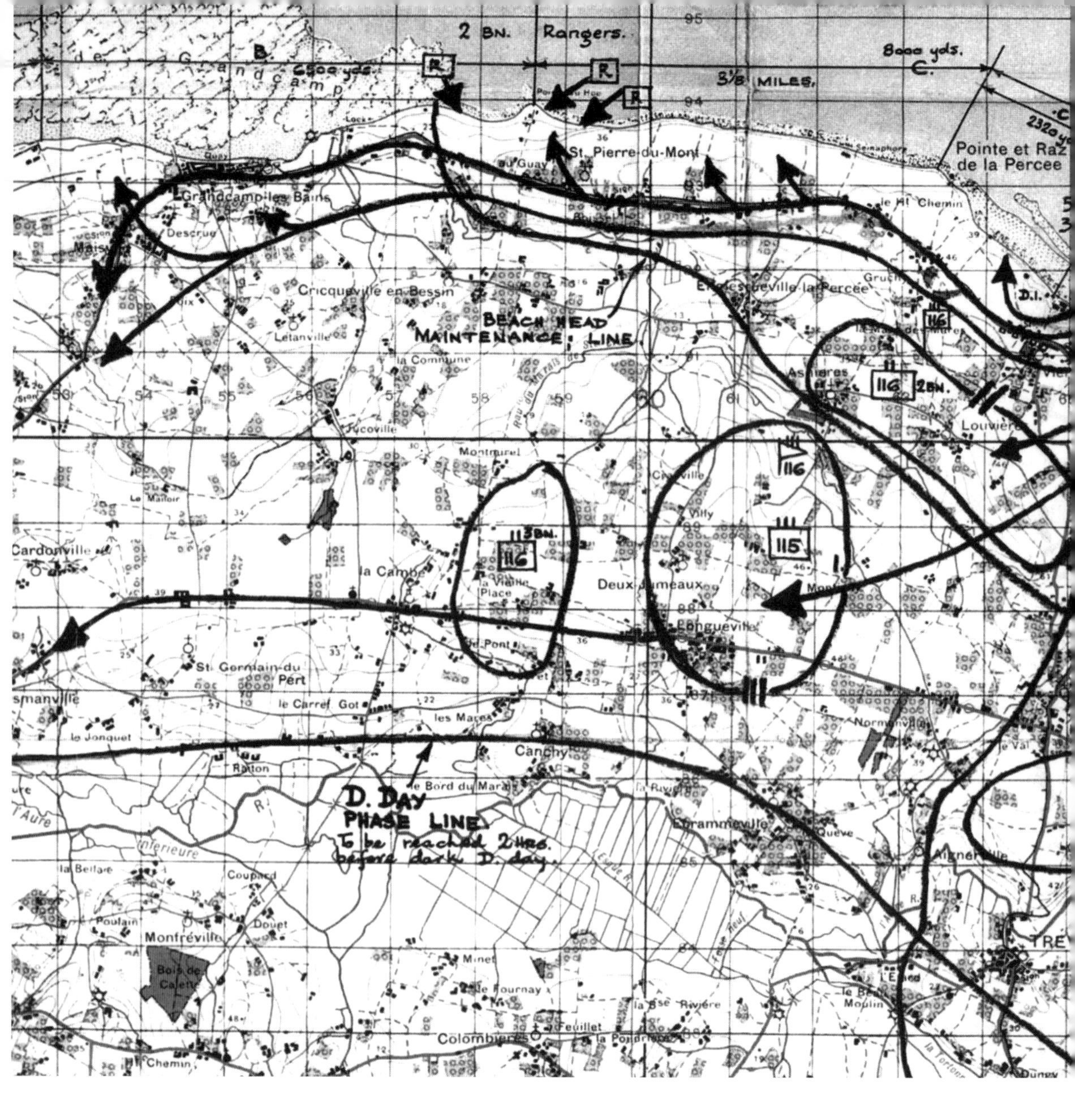


*V US Corps plan and D Day objectives.*

bunkers as a part of the process. A and B Companies (a part of Force C) would follow and they in turn would be followed up the cliff by Lieutenant Colonel Max Schneider's 5th Rangers (the remainder of Force C) some thirty minutes later. US Admiral Hall's intelligence officer, however, on being briefed on the plan of attack commented 'It can't be done. Three old women with brooms could keep the Rangers from climbing that cliff'.

But the Rangers were confident that it could be done and

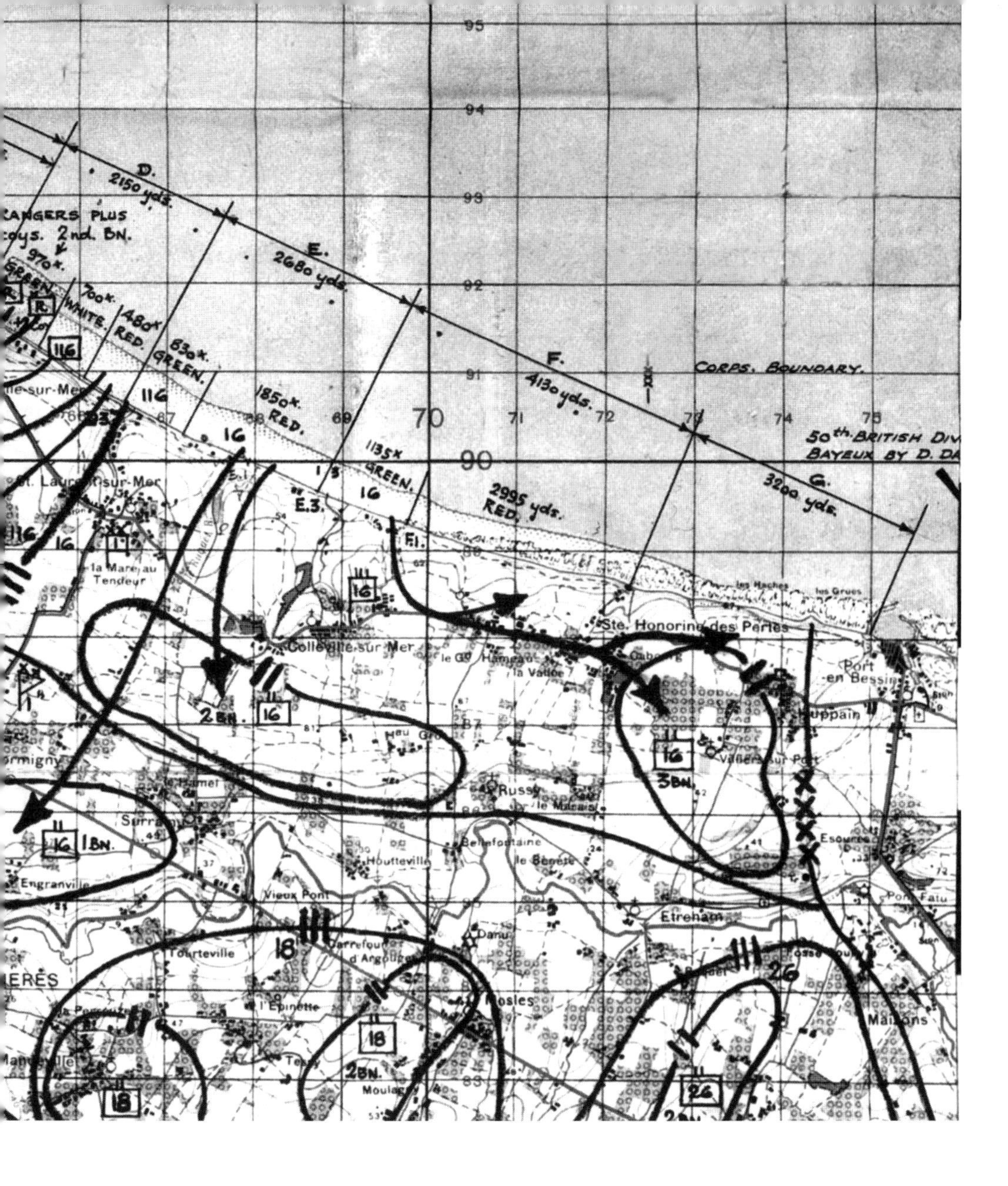


planned and trained in depth to succeed.

A total of 225 men including Ranger HQ would assault the cliffs having been landed by ten British-crewed LCAs. Companies E and F were to land at the foot of the eastern face of Pointe du Hoc, while Company D would assault the western face of the Pointe. Once up the cliff small groups were to fan out across the battery to take their objectives, clearing the numerous other concrete bunkers as a part of the process. On the codeword 'CROWBAR' being received, Force B followed by Force C would land, climb the cliff, and advance beyond the battery to block the coast road before advancing west towards Grandcamp.

Company C, 2nd Rangers had a separate mission of its own on OMAHA Beach where it was to land with the first assault wave of the 116th Infantry and destroy the German *Widerstandnest* 73 above the western end of the beach. They were then to advance westward along the coast clearing up known enemy positions, including the defended radar site near Pointe de la Percée.

## Special Equipment

The key to 2nd Rangers' plan was getting from the beach up and into the battery. The Rangers were of course trained to climb cliffs but those at Pointe du Hoc were particularly unstable and Colonel Rudder sought other means of scaling them that were more secure and quicker. Sixteen-foot sections of aluminium tube ladder were a standard piece of commando equipment in the Rangers' stores and sections would be taken, lashed to the upper sides of the LCAs as a matter of course.

A variety of launchers that fired rocket-powered grapples trailing a range of ropes and ladders were trialled. Two launchers per company were fitted to the gunwales of the LCAs and lighter versions for firing from the beach were also taken into use by the Rangers and in training enabled the first men to be on the cliff to within a minute of touching down on a beach at the foot of a cliff.

Four amphibious DUKWs were secured for conversion to help Force A's cliff assault. Code named SWAN 1-4, each vehicle mounted a hundred-foot London Fire Brigade escape ladder. At the top, a steel shield and mount for twin Vickers K guns were fitted to enable a gunner to engage the enemy with suppressive fire that would rake the cliff top, while the assault team climbed the ladder below him. The seven-man Ranger crews successfully practised driving the vehicles ashore, securing each with four jacks and using the vehicle's power to send the ladder up onto the cliff top. These ladders were allocated one per assault company with the fourth being a spare.

**The Run-in to the Beach**

Ten miles out to sea *Ben-my-Chree* hove-to and well before dawn the Rangers, fully kitted out, laden with ammunition and five-day supply of K Rations, made their way to the boat deck where the LCAs awaited them. The Rangers were lucky, as not all ships could lower LCAs with their three or four man crew and passengers into the sea; the unlucky were forced to climb down wet and slippery cargo nets into Landing Craft bucking erratically in the waves. At 0430, two full hours before H Hour, the LCAs were lowered and headed for the coast. With a moderate sea running, seasickness was an immediate problem for the 225 Rangers but the necessity of constantly bailing out waves that regularly broke over the bows provided a distraction from their misery for some.

The RAF night bombers and the Allied parachute transport aircraft that had been so active over Normandy during the hours of darkness had departed and at 0550 hours, nautical twilight, the guns of the Naval Bombardment forces opened fire up and down the invasion coast. Their targets were the coastal batteries and strong points. Pointe du Hoc received the attention of USS *Texas*, who according to the Schedule of Fires was to engage the cliff top battery with up to 250 rounds of 14-inch ammunition fired from her ten main armament pieces mounted in five turrets. The Hunt Class destroyer HMS *Talybont* added up to 300 rounds of 4.7-inch to the drenching fire falling on the Pointe. The smashed concrete and craters that still scar the area of battery seven decades after they were formed are testimony to the ferocity of the bombardment and the numbing effect on the enemy.

The naval bombardment paused at 0610 hours (H-20 minutes) to allow eighteen USAAF medium bombers to strike the battery

*USS* Texas, *under way at speed.*

with 36 tons of bombs. Due to the weather conditions, the majority of the Allied aircraft involved in similar strikes had time added on to prevent cratering of the landing beaches but in the case of Pointe du Hoc it is still a matter of debate as to what proportion of the medium bombers' loads hit the battery.

The problem with the early H Hour in the US sector was that there was little light and they did not have that extra hour for bombardment that the British enjoyed with their 0730 H Hour (due to tidal difference). The lack of light to accurately pick out features on the uniform wall of cliffs between OMAHA and Grandcamp was to compound critical failures.

Lieutenant Colin Beever RN was skipper of ML *304*, which

*The actual landing points of the surviving Landing Craft.*

was to guide the LCAs to the beach at the foot of the Pointe but an hour before their scheduled touchdown, both the forward-looking navigational radar and the equipment that read the lattice of radio beams that had been established across the invasion area failed. This left Lieutenant Beever in the dark having to navigate on dead reckoning and observation. As a result of this and a much stronger than expected eastward sea current the flotilla was set three miles to the east, heading for Pointe de la Percée. Further out to sea HMS *Talybont's* log, however, confirms that *Texas's* 14-inch shells could be clearly seen exploding on the battery. But low in the water and with numerous other naval gunfire engagements under way Lieutenant Beever's difficulties can be appreciated.

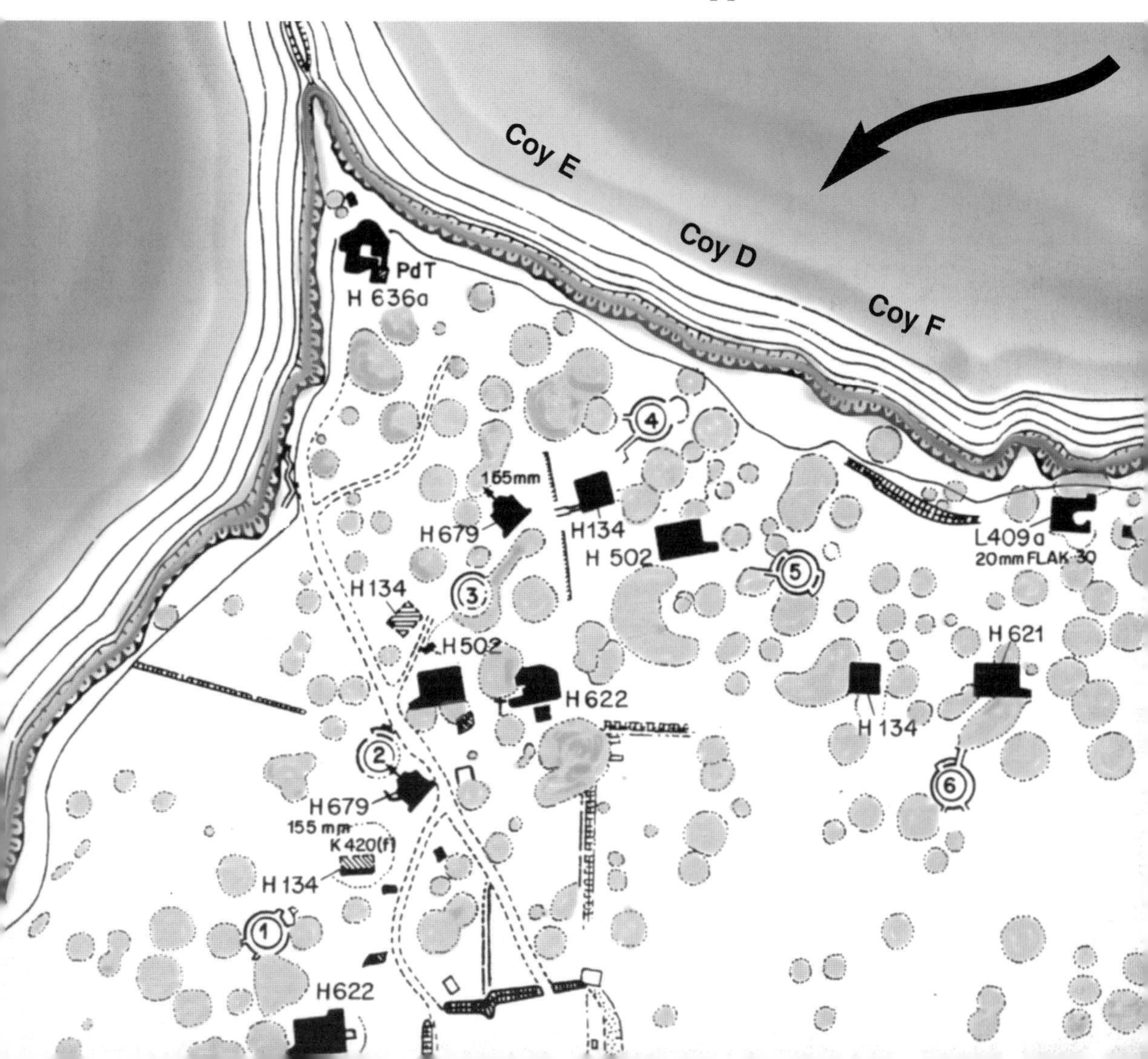

At almost 0630 hours, after the LCAs had left ML *304* for the final run-in and less than a mile from the cliffs, Colonel Rudder finally identified the error and ordered his coxswain to turn to starboard. Making just seven knots (about 8 mph), the flotilla would now not only be late but also be taking the seas broadside-on for much of that distance and be under fire from German positions between OMAHA and Pointe du Hoc.

German fire grew as the main, pre-H Hour bombardment switched targets and the coastal troops started to recover from the naval gunfire and bombing. The largest targets were the four DUKWs that had already been launched from their Landing Craft Tank (LCTs) prior to the change in course. HMS *Talybont* suppressed the enemy but a little later SWAN 2 was lost to automatic fire from the shore. Another casualty, probably to a combination of enemy action and the sea, was LCA *860* with the HQ of Company D aboard. Seven men lost their lives. This was followed by the loss of LCA *914*, a supply craft that also carried men of Company D, which had now lost over a third of its men.

Between thirty and forty minutes late, the Rangers touched down at the foot of the cliffs. Rather that waste additional time by sending the depleted Company D to the west face as planned, Colonel Rudder decided to concentrate all three companies with the three surviving SWAN DUKWs on the east-facing cliff.

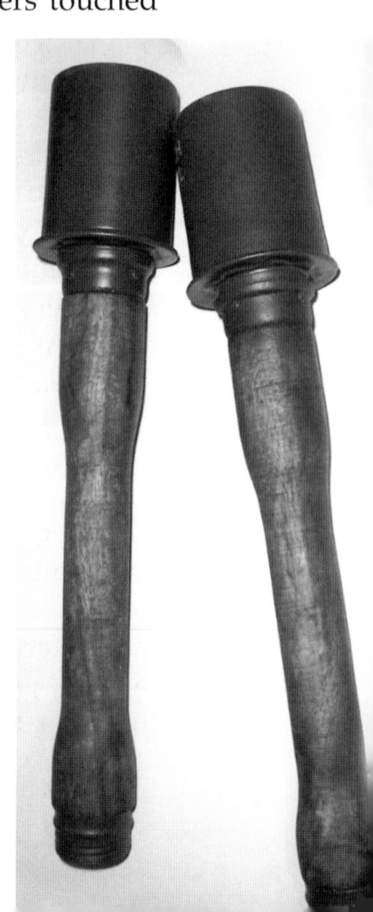

By the time Force A was approaching their landing at 0700, the numbing effect of the naval bombardment and air force bombing, all of which had stopped at 0625 hours, had all-but worn-off and the Germans were organising themselves on the cliff top. As the Rangers closed in on the beach the volume of fire plunging down on them from the battery increased and the low freeboard of just eighteen inches that had made the LCAs a small target was now negated. There was little protection available from rifle or machine gun fire. Casualties in every landing craft further whittled away the already slim ranks of Force A. The Rangers in LCA *884* had three men wounded during this period but had replied with its Lewis guns and the Rangers' BARs. The destroyer USS *Satterlee* returned fire and was joined by the guns of Lieutenant Beever's ML *304*, a 3-pounder, 20mm gun and a pair of machine guns. The enemy's fire was sufficiently suppressed for the final run-in to be not too costly in terms of casualties. The first of three codewords to be issued by Force A, 'CROWBAR', was received aboard HMS *Prince Charles* at 0709 hours, nine minutes after Force C had as per orders adopted the alternate plan and Colonel Schneider with the eight follow-on Ranger companies headed for OMAHA Beach.

**The Landing and Escalade**

As the LCAs approached the beach most of the craft fired the six rocket-propelled grapples per boat, at a range of about thirty yards, just as they had repeatedly practised in training. The hemp ropes, however, which had all been soaked by seawater during the previous two hours, were now so heavy that most fell short. 'In some cases not more than half the length of rope or ladder was lifted from the containing box.' Scaling means one had largely failed.

Conditions on the already rough and rocky beach were now also untenable for the three remaining SWANS. Shell and bomb craters littered the beach together with rubble blown down from the cliff. Consequently, the long fire brigade ladders could not be put up close enough to the cliff to provide a route up; the second scaling means had failed. To make matters worse the majority of the sectionalised commando ladders, lashed to the topsides of the LCAs, had been washed overboard in the heavy seas.

So heavily cratered was the beach in places, the Rangers had trouble in getting across it. In one case soldiers landing 'neck deep in water' found it hard to wade out because of the slick clay bottom. The chaotic state of the surface of the beach did, however, have some advantages for the Rangers; the craters provided cover from German stick grenades that were being thrown down from above and the rock rubble much reduced their effect. Only two casualties were recorded as being caused by stick grenades, which worked on the blast principle rather than the fragmentation of Allied grenades. German soldiers were seen peering over the cliff top and several were hit and plummeted to the beach along with rocks dislodged by the bombardment.

Waiting on the beach were two members of 506 Parachute Infantry Regiment who were the sole survivors from a Dakota that had crashed into the sea near the coast shortly after 0100 hours. Picking their way along the beach they had followed the landing craft westward and joined the Rangers below the battery. The two paratroopers were taken to Colonel Rudder and they remained with the Rangers for almost a week of hard fighting before rejoining the 101st Airborne Division.

### The Cliff Assault

The US historian wrote that …

> *… the assault went forward without check. Ranger casualties on the beach totalled about fifteen, most of them from the raking fire to their left. In something less than ten minutes from landing, the first Ranger parties were getting over the cratered edges of the cliff top.*

The first LCAs are recorded as landing on the thirty yard wide beach at 0708 hours:

> *The nine LCA's touched down on a front of about 500 yards, the right-hand craft just under the tip of Pointe du Hoe, and the others spaced fairly evenly. No great distance separated some of the boat teams, but according to plan they went into action as separate units, each facing its particular problems of escalade and opposition.*

Colonel Rudder's craft, LCA *888*, had been first to hit the beach, with fifteen Rangers of Company E and six men from his headquarters aboard. Enemy troops had been seen on the cliff 'but, when Sergeant Boggetto shot one German off the edge with a BAR, the others disappeared'.

With the failure of the rocket grapples two Rangers, 'best of the group at free-climbing', tried to scale the shell-scarred cliff without ropes. They were thwarted by the wet and unstable clay between the bands of crumbly rocks. A combination of wet weather and the shelling defeated this method of escalade, as the cliff 'gave way too easily to permit knife-holds'. The bombardment had, however, brought down a section of the cliff that formed a forty foot ramp.

A section of commando ladder, with a toggle rope attached, was carried to the top of the mound and set up.

> *A Ranger climbed the ladder, cut a foothold in the cliff, and stood in this to hold the ladder while a second man climbed it for another 16 feet. The top man repeated the process, and this time Tech. 5 George J. Putzek reached the edge. Lying flat, with the ladder on his arms, he held on while a man below climbed the toggle rope, then the ladder.*
>
> *From there on it was easy. As the first men up moved a few yards from the cliff edge to protect the climbers, they found plenty of cover in bomb craters, and no sign of an enemy. In fifteen minutes from landing, all the Company E men from LCA 888 were up and ready to move on. Colonel Rudder and headquarters personnel remained for the moment below, finding*

*A ramp of rubble caused by the strike of a 500lb bomb or a 14-inch shell on the cliff.*

*Part of the Normandy defences, a 'modified' Vickers machine gun.*

*shelter from enfilade fire in a shallow cave at the bottom of the cliff.*

Meanwhile, LCA *861* carrying a platoon of Company E, grounded twenty-five yards from the bottom of the cliff.

*Three or four Germans were standing on the edge, shooting down at the craft. Rangers near the stern took these enemy under fire and drove them out of sight.*

The platoon's smaller hand-fired, rocket-propelled grapples were carried ashore, and the first one was fired fifteen yards from the cliff and with a lighter rope to carry it went over the top of the cliff and bedded in.

Private Roberts started to climb up the thin hand-line:

*... bracing his feet against the 80-degree slope. He made about twenty-five feet; the rope slipped or was cut, and Roberts slithered down. The second rocket was fired and the grapnel caught. Roberts went up again, made the top (he estimated his climbing time at forty seconds), and pulled into a small cratered niche just under the edge. As he arrived, the rope was cut. Roberts tied it to a picket. This pulled out under the weight of the next man, and the rope fell off the cliff, marooning Roberts. However, a 20-foot mound of clay knocked off the cliff enabled Roberts' team to get far enough up the side to throw him a rope. This time he lay across it, and five men, including Lieutenant Lapres, came up. Roberts had not yet seen an enemy and had not been under fire.*

*Private Roberts, one of the first Rangers up the cliff.*

Without waiting for reinforcement, the first six Rangers up the cliff including Lieutenant Lapres headed off for their objective, the nearby battery Observation Post that had been built into the tip of the point.

About 100 yards to the left, LCA *862* touched down with fifteen Rangers and Lieutenant Johnson's Naval Shore Fire Control party aboard, who like many others on the narrow beach found themselves exposed to machine-gun fire from the east. One man was killed and another wounded by this fire; two more were injured by grenade fragments.

LCA *862* was, however, almost an exception to the failure of the other craft mounted grapples; they waited until touchdown to fire their rockets. Benefitting from the decreased range, three grapples reached the cliff top.

> *One plain and two toggle ropes reached the top, but one toggle rope pulled out. Tech. 5 Victor J. Aguzzi, 1st Lt. Joseph E. Leagans (commanding the team), and S/Sgt. Joseph J. Cleaves went up the two remaining ropes, arrived at the top almost together, and fell into a convenient shell hole just beyond the edge.*

About twenty yards left of Colonel Rudder's craft, LCA *722* landed with the usual complement of fifteen Rangers of Company E, five headquarters men, a *Stars and Stripes* photographer, and a British commando officer who had been the Ranger's training liaison officer. Touchdown was made at the edge of a crater, which the men could not avoid, but the crater gave cover from enfilading fire from the left.

Equipment on this craft included a 60mm mortar with ammunition, and some demolitions. 'All were got ashore without loss, though it took manoeuvring to avoid the deep water in the crater.'

As the ropes were drier two grapples reached the cliff top; one ladder and a plain rope. The single rope lay in a slight crevice, but the ladder hung from an overhang which was exposed to the flanking fire and was hard to climb. Tech. 5 Edward P. Smith tried the plain rope and found he could easily 'walk up it'.

> *On top three or four minutes after landing, he saw a group of Germans to his right throwing grenades over the cliff. Sgt. Hayward A. Robey joined Smith with a BAR. Robey lay in a shallow niche at the cliff edge and sprayed the grenadiers with 40 or 50 rounds, fast fire. Three of the enemy dropped and the rest disappeared into shelters. Pfc. Frank H. Peterson, lightly*

> *wounded on the beach by a grenade, joined up and the three Rangers went off on their mission without waiting for the next climbers.*

The mortar section in this boat team remained on the beach, according to plan, setting up their 60mm and offload ammunition from the supply craft, ready to deliver supporting fire but according to the after action report 'the beach was too exposed to make this practicable … About 0745 the mortar team went on top without having yet fired'.

Company D's craft had been planned to land on the western side of Pointe du Hoc but the two surviving LCAs now came in to the left of Company E, and in the centre of the Rangers' landing.

LCA *668* grounded on boulders short of the beach and the Rangers consequently had to swim about twenty feet to shore.

> *While 1st Sgt. Leonard G. Lomell was bringing in a box of rope and a hand-projector rocket, he was wounded in the side by a machine-gun bullet but reached shore and kept going. Despite the unusual distance from the cliff, and the very wet ropes, three rockets had carried the cliff edge with a toggle rope and the two rope ladders. All ropes were on an overhang, and only the toggle line proved practicable.*

But this was too slow and too exposed to the enemy's fire. Picking a spot high on the ramp of rubble at the back of the beach, Sergeant Lomell found that a pair of sectionalised commando ladders just reached the top of the vertical stretch, beyond which thee was a gap where the rock from the rubble ramp had fallen and the resulting slope was shallow enough to be managed without ropes. Meanwhile, two men had got up by the toggle rope and the other ten used the ladder.

Shipping enough water all the way in to keep the Rangers busy bailing, LCA *858* was two minutes behind the others arriving on the beach to discharge its men into a flooded crater. 'Despite the wetting, a bazooka was the only piece of equipment put out of action.' Three Rangers were wounded by machine-gun fire from the east flank.

Having received a thorough soaking only one of the hand-held grapples reached the top of the cliff and lay in a crevice that would give some protection from enemy flanking fire, but

approaching it was horribly exposed.

> *The Company D Rangers worked their way to the rope through the piles of debris at the cliff base. While one man helped the wounded get to Colonel Rudder's CP, where the medics had set up, all the party went up this one rope and found it not too hard going. They could get footholds in the cliff face, and a big crater reduced the steepness of the climb near the top. The group was up within fifteen minutes.*

With the insertion of Company D's two craft in the centre of the Pointe's eastern face the three Company F LCAs were pushed to the east all of them touching down beyond the area originally assigned them, though few of the Rangers realized this at the time.

> *LCA 887 had not been much bothered by either water or enemy action on the trip in. The craft grounded five yards out from dry*

> *beach, and the shorter men got a ducking in the inevitable crater. No equipment trouble resulted; even Sgt. William L. Petty's BAR, wet here and muddied later when he slipped on the cliff, fired perfectly when first needed. Some enemy fire, including automatic weapons, came from either flank. Two Rangers were wounded.*

Lieutenant Arman realized that the heavier ropes of the craft-mounted rockets had no chance of reaching the cliff from the edge of the sea. So, with ten minutes of heavy manhandling, four of the mounted rockets, together with the boxes carrying toggle ropes and ladders, were taken out on to the sand. When

the rockets were set up on the beach, the firing wire connection was found to be missing. Sergeant Cripps selflessly fired the rockets in turn by touching the short connection, three feet from the rocket base, with his 'hot-box'.

> *Each time, the flashback blinded Cripps and blew sand and mud all over him. The other Rangers saw him clean his eyes, shake his head, and go after the next rocket: "he was the hell-of-a-looking mess" But all the ropes went up, and made it possible for the party to make the top. Sergeant Petty and some other expert climbers had already tried the plain rope and failed; it was on a straight fall, requiring hand-over-hand work with no footholds possible, and the men had trouble with their muddy hands and clothes on the wet rope.*

Under fire 'from somewhere on the flanks' the Rangers began to climb the ropes and ladders.

*LCA 884* on the flank of the flotilla had been the target for considerable volumes of enemy fire from cliff positions on the three mile journey to the correct Pointe. Four grapples got over

*Rangers fight for a foothold on the cliff top.*

the cliff, 'but every rope lay in such position as to be fully exposed to the continuing enemy small-arms fire'. In addition the Rangers were so covered in mud from the cratered beach that the plain ropes would have been un climbable after the first man went up. Failing to get up any other way the group went over to the left, where they used *883*'s ladders.

LCA *883* was the last craft to reach shore, and according to the US Historian was 'nearly 300 yards left of its planned position and considerably beyond the edge of the main fortified area on Pointe du Hoe'. However, a rib of rock in the cliff protected the Rangers from the flanking fire that was causing so much trouble for the other climbers to the west. On a narrow bit of beach:

> *They made a dry landing, and had a perfect score with the six rockets. This gave an opportunity to use the climbing assignments on a full schedule, using every rope. Nevertheless, the going was hard, even on the ladders. 1st Lt. Richard A. Wintz, on a plain rope, found it impossible to get any footholds on the slippery cliff. The wet and muddy rope made it difficult for hand-over-hand pulling, and at the top Wintz was "never so tired in his life".*

At one point during Force A's assault on the cliffs there was a loud explosion which half buried Pfc Medeiros under rock and mud. It is thought that the explosion was a naval shell, or a mine that the enemy had hung over the edge, attached by wire to a pull firing mechanism and fitted with a short-delay time fuse. Only a few of these devices were found intact elsewhere on the coast, as most were probably detonated by the bombardment. Private Medeiros and four other Rangers from LCA *861* quickly reached the cliff top.

As elsewhere on the US V Corps landing front the Allied navies played a significant role in getting the Army ashore and keeping them ashore. The destroyer USS *Sattlerlee,* seeing that the Rangers were facing active opposition, brought her 5-inch guns to bear on the promontory, dashing at high speed to a matter of hundreds of yards from the rocky coast. Here, she was able to do more than anything else to subdue the defenders on the cliff top and enable the Rangers to complete their escalade.

Through the SWANs had failed to provide a quick and easy

way up the cliff, they were not entirely redundant and also provided some fire support. One under command of Sergeant Stiverson elevated its ladder to cliff level, with Stiverson himself manning the twin Vickers K guns mounted behind a steel shield. He bravely engaged the defenders and swaying in the wind some distance from the cliff top his inaccurate fire nevertheless contributed to the psychological effect on the enemy. Stiverson naturally attracted the return fire of the German defenders but the swaying target was equally difficult to hit. He was, however, forced to order the ladder to be lowered as the volume of fire directed at him grew.

With the Rangers at the top of the cliff, Lt Eikner, Colonel Rudder's signals officer could send his second signal, 'TILT' to Colonel Schneider but this message timed at 0725 and possibly also the earlier Signal, was undecipherable.

### The Fight in the Battery

Between twenty and thirty minutes after landing the Rangers were virtually all on the cliff top. From here Colonel Rudder's plan for the clearance of the battery was simple:

> *... in essence the attack followed a definite plan and order. As first objectives, each platoon ... had a limited part of the enemy*

*Set into the Pointe the Battery OP was difficult to hit during the bombardment and was still active.*

*defensive system to reach and deal with. Every man knew what this mission was, and where to go. The outcome was an action without clear pattern in detail, but with very clearly defined results.*

The principal and 'chief objectives' were the two commissioned casemates, the four open gun pits and the OP casemate at the tip of the Pointe. The OP and gun No. 3 were assigned to Company E; Company D was to clear gun pits 4, 5, and 6 at the western end of the battery, while Company F, was to head for guns 1 and 2 along with the machine-gun position at the edge of the cliff at the battery's eastern end.

*Once these objectives were taken, the plan had been to assemble at a phase line near the south edge of the fortified area. From here, D, F, and most of E would strike inland for the coastal highway about 1,000 yards south, cross it, and establish a road block against enemy movement from the west. A platoon of Company E was to remain on the Pointe with the headquarters group and arrange for perimeter defence of the captured fortifications.*

The scene that greeted the Rangers as they pulled themselves up onto the cliff top was unexpected and momentarily disorientated them. They were looking at a wilderness of torn earth and smashed concrete; only Casemates 1 and 2 and the two anti-aircraft positions to east and west were readily discernable. Using these as approximate references the small groups of Rangers set off with some difficulty to find their individual areas, not pausing to form up as a body. Company D having landing between Companies E and F to reduce the delay had furthest to go and had to cross the line of advance of Company F to reach its objectives and contributing to what is described as 'chaos' by those who seek to make ordered sense of what was a soldier's battle.

Sergeant Lomell described his advance from the cliff top:

*We didn't stop. We played it just like a football game, charging hard and low. We went into the shell craters for protection, because there were snipers around and machine guns firing at us. We'd wait for a moment and when the fire lifted, we were out of that crater and into the next one*

It was only a matter of twenty yards or so from the central area of the cliff top to the closest of the gun positions and even amidst the destruction it was immediately apparent that the guns were not in position in the open pits; what had appeared in air photographs to be the heavy 155mm gun barrels were in fact telegraph poles!

The surviving troop shelters and concrete machine gun pits, *Tobrukstände*, were cleared of Germans by groups of three or four Rangers who worked quickly and ruthlessly. Few of the enemy's coastal troops, infantry or gunners left on the battery, were disposed to put up a fight. Soon the first prisoners started to arrive at Colonel Rudder's HQ along with the news that the guns had not been in position. It was also became apparent from the number of prisoners, counts of enemy dead and wounded that the majority of the defending infantry from *III/726. Infanterieregiment* (coastal) had fled the bombardment and/or the assault.

According to the account in Small Unit Actions the only serious fighting in the battery took place around the westerly anti-aircraft position and the observation/command post on the Pointe. Corporal Aguzzi, from LCA *862*, saw a German soldier near the OP, lobbing grenades from a cliff top trench. The OP was not his objective, but his group decided to go after this active enemy. 'They threw grenades at the German and moved into the trench when he ducked under the entrance to the OP', while Aguzzi found a shell hole from where he could cover the main entrance. Meanwhile, three Rangers tried to skirt the OP and get at it from the rear.

They were not the only ones to tackle the OP:

> *Here, the first men up from LCA* 861 *found themselves about twenty feet to seaward of the massive and undamaged concrete OP. As S/Sgt. Charles H. Denbo and Private Roberts crawled five feet toward a trench, small-arms fire, including machine guns, started up from slits in the OP. The Rangers threw four grenades at the slits, and three went in.*
> *The machine gun stopped firing, but Denbo was wounded by a rifle bullet.*

Sergeant Yardley brought up a bazooka, and with his first shot hit the edge of the

firing slit; the second went through. While the Germans were reeling from the effect of the explosion in their casemate, a group of Rangers 'left Yardley to watch the embrasure and dashed around the OP without drawing enemy fire'. On the other side of the OP they came across Corporal Aguzzi.

Thus two groups of Rangers had attacked the OP and succeeded in getting a number of grenades and bazooka rockets through the embrasure. But the casemate was impervious to their attempts to subdue it and the demolition charges had been left down on the beach. In the prevailing conditions, they were too far away to consider retrieval. The enemy, however, were 'buttoned-up' inside and once the radio antenna had been shot away, without viable communications.

> *For the rest of D Day and through the following night, Yardley and Medeiros stayed in their trench on one side of the OP while Aguzzi watched the main entrance. Neither guard knew the other was there. Demolitions could have been used on Aguzzi's side, but nobody bothered to bring them up for use; there was no sign of action from the enemy in the OP.*
>
> *The following afternoon the OP was finally cleared when demolition charges were brought up cliff. Two satchel charges of C-2 explosives were thrown in the entrance, and Aguzzi, still on guard, figured the enemy must be wiped out. But eight unwounded Germans swarmed out with their hands up, and only one body was found inside. The Rangers were never sure how many enemy had been in the post, as the OP, like many positions in the battery area, was connected by tunnels, 'which the Rangers had neither numbers nor time to investigate fully'.*

## Destruction of the Guns

While the remains of the three companies fanned out across the battery, Colonel Rudder established his HQ at the site of a rock fall. Its ramp of rubble and cliff top crater and consequently short vertical section gave relatively easy access to the battery. It was here that Rudder hurriedly laid out the Stars and Stripes, as a squadron of fighter bombers summoned to give support to the escalade arrived and started their bombing run on the cliff top; one aircraft waggled its wings and dropped its load further

*The Stars and Stripes hang on the cliff marking Colonel Rudder's headquarters.*

inland. Although one friendly fire incident was averted, others from land, sea and air did cause casualties during the battle for Pointe du Hoc.

Finding the casemates and gunpits empty, most Rangers simply moved on to their next objective, blocking the road between Grandcamp and OMAHA, some 600 yards further inland. Making their way from crater to crater, tackling any enemy they encountered *en route,* the number of prisoners began to increase.

Amongst those leading the advance inland was Sergeant Lomell, in charge of a section of eleven men.

> *By this time we were taking mortar and heavy-88 fire, crawling fire to our rear. We moved out of that position fast, hoping to locate the missing guns, thinking they were in an alternate*

> *position and would soon be firing. It did not happen that way.*
>
> *We never stopped. We kept firing and charging all the way through their buildings area* [concrete troop shelters], *where they came out of their billets in a state of undress. We were confronted with them there on our way up the road from the Pointe to the coast road. Our orders were to set up roadblocks … We were to also destroy all communications along the road.*

Arriving at the road, Lomell saw a half-company of Germans marching down the road towards them. With the enemy already in close proximity, and the outnumbered Rangers not being in carefully sited ambush positions, the Germans were allowed to march onwards towards OMAHA.

With the enemy out of sight, Lomell positioned his men to block the road from the west and went out on a clearance patrol of his area. Only a short distance from his position he and Ranger Jack Kuhn noted tyre tracks in the mud leading from the tarmac surface of the coastal road onto a country lane running south:

> *Jack Kuhn and I started leapfrogging down this sunken farm road heading inland, following wagon tracks between the high hedgerows with trees, not knowing where it was going. It led to a little swale, or draw, in an apple orchard. There was camouflage netting all over it... I peeked over this hedgerow and there were the guns, all sitting in proper firing condition, the ammunition pilled up neatly, everything ready. But they pointed at UTAH Beach. They weren't pointed at OMAHA Beach.*

The gun crews were apparently being briefed further down the field and the guns unattended.

Of the six guns, five had been moved from the open gun pits

*An indication of the size of the 155mm guns can be gathered fom the man standing alongside.*

and unfinished casemates after a pre-D Day bombing raid that had damaged the sixth. It can only be supposition but it is probable that the guns, an hour after the American H-Hour, even though they appeared ready for action, were not in radio or telephone contact with a forward observation officer in the target area around UTAH Beach. The old Gunner adage 'No comms, no bombs', holds true!

> *I said 'Jack, you cover me, I'm going to destroy them.' So, all I had was two thermite grenades* [AN-M14 TH3]. *I went in, he covered me. I said, 'Keep your eyes on these people. I won't know if anybody comes and keep your eyes open'.*

Placing the thermite grenades in the elevating mechanism of the nearest two guns, Lomell retired to the hedgerow as the grenades did their work of effectively melting the gun components together with their nearly 4,000 degree burning temperature. Without an explosion and with the nearest Germans some hundred yards away Lomell and Kuhn retired from the hedgerow and enterprisingly went to get more grenades:

> *… we ran back to the road, which was a hundred yards away, and got all the other thermite grenades from the remainder of our guys. So we stuffed our jackets and rushed back, and we put thermite grenades, as many as we could, in traversing mechanisms …*

By 0830 hours, without the Germans noticing, the five 155 mm guns were effectively put out of action. Lomell returned to his position and a runner made his way back from Company D to Rudder's HQ with the news that the mission had been accomplished. Shortly afterwards another runner arrived from Company F claiming that the guns had been destroyed by them! Patrols of the two flank companies had presumably approached the guns from opposite directions and, as thermite works without causing a great deal of obvious damage, it is conceivable that both companies contributed to their destruction.

Later another patrol of Rangers pushing forward south of the road located the main stock of ammunition, which had also been removed from the site around the Pointe for the guns and blew it up in a massive explosion.

As Rangers arrived in small groups at the road, their commanders put them into position:

> *Along the road they found enemy dugouts and fox holes conveniently prepared on the north side of the hedge. The contingents from Company E and Company F occupied this line for a distance of four fields, two to each side of a lane that ran from the highway down to the creek.*

In their appointed location the Rangers awaited the arrival of 116th Infantry from OMAHA beach, confidently expected some time around midday. It was, however, to be a long wait with little information and a growing sense of isolation. To make matters worse ammunition of all types was running short and the Rangers were already resorting to the use of enemy weapons particularly the *Spandau* machine gun to replace the ammunition hungry Browning Automatic Rifles (BAR). The sound of the concussion of German stick grenades also started to replace the sharper crack of the American fragmentation grenade.

*Destroyer USS* Satterlee *in May 1944. This destroyer supplied covering and support fire with her four 5-inch guns for the Rangers assaulting Pointe du Hoc.*

**Counter Attack**

The destroyer USS *Satterlee*, whose fire had been instrumental in getting the Rangers up the cliff, now played a significant part in preventing the enemy pushing the Rangers off again. With Lieutenant Johnson's Shore Fire Control Party able to communicate with the ships by radio, and Lieutenant Eikner using a heliograph to send Morse coded requests for fire, *Satterlee* had fired off 70 per cent of her entire stock of 5-inch ammunition within twelve hours, with the longest gap between calls for fire being twenty minutes. This contribution should not be underestimated. At 1900 hours, however, the USS *Thompson* took over close support duties for the Rangers. Perhaps the greatest contribution of these ships was to break up counter-attacks that grew in strength during the night.

Having engaged a significant number of marching troops on the road, as well as a variety of vehicles, the surviving Rangers were deployed forward into the hedgerows south of the road. Without reinforcement, this was a very thin line with just eighty men of the original 225 and no reserves. Each company deployed forward listening posts to give warning of the approach of the enemy.

Up to nightfall, enemy action directed against the Rangers at Pointe du Hoc had been limited to action by the remains of the

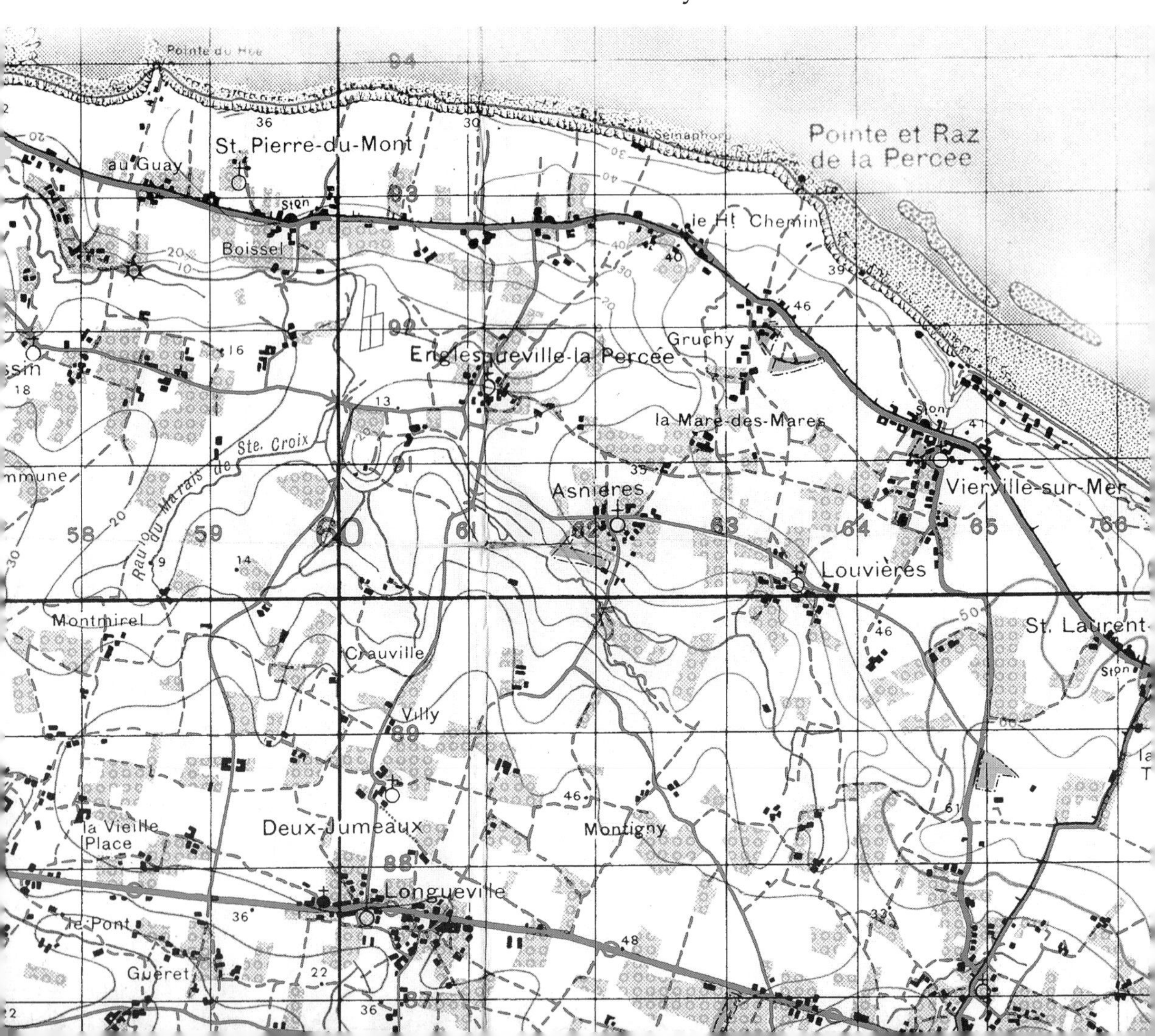

garrison and encounters with and ambushes of enemy troops moving towards OMAHA. Plans were, however, being made by the Germans to attack both the slim American beachhead at Colleville and that at Pointe du Hoc. *I/914 Regiment* was given the task of destroying the isolated toehold that the Rangers held around *Stützpunkt* 75. Seriously outnumbered but with the enemy being forced to operate at night thanks to Allied air superiority, the odds still seemed in favour of the Germans.

*Oberstleutnant* Ziegelmann the S1 or Chief of Staff of *352. Division* recalled that for General Kraiss the Rangers at Pointe du Hoc represented another beachhead that could be developed to threaten their attempts to contain the Americans at OMAHA and of course the Rangers were blocking an important route. These factors help explain why the Germans committed

*Colonel Rudder's HQ was established on the cliff top.*

precious resources to regain Pointe du Hoc, when they surely knew that the guns had been destroyed.

Just before midnight the first of *I/914 Regiment's* attacks fell on the Rangers' positions. These were not 'the elderly gentlemen of Hitler's last reserves' found in the coastal divisions but field grade infantry and they knew their business. In a silent approach through the thick country, they got to within thirty yards of Rangers forward outposts before attempting to rush the Americans. Sergeant Honhart and his BAR gunner were lucky to make it back to the line. The appearance of the Germans had prompted return fire from the main defensive line. The Germans withdrew having driven-in the outposts and gained a better knowledge of the Rangers' positions in the hedgerows.

The Americans were shaken and there had been some calls to withdraw but sufficient men remained in the line although few knew little about the situation other than what was going on within their own few yards of night vision.

The enemy's next attack, at about 0100 hours, was altogether more serious. Again the Germans approached silently to within 100 yards before 'going noisy' with their attack; off to a flank, whistles blew and names were shouted, all accompanied by high volumes of mortar and machine-gun fire, which included tracer. The whole was designed to intimidate the defenders and break their morale but the Rangers stood their ground and returned fire. The Germans withdrew again.

The next attack came in at 0300 hours along the Rangers' front but the main effort appears to have been further east along the line than was the case in the previous attacks. The Germans this time used an old Eastern Front trick: again there was plenty of machine-gun fire but the Americans noticed that the fire was slightly high, with the bullets cracking through the hedgerow above them, that the enemy infantry crawling forward under its cover. This time the Germans reached the hedgerow and having gained a foothold in the Rangers' position proceeded to break their hold. About fifty exhausted Americans withdrew in some confusion to the road before being pulled back to a tighter defensive position within the area of the battery. The Germans had not been able to press home their advantage during the withdrawal, being as disorganised after the fight in the darkness as the Rangers.

With the failure of the German counter-attacks to destroy the Rangers, during 7 June the *352. Division* began to withdraw to the line of the Aure River. Rommel's strategy of destruction of the enemy on the beaches had failed. However, the Rangers were not left alone at Pointe du Hoc; delaying forces remained forward to engage any movement and keep them under fire from mortars and artillery. These inflicted further casualties.

## Relief

Repeated radio requests for reinforcement by Colonel Rudder were brusquely turned down without explanation; passing details of the parlous situation at OMAHA was not practical and anyway the focus was on bigger issues. With the Pointe du Hoc guns destroyed, not diverting resources away from US V Corps's main effort to establish a beachhead, to a small and expendable group, was a hard but plain military decision. The first relief to reach Rudder came from OMAHA Beach. They

*Wounded Rangers and German prisoners being brought aboard USS* Texas *following the fierce fighting behind the OMAHA beachhead.*

were twenty-three men Lieutenant Parker's platoon from Company A of 5th Rangers who had become separated from the rest of his company during the chaos of the landing on OMAHA. Believing that the remainder of his battalion was ahead of him, Parker followed his original mission and headed across country to Pointe du Hoc. Arriving at 2100 hours he brought with him twenty prisoners. These Rangers made a small but in the circumstance very welcome reinforcement.

Monitoring the increasingly serious situation at Pointe du Hoc, a Ranger staff officer in Admiral Hall's HQ, Major Street, gained permission to send help. Admiral Bryant made available food and ammunition from the USS *Texas*, while Street recovered two isolated groups of 5th Rangers from OMAHA. Two landing craft laden with thirty men and supplies headed for Rudder's beleaguered command. It goes without saying that this slim re-reinforcements not only helped the physical needs of the defence but also provided a much needed psychological boost to ease the feeling of isolation and betrayal that had grown in the minds of the Rangers.

The parlous situation on the evening of D Day at OMAHA where General Gerow's V US Corps had fought hard to get ashore and were now fighting even harder to stay ashore, let alone advance, had recast the role of the nine Ranger companies who had been diverted to OMAHA. The detail of their beach landing and their battle on the bluffs will be told in the next chapter.

With the changed situation, Colonel Canham of 116th Infantry, stopped Company B, 5th Rangers from attempting to break through German positions in the area of Vierville. This latter village had to be held for the sake of the overall situation at OMAHA and despite Schneider's protestations the Rangers were put into defensive positions on the evening of 6 June.

The following morning, however, a task force was assembled to drive west. It was made up of survivors of 1/116th Infantry (about 250), the remains of Companies A, B and C 2nd Rangers (totalling about eighty-five men) and Companies C and D of 5th Rangers, plus eight Shermans from 743 tank battalion.

*Rudder's men awaiting relief from off the Pointe.*

Initially opposition was light, with many isolated groups of Germans being mopped up, presumably having been left behind during the withdrawal of their division. Their four mile advance in four hours is considered very good progress in such thick hedgerow country with an *ad hoc* force. Resistance on the axis of the coastal road, however, stiffened as the Rangers reached the village of St- Pierre-du-Mont at midday. To make matters worse a mined demolition crater on the road separated the tanks from the infantry they were supporting. As the afternoon wore on, the westward advance stalled less than a mile from Pointe du Hoc and the tanks were ordered back to the beachhead.

Overnight on the 7th/8th, patrols were sent out to slip through the German outposts to reach Colonel Rudder. One patrol commanded by Sergeant Raaen got through and not only reached 2nd Ranger's HQ but came back having laid-out a telephone cable. Direct contact with the depleted Rangers at the Pointe had been made!

On the morning of 8 June, with the pressing danger of V Corps being thrown back into the sea past, 116th Infantry promptly went over to the offensive. The relief of Pointe du Hoc by Schneider's Force C and 1/116th Infantry was just a part of a larger scheme to drive 29th US Division westward in accordance with the original but much delayed plan.

The operation to relieve Colonel Rudder's Force A was complete by midday, some forty-eight hours behind schedule but was marred by a final friendly fire incident when 3/116th advancing south of the relieving force heard the sound of German weapons coming from the Pointe and engaged, with tanks and mortars. The US Navy had to be prevented from joining the 'battle', which was only stopped by a Ranger jumping up onto a tank and explaining the situation.

Thus ended an epic of American military history of which the Rangers are justifiably proud. They defied the staff offices analogy of 'an old woman with a boom', having scaled the cliff in the face of opposition and destroyed a gun battery that posed a significant threat to the US landings. It was a plan that had gone wrong at a number of points and relief was 48 hours late, but the small group of Rangers had persevered, overcome challenges that would have been insurmountable for lesser soldiers and held out against all the odds.

### Visiting the Battlefield

A tour of the Ranger battlefield at Pointe du Hoc is dramatic, being in a preserved setting that is easy to visit in a relatively short time. Although to walk the actions subsequent to the landing and capture of the battery may take some time.

The Pointe du Hoc battery is located just off the D514 to the west of OMAHA Beach between the coastal town of Grandcamp-Maisy and Vierville. If travelling west from OMAHA it is an easy matter to follow the action of 5th Rangers fighting towards Pointe du Hoc

Follow the signs and turn off the D514 on the approach road and park (this area was formally a part of the minefield). The route into the battery area, via the visitor centre and facilities, is best and takes one through the then barbed wire protected minefields into the eastern portion of the battery. Follow the path to the cliff. It is below the anti-aircraft casemate, with the viewing platform where Colonel Rudder established his HQ in a cleft caused by a bomb or shell. From here it is possible to work out, using the maps in this chapter, where the various boat loads of Rangers landed. Sadly it is not always possible to visit the command post bunker built into the pointe or the Ranger memorial due to the unstable cliff face. The remainder of the site speaks for itself!

To reach the place where the guns were found and destroyed, retrace steps back to the car park and to the roundabout. Turn left and less than fifty yards on the right there is a track. Follow this for 200 yards and you will be in the area of the orchard and the Rangers' defensive line. The orchard has long gone and there are now fewer hedgerows. This is private land and the farmer takes a dim view of visitors on his property without permission.

The relief Force arrived from the east between the church of St-Pierre-du-Mont and the D514. The Ranger Museum in Grandcamp-Maisy is worth a visit, as is the nearby battery (signed from the D514 south of Grandcamp-Maisy), which has recently opened to the public and is steadily being improved as an attraction. It is worth noting that this battery was always planned to be the subsequent objective for the Ranger Force.

## Chapter Four

# OMAHA Beachhead

Company C, 2nd Rangers (Force B), having a separate mission of their own, was always intended to be landed over the very western end of OMAHA Beach in CHARLIE Sector. They were to land just behind the first assault wave of the 116th Infantry at H+3 minutes and destroy German strongpoint *Widerstandnest* 73 above the western end of the beach. This task completed they were then to advance westward along the coast clearing up known enemy positions, including the defended radar site near Pointe de la Percée. (*WN 74*) Then rejoining the main body of 2nd Rangers, they would continue the advance west with the battalion clearing the coastal strip as a part of the drive to link up with amphibious and airborne forces around UTAH Beach.

The other two companies (A and B) from 2nd Rangers who were not involved in the initial assault on Pointe du Hoc *Stützpunkt 75* (*S 75*) and all six companies of Lieutenant Colonel Schneider's 5th Rangers (together making up Force C) were only to land at OMAHA in the event of a failure of Force A to seize the battery form the sea. In the event without receiving the code word from Colonel Rudder by 0700 hours, in accordance with orders, Force C set off to OMAHA, with a view to getting ashore at H Hour+70 minutes and slipping through the German defences, marching five miles to the west to attack *S 75* from its equally formidable landward side.

### *Widerstandnest* 73

*WN 73* was the western-most of thirteen German platoon- or company-sized defensive positions that on the bluffs covered the beach, or lower down blocked the valley exits (draws) running inland. Each *Widerstandnest* contained of a mix of rifles, machine guns, mortars, anti-tank guns and artillery pieces, as appropriate to cover their bit of ground with overlapping and interlocking arcs of fire.

*WN 73* sited on the cliffs was ideally sited to cover the length of what was to become Dog Sector of the beach with fire. When

*A German NCO uses a specially designed periscope to scan the foot of the cliffs for any sign of an intruder, saboteur or invader.*

*352nd Division* took over defence of Coastal Sectors 1 to 3 during April and May 1944, the coastal infantry of *III/726* were left in place and it was *Kompanie 11* that was responsible, with attached artillery etc., for the Vierville area at the western end of the beach, encompassing *WN 70–73*. These three positions, in a defensive scheme that was medieval in its simplicity, covered virtually every inch of beach and bluff with cross fire of every type. Landing in the first wave was a terrible proposition for those leading the assault but without the removal of *WN 73* from the matrix of the German defences, breaking into *Festung Europa* via the Vierville draw (DOG 1) would be all but impossible.

The network of *WN 73's* trenches, on the upper slopes and top of the bluffs, extended for several hundred yards and included troop shelters, a 75mm gun, numerous machine guns and three 81mm mortars. The position was surrounded by mines and barbed wire on the landward side and the whole position was built around what was referred to as the 'Fortified House', which was set in a cleft in the cliff, Although this stone-built house was built looking out to sea it offered little in the way of a useful field of fire but it was used by the Germans as accommodation, etc.

### Run-in and Beach Assault

With an H Hour of 0630 hours and a long twelve mile run-in from the Transport Area, Captain Groranson's Company C of 2nd Rangers shared the misery of sea sickness with the rest of the assault force. They were in three British-crewed LCAs on the

*US Landing Craft approach OMAHA Beach 6 June 1944.*

*The run-in to OMAHA Beach.*

left flank of the assault flotilla due to touchdown just eight minutes after the amphibious Sherman DDs of B Company 743 Tank Battalion (H-5 minutes) and three minutes after Company A of 116th Infantry (H Hour).

The weather was as rough as predicted and the three to six foot waves were obviously too much for the low freeboard of the barely seaworthy DD tanks, so the decision was taken to run the tanks to within wading depth of the beach. One of the four Landing Craft Tank (LCT) was hit by artillery and it with its cargo of four tanks was lost. The other three LCTs made it and discharged the remaining twelve tanks onto the beach, where four were knocked out in short order by German anti-tank fire from the 75 and 88mm guns in *WN 72*. At H Hour the surviving eight tanks were too busy fighting for their own lives to play the role of mobile pill-boxes for Company A of 116th Infantry running out onto the open beach. Despite the strong easterly current that displaced most of the invasion fleet about 800 yards to the left of their correct landing, aided by the rising cliffs and buildings, Company A touched down correctly but this meant that there was a large gap to their east and they were in effect isolated, along with some beach clearance engineers who had landed earlier.

Company A had come under fire as they approached the beach but as the landing ramps went down on DOG GREEN, the enemy fire redoubled and men fell. Ahead of them was just less than three hundred yards of open sand with no cover and only a few beach obstacles. Casualties mounted, particularly amongst officers and NCOs, as bullets cracked and mortar bombs and shells exploded about them. The largely leaderless survivors of Company A 116th Infantry were driven back to the cover of the surf and obstacles. The hell of OMAHA had begun!

Nine minutes behind Company A came Company C of 2nd Rangers landing at 0645. On the run-in they lost a third of their strength when one of their LCAs was swamped and sank. Some overloaded men drowned but others were picked up by the US Coastguard and evacuated. They touched down slightly east of their intended location but with the cliffs still rising at the back of the beach to *WN 73*. The cliffs were an unlikely assault route compared with the sloping bluffs just to the east, the German fire that covered this part of CHARLIE Sector of the beach was less heavy here than further east. This saved the remains of Company C from sharing the fate of other early landers on the adjacent Dog beach.

*US Infantary struggle ashore into the hell of Omaha Beach.*

The specially selected and trained volunteers had had the mantra of the Commandos and Rangers drummed into them to 'Get off the beach' and they kept going. It is, however, estimated that some nineteen Rangers lost their lives on the beach and only half of the company reached the sea wall.

The wounded that survived to tell the tale describe a hell of



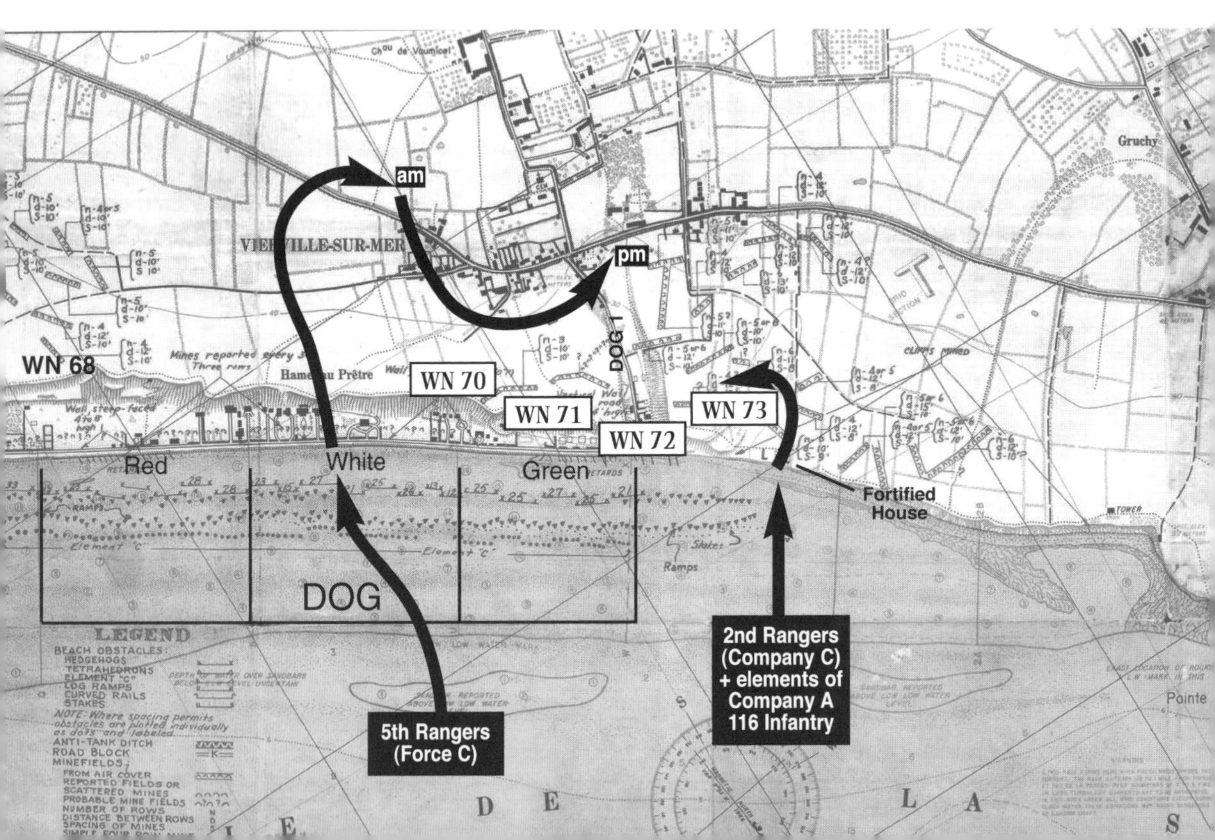

noise and destruction, sand being thrown up by repeated explosions of mortars and shells, the crack of bullets as they passed overhead and the distinctive strike of bullets on the steel hedgehog obstacles. All was laced with screams of the wounded and dying men, as well as the rush and blast of incoming naval gunfire passing just overhead.

**The Attack on *WN 73***

Somehow the Rangers made it to the foot of the cliff and out of the arc of fire of small arms but mortars continued to seek them along with a new threat, grenades being thrown from the cliff top. As at Pointe du Hoc these blast grenades were less than fully effective on the rubble-strewn beach. Captain Goranson was lucky to survive the blast of a stick grenade that landed between his legs.

Where the Rangers were, alone with a handful of infantrymen from Company A, the cliff was not scalable, so they moved west along the foot, beyond *WN 73*, to a cleft that had been identified on air photos two hundred yards away. Here Private Stephens climbed the loose cliff using his bayonet and Commando knife and trailing a climbing rope from his waist. Reaching the top he tied off the rope to a barbed wire picket and the others climbed up hand-over-hand, slipping and sliding on the damp and loose cliff. Amongst those making it to the top of the cliff were Lieutenant Salomon who had a piece of mortar splinter removed from his shoulder at the base before making the climb.

At approximately 0700 hours, with the Rangers, undoubtedly the first to get from OMAHA to the top of the bluffs, making their way up the cliffs they came under fire from *WN 73*, less than two hundred yards to the east. The Rangers started to probe forward to identify the German positions with about twenty men from the 116th's Company B climbing the cliff to join the Rangers. The infantry gave covering fire while the handful of Rangers stormed the 'Fortified House' and trenches. The house, not really a part of the German defences, was quickly taken but the trenches were a maze and the Germans had the advantage of knowing how to outflank the Rangers in a deadly game of cat and mouse. Lieutenant Salomon and his men cleared German

*Landing craft disgorged troops onto fire-swept beaches. The smoke-shrouded bluffs rise beyond.*

bunkers and weapons pits with grenades including white phosphorous and occupied them, in the process denying some excellent fire positions to the Germans, from where the Rangers were also able to bring fire down onto *WN 71* and *72* blocking DOG 1. The extent of this fire was of course limited by the number of men occupying *WN 73* and resources that could be spared from keeping the German counter-attacks at bay, as well as a lack of ammunition. But it helped.

**Force C Arrives**

Staff Sergeant Miller described the 5th Battalion's run-in to the beach:

> *The sea was pretty rough. We were each issued two puke bags, and in our boat of 30-some men, there were only two of us that didn't use them. Probably most of them used both. We were really crammed into these assault boats, there was absolutely no room back or front. The boat pitched quite a bit which made ideal circumstances for seasickness.*

Five minutes late, Lieutenant Colonel Schneider's eight companies of Rangers from his own 5th Battalion, plus two from the 2nd arrived on OMAHA amidst what many who were there described as 'a hell of confusion and death'. The plan stated that at H+70 minutes the beach should be clear, with signs set up to mark routes through the beach obstacles and the mined sand dunes at the back of the beach. But this was clearly not the case. As each successive wave of landing craft approached the beach it was greeted with a deluge of fire from machine guns, artillery and mortars, while anti-tank fire swept the beach, which was dotted with burning hulks that billowed thick black smoke until the fires were doused by the rising tide.

Landing on DOG White, with the tide rising amidst the mine-tipped obstacles, 5th Rangers stepped out into a blood-tinged surf, where bodies washed backwards and forwards with the waves. Driven on by their officers and NCOs, the Rangers dashed to get off the beach, charging through surprised soldiers of the 116th who were sheltering in the surf and amongst the obstacles. 5th Rangers reported that,

> *The LCA's slowly threaded their way through gaps in the lines of obstacles and at H+75, 0745, the first wave consisting of one half Battalion Headquarters, Companies A, B, and E, landed on Omaha Dog White Beach at a point approximately 800 yards east of Exit D-1. The Battalion Commander, Lieutenant Colonel Max F. Schneider, had ordered the flotilla commander to touch down his craft east of the intended landing point, Dog Green, because the tremendous volume of fire which covered that portion*

*One of the sixteen iconic pictures of Omaha.*

> *of the beach was inflicting a large number of casualties on the preceding wave.*

Staff Sergeant Miller recalled the landing:

> *The tide was now coming in a bit and this started to be a serious problem for a number of wounded that were scattered along the beach at the places they had been hit. They were crying out to us, but if they couldn't move themselves there was little we could do for them, at least from our point of view. Most of them eventually drowned.*

Landing on DOG WHITE the experience of 5th Rangers was entirely different from that of the 2nd, who had touched down just a few hundred yards to the west. Colonel Schneider led his 450 men across the beach losing fewer than ten.

This totally different experience was by no means unique. For example, on JUNO Beach, B Company of the Canadian's Winnipeg Rifles was virtually destroyed, while two hundred yards away, A Company crossed the beach virtually unscathed. The reasons for the lack of fire on Dog White spotted by Colonel Schneider can only be guessed at: obscuration by smoke, effective neutralisation of enemy artillery by naval gunfire, or the defenders simply engaging closer targets which represented the greatest threat to them.

**Advance up the Bluffs**

Meanwhile, realizing that they had reached the sea wall too far east, the 2nd Rangers turned right and followed the wall, before crossing the beach road and heading up the bluffs in a south-westerly direction towards their route to Pointe du Hoc. Once off the hell of the beach, moving on the bluffs was not as dangerous as it might seem, as the ground there was more broken, pock-marked with shell-holes and wreathed in smoke from grass fires started by the bombardment. This confirms the validity of Colonel George Taylor's statement made just a little later at the eastern end of the beach, 'Two kinds of people are staying on this beach, the dead and those who are going to die. Now let's get the hell out of here!'

The advance up the hundred foot high bluffs took the two 2nd Rangers companies to the crest between *WN 70* and *WN 71*, which they reached at 0824. This was not a speedy process taking just under an hour and a quarter from landing to achieve. With them were some stout hearts from Company D of the 116th Infantry.

5th Rangers' After Action Report recorded:

*At a signal of the Battalion Commander the leading echelon scrambled over the wall, blew gaps in the protective wire, and protected from enemy observation by the curtain of rising smoke advanced unhesitatingly to a point near the top of the hill. Here the smoke had cleared and the topographical crest was being swept by effective automatic weapons fire. First Lieutenant Francis W. Dawson, Company D, led his platoon over the top and wiped out a strongpoint thereby enabling the battalion to advance.*

Staff Sergeant Miller recalled how it happened:

*The officers finally decided that we had to forget about our original mission for the moment and had to concentrate on creating a beachhead, since the infantry (the 116th Regiment) that had proceeded us on the beach had not made any progress so far. The engineers brought in the Bangalore torpedo's and shoved them under the barbed wire that was running along the seawall at the top of the beach. When a breech was blown in this seawall, we could start our ascent on this very steep hillside, which was still obscured by smoke.*

General Norman Cota

In fact the smoke that covered them on the climb up the slope was so heavy it forced some men to put on gas masks. By the time the crest was reached, platoon formations were disorganized and contacts between companies was lost. Colonel Schneider's report described the advance up the upper slopes and crest of the bluff.

*Because of numerous minefields the battalion now changed into a column formation and, after winding through their intricate pattern, the leading*

> *unit, Company B, reached the St. Laurent-Sur-Mer – Vierville-Sur-Mer road at a point approximately one (1) Kilometer east of Vierville-Sur-Mer. During the advance, numerous Germans, well concealed in weapons pits constructed in hedgerows, were killed.*

Again Staff Sergeant Miller adds detail to the report:

> *While going up the Bluff, I suddenly realized that one of my squads was missing. Both squads had been by my side the whole time, but now one was gone. I decided to go back down the hill and there I found my men. When I asked for an explanation why they weren't yet on their way to the top, they told me that someone had told them that there was a minefield on the road to the top. I drove them up the hill and once there they too realized that they were safer there than on the beach. We could hear the* [enemy's] *shells go overhead on their way to the beach.*

By 0900, 5th Rangers and a mixed bag of infantry from the 116th and some engineers, altogether totalling approximately 600 men, were also ensconced on the crest of the bluffs in the gap between *WN 68* and *WN 70*. With the powerful presence of Brigadier General Norman Cota, the Assistant Divisional Commander of 29th Division, they were pushing inland, with the assistance of suppressive fire from destroyers which came dangerously close inshore, towards the coast road between Vierville and St Laurent. Here they were checked around midday by a virtual wall of machine gun fire from mutually supporting enemy positions dug into the hedgerows. Attempts to pursue a southerly advance were eventually abandoned and Schneider took his Rangers westward to Vierville with a view to breaking out towards Pointe du Hoc. 5th Rangers' report describes the situation:

> *Company E attempted a penetration to the South but was halted by intense machine gun fire. An 81 mm mortar concentration fired by Company C knocked out several of these positions but they were rapidly replaced and the advance remained halted. Company B advanced toward Vierville-Sur-Mer receiving heavy sniper and machine gun fire. Several direct hits from enemy artillery on the rear of the battalion column caused numerous casualties.*

Having shifted its weight of attack toward Vierville the battalion had to overcome what it describes as 'considerable sniper resistance'. They advanced through the village to the western outskirts 'where it was again held up by a large volume of concentrated machine gun and sniper fire'. At this juncture, contact was established with the Commanding Officer 1st 116th Infantry and approximately 150 men of his unit. As night fell, the Rangers were ordered to dig-in a perimeter defence for the night west of Vierville. Companies A, B, and C of 2nd Rangers, numbering about eighty men, also took over a part of the defended area. Surviving Shermans of the 743rd Tank Battalion moved up to support the thinly spread Rangers. Except for occasional exchanges with enemy snipers and machine guns, the night was relatively quiet.

The 5th Battalion's history records that 'The results for the first day were about 100 prisoners taken, 150 enemy dead, and approximately sixty Rangers killed and wounded.'

Landing on the western end of OMAHA Beach, Ranger Forces B and C had made all the difference amongst the inexperienced National Guardsmen and GIs of 29th US Infantry Division. The Rangers had led the way across 'the hell and chaos' of the beach to be the first, in the case of Company C, 2nd Rangers, up onto the bluffs and in case of Max Schneider's 5th Rangers amongst the first in the central area of DOG SECTOR to reach the top. Grandoson's Company C had got into an excellent position in *WN 73* but had been too weak to exploit it to its full potential Nonetheless, the sheer guts, determination and examples of small groups of Rangers from companies of both battalions had made all the difference and contributed significantly to the unhinging of the German positions between the crest of the bluff and Vierville that dominated a large part of OMAHA on D Day and in so doing graphically showed their mettle. Only orders to dig-in and hold a sector of the ever-so-slim beachhead's perimeter against expected counter-attack prevented Schneider from marching west to relieve Colonel Rudder's force at Pointe du Hoc.

## Visiting the Battlefield

The Ranger Battlefield is confined to the western end of OMAHA Beach and these instructions are similarly confined to this area.

If coming from Pointe du Hoc on the D514 take the turning down the Draw (Dog 1), past the pieces of floating roadway from the Mulberry Harbour and park in the area at the bottom of the Draw. The exit from the beach was blocked by a thick concrete wall and covered by the selection of large casemates in front of you and by strong points up on the bluffs (*WN 72 & 71*) to the right and left. Look carefully and you can see the 'murder holes' in the cliff.

Walk down to the 88-mm casemate with the US National Guard Monument built on top of it and look at the gunners' view down the length of the beach. It is easy to understand how any vehicle that managed to get ashore within 2,000 yards of this point would fall victim to this powerful gun.

Still looking east down the beach, immediately in front of you is where Companies A and B of 2nd Rangers and the whole of 5th Rangers landed amongst the remains of 29th Division's 116th Regiment. They were instrumental in forcing their way up the bluffs between *WN 70* and 71.

Walk west past the double anti tank casemate, past the remaining piece of Mulberry Harbour pierhead washed up on the beach. You are now crossing from DOG onto the precipitous CHARLIE Sector. As the cliff rises there is a concrete track with an obvious square faced opening. Walk up this track. The casemate contained a French 75mm gun that fired HE shells down onto the beach.

Just beyond the casemate is a narrow set of steps leading up to the cliff. While these steps do take the visitor up to the cliff top, and do not lead close to the edge, the visitor should, however, seriously consider his, her or the group's abilities and the weather and ground conditions before deciding to go on up to the main part of *WN 73*.

From the trenches half way up, it is easy to fully appreciate the almost 'medieval simplicity' of the German defences and the vulnerability of the GIs disembarking on to the beach below. Follow the fence line or trench past the remains of a bunker position and on to the top of the bluff. Depending on the state of the vegetation it is possible to see or get into a variety of concrete positions which were all cleared by the Rangers. In the campsite a *Tobrukstand* machine gun position can be seen – converted into a large flowerpot! Follow the wooden cliff top fence. In the cleft in the cliff on can see the remains of the ruined 'Fortified House', through which Company C fought to gain access to *WN 73*.

CHAPTER FIVE

# Operation AUBERY – 47 Commando's Attack on Port-en-Bessin

47 Commando Royal Marines was formed from 10th Battalion RM at the Depot Barracks in Dorchester on 1 August 1943, under a new commanding officer, Lieutenant Colonel CF Phillips. A hard core of experienced Commandos posted in from other Commando units formed a solid foundation. Having completed basic training, the unit moved to the Commando Training Depot at Achnacarry, where the Marines earned their coveted green berets following a course pioneered by the Army Commandos that tested their determination, fitness and stamina; all in addition to high standards of soldiering. They became a fully fledged if inexperienced Commando in January 1944.

Rapidly emerging as one of the best Commandos units, 47 was allocated what arguably, proved to be the most difficult objective of the eight Commando units in action on D Day. Port-en-Bessin was a small port in the centre of the fifteen-mile gap between the British 50th Division on GOLD Beach and 1st (US) Division on eastern end of OMAHA. 50th Division's historian described the Commando's objective:

> *The small fishing port formed the right hand boundary of the 50th Division sector, and its capture as early as possible was considered vital to the security of XXX Corps' right flank and to effectively link-up with the 1st US Division, which was our right hand neighbour. The town is in a hollow between cliffs approximately two hundred feet high. It is fronted by a promenade and backed by closely packed houses with narrow streets. Towards the south-east and southern part of town the houses are less closely packed and are interspersed with gardens and small fields. Approaches to the town are very open and exposed, particularly the south-east approaches.*
>
> *Like other ports on the Normandy coast, Port-en-Bessin was well defended by a system of strong points on the cliffs overlooking the town and including emplaced guns sited to fire*

*seawards, guns and machine guns in open embrasures capable of firing both to sea and inland, trench systems, surrounded by minefields and wire at the various strong-points, and fortified houses and pillboxes on the mole and in the town itself.*

*The garrison was thought to be approximately one company, with some fifty naval personnel in the town and port defences.'*

Colonel Phillips was given a free reign as to how he would carry out his mission. However, he ruled-out a direct amphibious assault on the heavily defended port as being 'too great a risk to entertain'. Instead, he elected to conduct an organised landing, before marching across country to attack the port and its defences from landward. Therefore, 47 Commando would be under command for landing of 50th Division's right assault brigade, 231 Brigade, and touch down in Normandy behind the assault infantry at H Hour + 2 Hours (0925 hours). Once concentrated ashore they were to strike across enemy held country on foot, to reach Port-en-Bessin, fifteen miles away. Lieutenant Colonel Nevill, CO of the Devons in 231 Brigade, describes an incident at the first 50th Division OVERLORD briefing in April 1944:

*There was a tense moment at the Divisional Commander's Conference when General Graham asked Colonel Phillips whether in addition to his other tasks, he could mop up the odd position, which was known to exist between Port-en-Bessin and Longues. Colonel Phillips replied that General Dempsey had personally instructed him to capture the Port; that he would then be relieved by 50 Division, thus enabling him and his unit to return to England (laughter). He respectfully regretted therefore that he would be unable to assist in this small matter (loud laughter).'*

47 Commando's mission was eventually confirmed in 231 Infantry Brigade's operation order as follows:

*PHASE IV: STRAWBERRY*

*R Marines - 47 RM Commando will land approx H plus 2 hours on JIG Sector under Op Control of 231 Inf Bde and will capture Port-en-Bessin.*

*Phase 1. Land H+2. Assembly area just W of La*

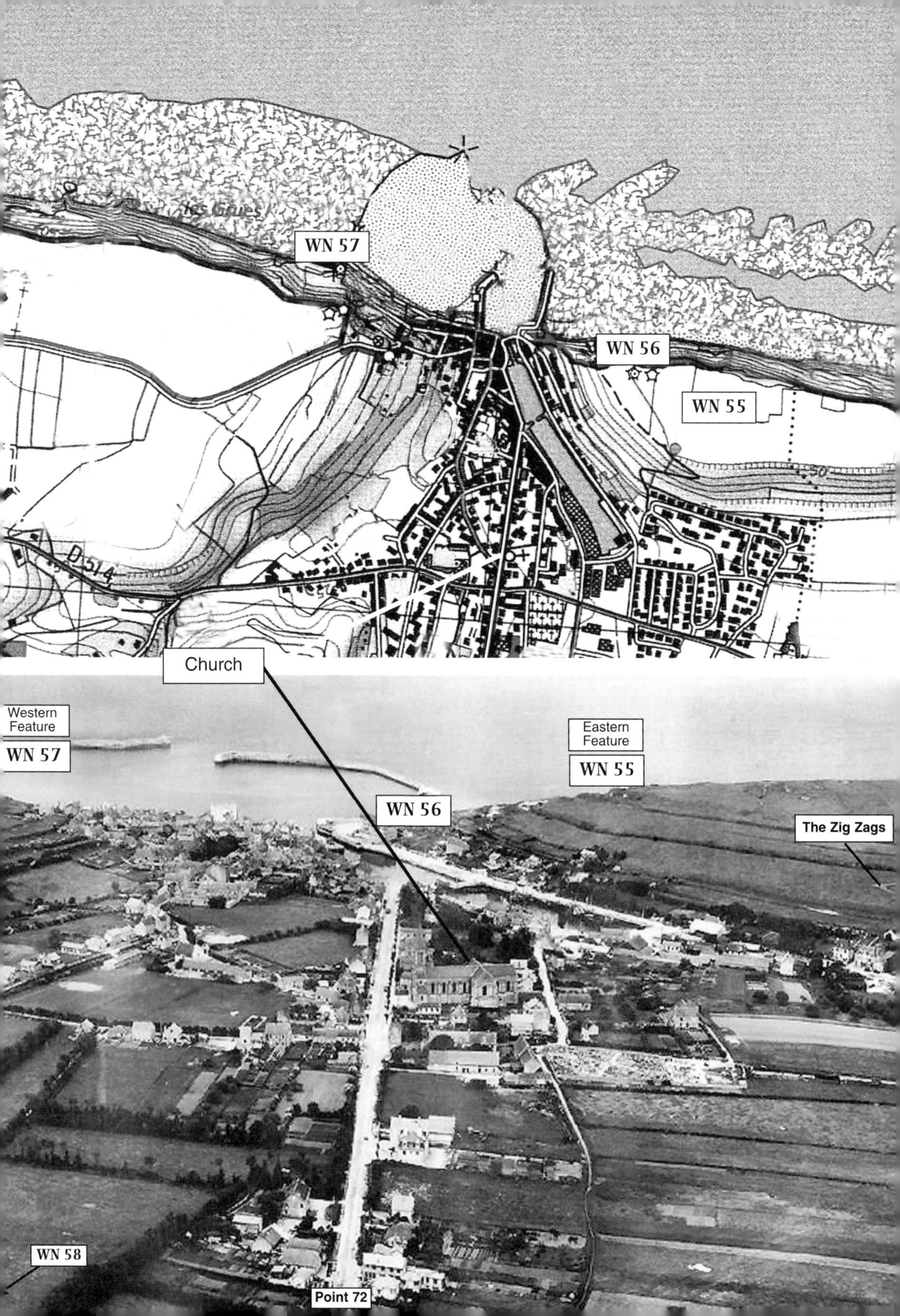

les Gues
WN 57
WN 56
WN 55
D 514
Church
Western
Feature
WN 57
Eastern
Feature
WN 55
WN 56
The Zig Zags
WN 58
Point 72

*Rossiere by H+3 via check pt 876859.*

*Phase 2. Seize Pt 72 by H+5, later if en positions have to be bypassed.*

*Phase 3. Capture high ground feature E of the basin in Port-en-Bessin, not before H+6, subject to time of air support request.*

*Phase 4. Capture of high ground - W of Port-en-Bessin.*

In common with the other units attacking coastal objectives, a considerable range of fire support was available to 47 Commando. This included one US destroyer that was to suppress the defences of Port-en-Bessin up to H+6 hours. In addition, a Forward Officer Bombardment (FOB), who would accompany 47, was to call for fire from the French cruiser *Montcalm's* nine six inch guns, which were on call from H+4, in a forty-minute bombardment. A Forward Observation Officer (FOO) from 147 Field Regiment was to have fire from his regiment's 25-pounders available to 47 from H+3. Finally, a US Artillery FOO, having landed at OMAHA was planned to join 47 in the area of Point 72. Superimposed on this very heavy naval and ground fire was close air support sorties for fifteen minutes before 47's attack on the main enemy position on the high ground to the east of the port. By any measure, this was an impressive range of firepower.

*French cruiser* Montcalm.

**Run-in and Landing**

Captain RE Jefereys Task Force J4 bearing the Commando Group crossed the Channel in LCIs from Warsash and Landing Ships Infantry (LSI) from Southampton. Like the US Rangers, 47 embarked on two of the larger LSI 'mother ships', the converted merchantman SS *Victoria* and HMS *Princess Josephine Charlotte* and transfer respectively to the six LCAs of 508 Assault Flotilla and the eight landing craft of 502 Assault Flotilla. Medical Office

John Forfar, was aboard the SS *Victoria*:

> *There was still a swell following the previous day's storm and the ship headed south through the Solent in the gathering dusk, only the droning of planes overhead and the swish of the ship's movement through the water disturbed the throb of its engines. Below decks the final briefing of the troops and careful and somewhat anxious, re-examination of weapons and equipment was taking place. There was a sense of relief and a certain amount of badinage, but there could have been few who did not with some apprehension, have a concern that their courage, their determination, their will to fight would match up to what lay ahead.*

The crossing went well and the two ships hove-to six miles out in the Transit Area on time. With a landing time of H+2 Hours the Commandos had a grandstand view of the bombardment and departure of the LCAs containing the assault troops of 231 Brigade: 1 Dorset and 1 Hampshire. Also going in behind the assault troops were the Royal Naval Beach Commandos, with their task of marking exits and calling in landing craft to unload. Petty Officer Eric Gear of Q Commando was with them, fortuitously landing at the Pointe, on the boundary of KING and JIG sectors where the enemy fire was at its least effective:

> *It was a very windy day, and the sea was quite rough. We unloaded into assault craft-off the French coast and began our run in. The noise was deafening, rocket firing craft, gunfire from a Royal Navy destroyer, and a good deal of gun and rifle fire coming from the beach. The whole length of the beach was covered in smoke, with the beach below the waterline filled with great iron obstacles. We had a fairly dry landing and we were only wet to the knee. Getting ashore was fairly comfortable. The beach in front of us was completely filled with tank traps and it was difficult to see where we were going, what with the smoke and the continuing noise.*
>
> *A few men around me were falling over hit and staggering to get on their feet. It didn't take us long to get to the back of the beach, and it took an even shorter time to realise we were in the wrong place. We also realised that we were under fire from positions along the end of the beach* [WN 37 Le Hamel]. *We*

*returned the fire, but I did not have a clear target as we could not make out where the fire was coming from.*

*It was then that I saw Petty Officers Williams and Hodgetts returning from their encounter with an enemy pillbox. Hodgetts was carrying Williams, who was wounded. They were both from Q Commando, and we heard later that one had provided covering fire as the other jumped on top of the pillbox and threw grenades through the slits* [WN 35] . *We then made our way along the coast towards Le Hamel. There we came face to face with a couple of Jerries in a trench* [WN 35A a section position west of WN 35]. *I was with two other blokes and when we ran towards them they surrendered. By the time we got to where we were supposed to be the whole beach was an organised shambles with abandoned craft, further craft coming in, and some vehicles stuck in the sand. There were the injured, the wounded and a few prisoners.*

It wasn't, however, until well after 47 had landed that the Beach Commando's signs were in place and the exits marked, as they were 'still under fire from points at the back and the ends of the beach'.

In common with British practice, the Transit area was six miles out to sea rather than the US twelve miles, with the obvious benefit to the condition of the assault infantry landing at H Hour. The familiar transfer of 47 to their LCAs also went well and with the mother ships' two flotillas of LCAs forming up in full light, at 0800 hours the run-in to GOLD beach began. Colonel Phillips, however, unlike most of 231 Brigade amongst whom he was landing, realized that he was heading for the wrong point on the GOLD. They too had been set to the east by the tide. Lieutenant Peter Winter RM recalled the correction made to take them into their appointed position on JIG GREEN Sector:

*Our fourteen landing craft came inshore in line astern but the CO did something he shouldn't have and turned parallel to the coast to get to our correct landing beach and made a good target for the Germans.*

Not only were they a target for the unsuppressed enemy but high water was at 1030. This meant that unless the beach obstacles had been cleared by Naval and Royal Engineer clearance teams, 47 would be landing amidst Rommel's 'devil's garden' of obstacles sited on the beach to impede craft attempting to land either side of high water. As the Commandos soon found out, the planned lanes through the obstacles had not been fully cleared.

231 Brigade had a series of problems. Chief of these was that the German defences in le Hamel (*WN 37*) had been missed by the naval bombardment through poor liaison. The air force bombing-run also missed due to the added time of flight because of the poor weather. And finally, the motor launch that was to have controlled the 'drenching fire' of the Royal Artillery's self-propelled Sexton 25-pounders broke down. Consequently, *WN 37* was un suppressed and a 75mm anti-tank gun in a low concrete casemate, joined by machine guns, was able to dominate the beach. Very quickly the beach had become dotted

*47 RM Commando landing on Jig Green East; with orders to pass through the enemy lines, bypassing Arromanches, and capturing Port-en-Bessin ten miles to the west.*

with the knocked out vehicles of 79th Armoured Division's assault armour, the first waves of infantry suffered cruelly and so it went on. Two hours after H Hour, JIG GREEN was still swept by enemy fire that had prevented the clearance of the beach where Colonel Phillips had intended to make his 'well organised landing'. This factor coupled with Colonel Phillips's intention to navigate parallel to the coast to land where 47 should have been, led to a disastrous landing on a scale from which lesser units would have been hard put to recover.

The fourteen LCAs made their way along the coast under enemy fire, through the uncleared and beach obstacles, studded with mines, in a heavy sea. John Forfar recalled:

> *For many in 47 RM Cdo the first hostile shots of war were now sounding from a battery on the high ground above le Hamel and the battery of 6-inch guns at Longues ...both now ranging* [they had lost their rangefinder and were firing blind] *on the approaching assault craft. Spouts of water from exploding shells began to dot the stretch of sea between the LCAs and the coast.*

One of the first craft to be hit bore Q Troop. Men jumped overboard; many overloaded men sank. A total of twenty-six out of the thirty-six aboard drowned. Some survivors, under the circumstances lucky to have been picked up, knew nothing of their experience until they woke up in hospital in the UK.

> *Next the LCA containing half of Y Troop struck a mine and the front of the craft was blown off. As a cloud of spray engulfed it, and then settled, this LCA too was seen to be sinking and men were in the water. Eight in the LCA had been killed and others including the Troop Commander were wounded.*

The increasing numbers of men in the water, attempting to reach the shore, were in danger of being run down by incoming craft whose coxswains were concentrating on avoiding the mine studded beach obstacles that were only now just showing above the rising tide.

47 Commando eventually landed around 0930 hours; the worst time possible for obstacles, mines, sea conditions and congestion in the water and on the beach. Five LCAs had been sunk and another five were damaged, causing casualties and

*Concrete* Tobrukstand *with a single MG 34.*

*Coastal artillery observers at WN37.*

*German defenders in positions on the beach or futher inland were still in action.*

capsizes. The remainder and survivors were scattered across a thousand yards of fire-swept beach, pinned down in the sand dunes. Lieutenant Peter Winter told of his experience:

> *My landing craft hit a mine and I was knocked unconscious for a while. When I woke up, I found myself in the water. I had a broken leg and a broken arm and attempted to swim ashore but*

*Men of 1 Dorset pinned down on the beach amid the wreckage of their carriers.*

> *only ended up going around in circles. A sergeant saw me and despite the awfulness of the situation said "You won't get anywhere fast like that Sir. You had better think of something better." I eventually made it ashore where my MOA* [Marine Officer's Assistant – batman], *Marine Woodgate, met me on the beach with the words "I thought you'd like a cup of tea Sir". I can tell you that no cup of tea ever tasted better. The doctor could do little for us wounded, as he had few orderlies and they had lost all their medical equipment when their landing craft was sunk. It took me three days to reach hospital in England.*

Amongst those who found themselves unwounded in the sea was Sergeant Donald Gardner. 'We swam ashore, about fifty yards, under machine gun fire and at one point I heard someone say "Perhaps we're intruding, this seems to be a private beach". Humour in adversity has always been a feature of life in the Commandos. Many others from the four mined craft were able to swim ashore but invariably they had lost their eighty-eight pounds of weapons and equipment in the process. Once ashore, 47 'concentrated at the back of the beach during clarification of situation ... Mortar fire and shelling of the beach continued'. Initially, only about three hundred of the four hundred and seventy Marines were present. Amongst the missing, was Lieutenant Colonel Phillips. In an often unrecorded loss, only two of the fourteen LCAs, each crewed by two Royal Marines, made it back to the 'mother ships' SS *Victoria* and HMS *Princess Josephine Charlotte*. Most of the crews had been killed.

Not all the Commandos had a wet landing. In an oft-regaled story, 47's veterans recount how the padre, the Reverend Reginald Haw, 'arrived looking very spruce'. He was:

> *... chaffed at being one of the few to land dry, he explained that one baptism a day was enough for any chaplain and that as he had started the day with a baptism of fire there had been no need for him to engage in any further baptismal rites. He described his untroubled run-in. As he had no duties to perform, he sat low down in the LCA and could see nothing. As the boat moved in he heard all manner of crashes and bangs and felt 'reassured' by this intensity of 'covering fire'. His LCA passed clear through the coastal minefield and he stepped ashore dryshod and in the best of spirits to see, suddenly, so many sinking damaged craft, and men swimming in the water, and realised that most of the encouraging noise and explosions which he had heard were missiles coming in the opposite direction from what he had supposed.*

## Assembly and the Move Inland

The citation for Major Patrick Donnell's *Croix de Guerre* with Vermilion Star describes how, with the CO forward on a recce, he

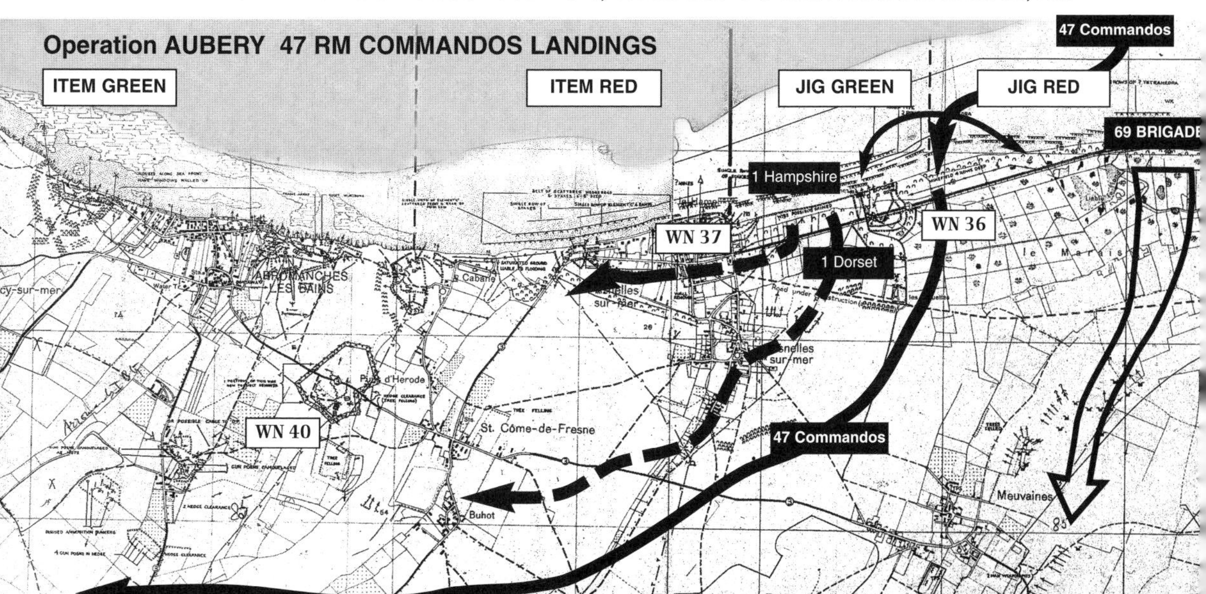

gathered the Commando together and led them off the beach, reporting to commander 231 Brigade, Brigadier Stanier, that they had lost much of their equipment. Advancing behind the Devons, who were beating-off repeated counter-attacks, 47 Commando started its reorganization in the area of Asnelles, which, at the time, was far from secure. Soldiers of 231 Brigade donated items of equipment, as recalled by Private Powis of 2 Devons:

> *A drenched and dripping Commando unit now joined us at the side of the road, they were almost completely unarmed and looked a very sad sight. They explained that they had come in on the high tide and their landing craft had either hit the ramps or bottle mines, so the were forced to throw off their equipment and swim ashore. Having armed themselves with whatever they could from*

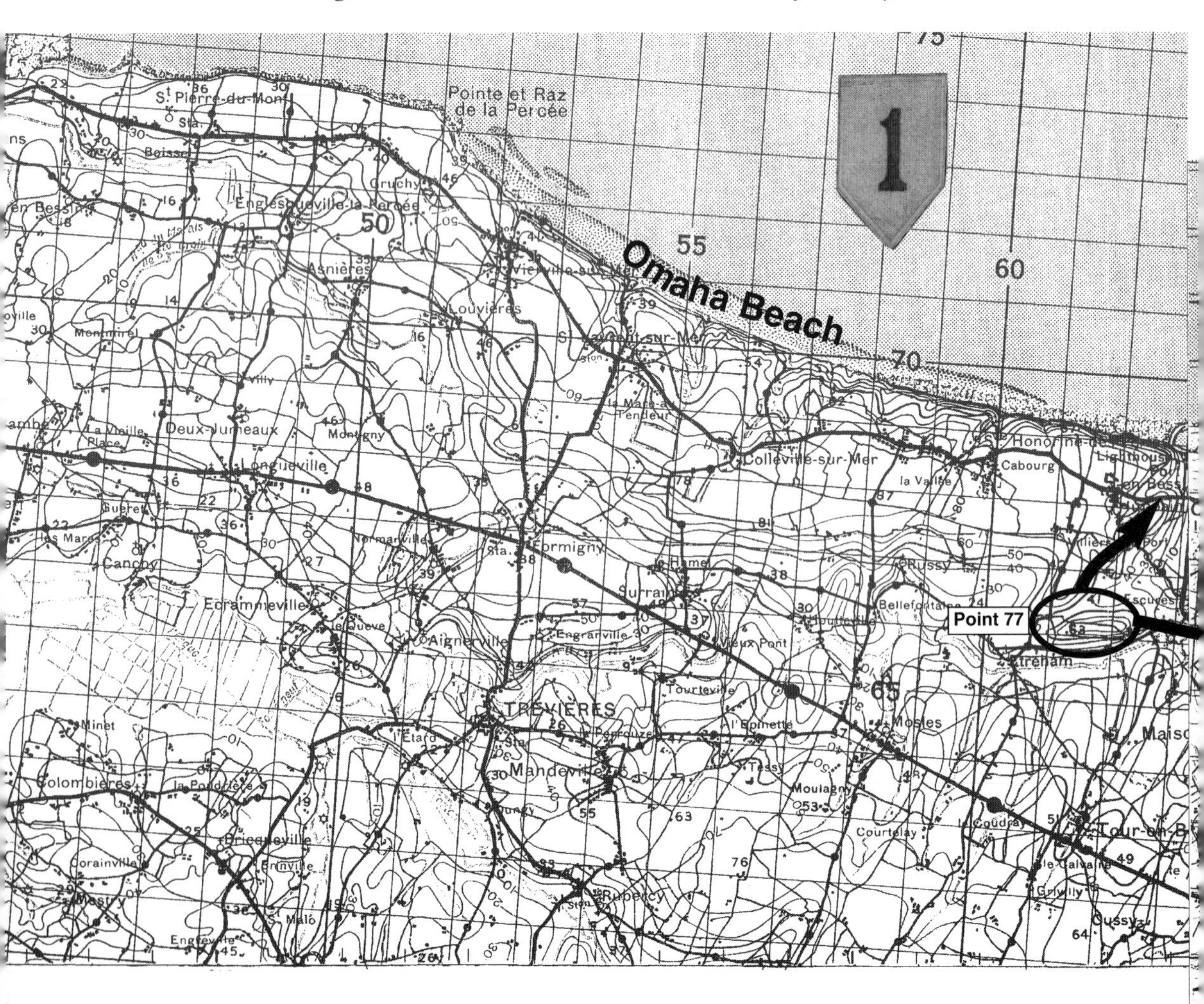

*dead soldiers, they welcomed anything we could spare in the way of armaments and ammunition. I gave them one of my two fifty round bandoliers of rifle ammunition, a grenade and two magazines for the Bren gun.*

*The Commando went along the road furnishing themselves with small arms and ammunition from the German and British soldiers now lying dead there. They filtered through the leading Devon company, engaging the Germans with their captured and borrowed weapons.*

Delays in getting away from the beach area had been considerable but having reorganized, the Commandos now had to slip through the enemy positions on the ridge of high ground, between Ryes and le Buhot, to the south of Arromanches, rather than following up behind 231 Brigade. They infiltrated through the battle lines as planned in the area of la Rosière, two and a half miles further on.

While crossing the ridge, the Royal Marines 'had one brush and two small battles with the Germans'. However, on reaching

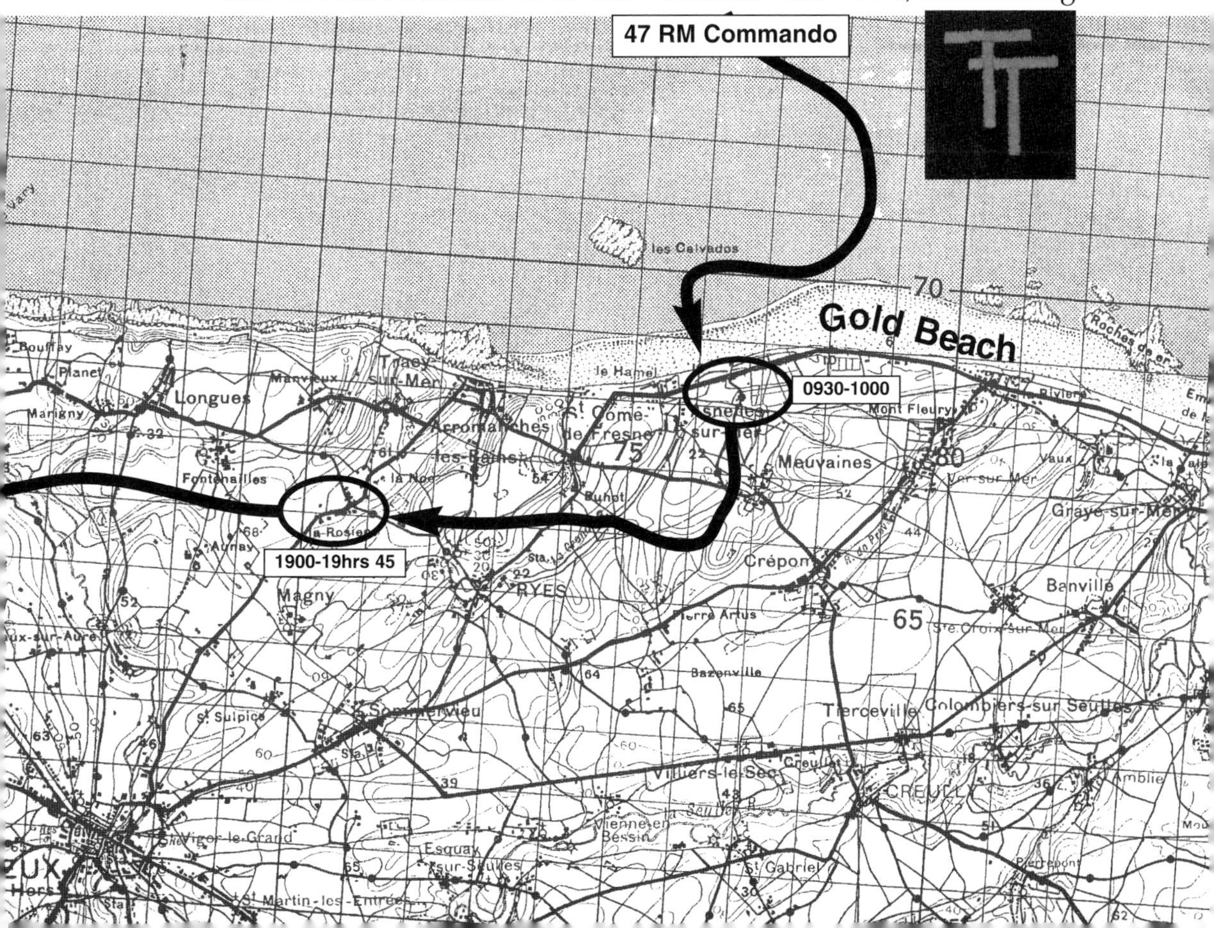

the area where they were originally planned to have assembled, the Commando found that la Rosière was still occupied by a weak company of German infantry.

An attack was quickly arranged, without fire support, as most of the radios had been lost along with much of the other heavy equipment during the landing. B Troop led the attack under the cover of smoke laid by the Commando's remaining 2-inch mortars.

Marine 'Shock' Kendrick was attempting to treat the wounded:

> *A machine gun opened up on us injuring some of the lads. "Shock!" The cry rang out from one of the wounded. As I tended to the lad, I realized I couldn't do all the necessary first aid in a prone position, but as soon as I stood up the machine gun opened up again. I could see the bullets hitting the hedge but as they came nearer to me, the gun must have lifted. Although the firing continued, the bullets were flying about above my head. We put in a flank attack and captured the machine gun crew. The gunner had a right shoulder injury. I had to treat him and when I finished, he hugged me. A scout car with six Germans in it suddenly rounded a bend in the road. We dealt with it. Soon afterwards, we heard a horse galloping down the lane and as it came into view we saw that it had a German rider. Sergeant Hooper stepped into the lane and fired his Tommy gun. The horse galloped off with the dead body still on his back.*

At 1900 hours, it was reported to Corps Headquarters, aboard HMS *Bulolo*, that 47 Commando was 'now in la Rosière' but it was not until 1945 hours that 47 was ready to set off towards Port-en-Bessin and Point 72, having suffered a further eleven casualties. They were running some six hours behind schedule at this stage.

During encounters with both friends and enemy they had taken every useful weapon and piece of ammunition from the dead, the wounded and from prisoners in order to make up for their losses on landing. These were not the kind of soldiers to be deflected from their mission by 'mere administrative inconveniences'.

Commander Kenneth Edwards in his Royal Naval history of

Operation NEPTUNE records that:

*After fighting another battle with German detachments, and crossing a small river, the Commando arrived on Point 72, a prominent hill immediately south of Port-en-Bessin. There they dug in for the night. They were in a dangerous position, between the defences of Port-en-Bessin and a fortified German camp at Fosse Soucy, about a mile south of Point 72.*

From a prisoner it was discovered that the enemy in Port-en-Bessin were the coastal infantrymen *1 Kompanie* of *I/726 Grenadier Regiment* and that just half a mile to the south, in Chateau Maisons, was their battalion HQ and to make matters worse the *352nd Division Sniper School* was even closer in la Fosse de Soucy. There was no sign of the Americans from OMAHA.

The capture of Port-en-Bessin and the link up with the US Army from OMAHA scheduled for the afternoon of D Day would now have to wait for D+1 and significant opposition could now be expected.

**The Plan Revised - D+1**

Nestling in the solitary break in the cliffs between Arromanches and OMAHA Beach, Port-en-Bessin was flanked by two significant German positions. On the flat topped feature to the east was a full-blown *Stützpunkt* (S 55); on the western feature *WN 57* provided mutual support across the port; while down at the port side were the defences of the small *WN 56*. A further defended location (*WN 58*) was on the forward slope overlooking the south-west quadrant of the village.

The original plan was to focus on capturing the high ground of the *Stützpunkt*, assisted by the prodigious firepower that was to be available. The village itself was not to be attacked for two reasons: firstly, once embroiled in clearing buildings, Colonel Phillips believed that the 450 men of a Commando would have been 'absorbed like ink on blotting paper'; and secondly the village and port were wanted intact to handle the fuel of the two armies that would come ashore at Port-en-Bessin.

See map on page 118

At dawn on 7 June, 47 Commando sent out patrols westward to locate the Americans who should by now have closed-up to the Army boundary just west of Point 72. The Commandos did

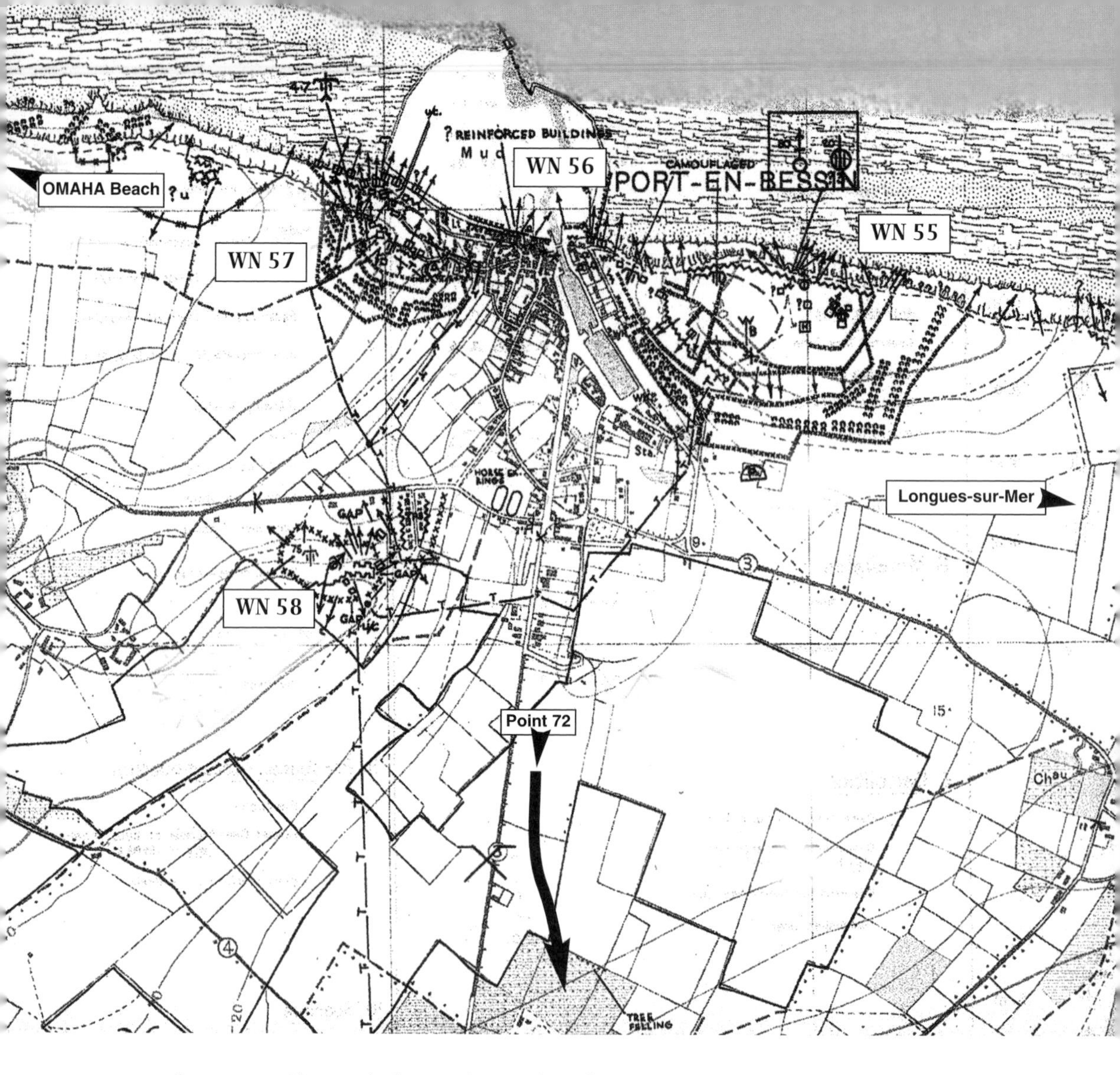


not learn until much later that, also facing 352nd Division, the 1st US Division, at OMAHA beach, had fared even worse that 231 Brigade. On their other flank 2nd Devons were preparing to attack the Longues-sur-Mer battery two and a half miles east. 47 Commando were on their own

Lacking contact with contacting the Americans, the Commandos had to face the prospect of attacking the port and its dominating cliff top defences with the available fire support from the Allied navies, artillery and airforces, co-ordinated over its single remaining radio; this would take a considerable time to arrange. The plan to assault the enemy held, flanking cliff top positions, avoiding the town, was abandoned as impractical.

Instead, Lieutenant Colonel Phillips decided that the Commando would bypass *WN 58* on the southern outskirts of the village and infiltrate into the streets and houses. Once in Port-en-Bessin, the Commandos would clear the village and port area before attacking the defences on the cliffs to the east and west. However, before the attack could begin the Marines needed more ammunition. To their support came 522 Company Royal Army Service Corps. Captain Brian Lindon's Military Cross citation records the resupply operation:

> *On 7 Jun 44 it was essential that the 47 Commandos, who were assaulting Port-en-Bessin, be supplied with ammunition, water and food, although well in enemy territory. Captain Lindon set out with two 3-ton vehicles to perform this task.*
>
> *He passed through the leading elements of 2 Devons in the area of Longues being told by them that the enemy were ahead. In spite of this he carried on in order to contact 47 Commando at Point 72 near Escures.*
>
> *Although he had to run the gauntlet of considerable small arms fire from enemy infantry who were flanking his route, his vehicle being hit several times, he succeeded not only in the delivery of his loads, but in safely getting back the empty vehicles.*
>
> *It was largely due to Captain Lindon's determination to get these essential supplies through, his disregard for personal safety and skilful handling of his vehicles, that 47 Commando received the necessary ammunition to enable them to continue the operation in which they were involved.'*

Actions by logistic troops can often be overlooked but in this case, it is clear that without the supply, 47 Commando would not have been able to take the town of Port-en-Bessin. Operations in built up areas are notoriously heavy consumers of ammunition.

Re-supply completed, the attack would begin at 1600 hours. However, destroyers began engaging the port and its defences at 1400 hours, with the cruiser HMS *Emerald* of Bombarding Force K, turning her seven 6-inch guns landward and sending her hundred-pound shells into the German positions at 1500 hours. Ten minutes before H Hour, three squadrons of RAF Typhoons 'came in and plastered the three German positions with extreme accuracy' and finally, the 25-pounders of 431 Battery of 147 (Essex Yeomanry) Field Regiment RA fired HE and smoke. The Commandos had been joined by a Forward Observation Officer, who had made his way across the two and a half miles of No Man's Land to reach them. He was to control the fire of the guns, which were in positions around Arromanches, in close support of 47 as they approached the town from the south.

**The Attack on Port-en-Bessin**

As the advance towards the village began at 1500 hours, the Commandos of A, B and X Troops were engaged by '*Spandaus*' firing on them from their left rear. This fire caused some casualties and a delay while the enemy were neutralised. Barring the way into Port-en-Bessin from Point 72 was the 'Southern Strongpoint' (*WN 58*), which was described as being:

> *… on the slope of the high ground south of Port-en-Bessin, covering the southern approaches to the town and docks. It is surrounded by a thick belt of wire, with two small gaps. There is one pillbox facing NE, and one concrete shelter. Several weapon pits give all-round fire, and a trench system is dug just south of the pillbox.*

This position having been 'plastered with extreme accuracy by the guns of the Essex Yeomanry', the leading elements of 47 bypassed it to the east. Guided by a local Gendarme, A and B Troops headed for the beach, leaving X Troop to deal with *WN 58*.

Under cover of the artillery fire Captain Walton led X Troop west, off their axis of advance, along the hedges to a position from where they could assault the enemy trenches and bunkers. With the artillery fire lifting, the Troop charged and the sight of 'the fearsome howling Commandos' was enough for the Germans 'whose hands went up in surrender before we came to grips with them'.

Meanwhile, A and B troops entered the town and were immediately embroiled in 'confused street fighting'. Fighting their way through the narrow roads and stone buildings was a slow business. A Troop, however, bypassed the worst of the fighting and was able to mount an attack up the western slope from the town to *WN 57*. Here the fighting was not at all straightforward, with mines and wire barring their way and trenches and bunkers, containing about a platoon of infantry having to be cleared. The German coastal troops were, however, no match for the determined Commandos.

Having broken in to *WN 57* through the Rue du Phare, A Troop split into its two sections. While one cleared the defences on the terraced slopes above the port, the other, in a flanking move around the south, took on the rearmost defences on the top of the feature. Initially all went well but as the screening smoke cleared and the enemy across the valley in *Stützpunkt 55* were able to engage A Troop, as was one of the enemy Flak barges in the harbour below. This slowed down clearance operations until they were neutralised. Casualties had been so heavy, with almost fifty per cent of the attackers being wounded. At around 2000 hours, the remnants of A Troop were forced to fall back into the town, where X Troop were fighting to mop up resistance.

Lieutenant Peter Winter RM recounted that:

*During the attack on the Western Hill, Cpl Amos stopped to put a first field dressing on a wounded friend. While he was doing this, he was taken prisoner and marched off to a bunker where on the wall, was Hitler's order that "All Commandos are to be shot". Corporal Amos spent a very uncomfortable night with a Gestapo man standing around supervising. As our final attack on the Eastern Hill was going in and the Marines could be seen on the German position, the Gestapo man,"seeing the writing on the wall", left the bunker. As soon as he had gone, the German military commander got out a cigar and offered it to Corporal Amos saying, "We would very much like to surrender". Corporal Amos fell the Germans into three ranks and with a large flag marched the Germans down the hill and that was that. Except when he got to the bottom of the hill, his troop commander said "Amos, where have you been?" Looking closely at him and ignoring the ranks of his prisoners, he added, "You haven't had a shave!"*

For the garrison of *WN 57*, a night contemplating what the

morning would bring proved enough to prompt them to surrender on the morning of 8 June.

**The Eastern Feature *S55***

The German *Stützpunkt* positions on the plateau above Port-en-Bessin to the east of the port were well developed and dominated the town and the slope up from the harbour. It was not until several hours after H Hour on the afternoon of 7 June that B Troop reached the foot of the eastern feature, as they had borne the brunt of the fighting in the town up to this point and had suffered twenty-five per cent casualties. Their initial probing attacks up the mined and wired slope were quickly halted by *'Spandaus'* in concrete *Tobruk* casemates. However, Captain Cousins of A troop had further inland identified a possible route up into the enemy position. As the war diary records 'Captain Cousins led two probing attacks up the zig-zag path on eastern feature, which were beaten back'. The attacks came to a halt before dusk, when the enemy mounted a limited counter-attack, supported by fire from two German Flak ships lying alongside the wall of the Port's outer basin, which drove the Commandos from the lower slopes of the eastern feature. According to his DSO citation, Major Donnell promptly dealt with the Flak ships when:

> *... he went forward and quickly sizing up the situation, assembled as many of B Troop as he could find. Taking cover in the houses and with complete disregard for his own safety personally led the attack on these ships.*

The already half-sunk ships duly surrendered.

To hold onto his foothold in the town Lieutenant Colonel Phillips and his Tactical HQ summoned Q Troop and elements of the Heavy Weapons Troop forward from Point 72.

Meanwhile, 231 Brigade appreciated the difficulties that the Commando was having, With a number of overloaded Royal Marines-crewed ammunition carriers having broken down, Lieutenant Colonel Nevill, with 2 Devon at Longues-sur-Mer, records that:

> *In the meantime news had filtered through that the 47 Marine Commandos were having a very stiff battle at Port-en-Bessin and*

OMAHA Beach
Longues-sur-Mer
WN 56
Stützpunkt
WN 57
WN 55
The Zig Zags
WN 58
Point 72

*were being hard pressed. Our Carrier Platoon therefore went to their immediate assistance and got seriously embroiled on the outskirts of the Port.*

The eight Bren gun carriers, accompanied by Lieutenant Bennett and some of his Marines, were the Devons' mobile reserve loaded with ammunition. Their light armour and speed gave protection to the crews and enabled the West Countrymen to drive through the three miles of enemy held territory between the Longues-sur-Mer battery and Port-en-Bessin. Sergeant Sear, one of the Carrier Platoon section commanders, was awarded a Military Medal during the infiltration to Port-en-Bessin, when a platoon of *Wehrmacht* infantry attempted to block the route two miles from the port and:

*... showing a complete disregard for his dangerous situation, with great skill and determination slowly and methodically disengaged his section, inflicting many casualties on the enemy. Sergeant Sear covered the move of the remainder of his platoon past the enemy with his Bren gun and 'carefully controlled his men and their fire'. The Carrier Platoon 'broke clean' of contact with the enemy and reached Port-en-Bessin in the early evening of D+1. The Devons carried additional ammunition in the carriers and used their machine guns and light mortars to support the Commandos attacking the Eastern Feature and themselves became heavily embroiled in the fighting around the Cemetery on the outskirts of the town.*

Private Jim Wilson identified the platoon's problem:

*We came down the hill, past a small Chateau that the Platoon Commander expected to be defended but there were no Germans in sight. My Sarge thought they may be ones that tried to ambush us earlier on. Further down the hill to Bessin, we got more* Spandau *fire from the high ground into the* [open] *top of the carrier, which didn't give us much cover. We fired back with Brens but later when we went up the hill we saw that the* Spandau *were in concrete Tobruk nests, so we were probably wasting our time.*

*We were under fire on the edge of Bessin all night but we got some Jerries who were trying to get out of the town and up our side of the hill to join the* Spandau *boys.*

With 47 earlier repulsed from the Eastern Feature, at dusk the remnants of A and B Troops were sent forward to probe the enemy's defences to find a weak spot and consequently the battle went on into the night. Commander Edwards wrote:

> *It was becoming very doubtful if the strong position on the height east of the town could be taken that night, but Captain TF Cousins said that he found and reconnoitred a zig-zag path up the hill and thought that he could get up to the German position with twenty-five men by that route.*
>
> *Captain Cousins was given between forty and fifty men* [an amalgamation of A and B Troops] *and set out* [at 2200 hours]. *It was like a miniature replica of the storming of the Heights of Abraham at Quebec by General Wolfe. At dusk Captain Cousins and his men reached the skyline and they at once assaulted the German defences. These they penetrated, while at the same time another troop attacked from the extreme right. This troop also penetrated the German defences, and captured the German commander in his dugout. The German company commander was induced to lead the Marines forward through the mines and summon the remainder of the German Garrison to surrender, and this they did.*
>
> *It was found that the whole top of the hill was honeycombed with dugouts and trenches. Mopping up was therefore a slow business and Captain Cousins unhappily lost his life in the process.*

In a silent attack (all the fire support earlier available had been re-tasked) Captain Cousins who had led the Commandos up the zig-zap path using its banks as cover, was killed during the fight to break-in to the *Stützpunkt*. Lieutenant Forfar recalled that the assault force was well up the path when:

> *Nearing the west end of the hill, the group came under heavy fire from a concrete blockhouse at close range. Cousins halted his men and told them to get into some unoccupied trenches. Taking his Bren gunner, Marine Delap, and Marines Howe and Madden with him, Cousins led this group through a gap in a wire fence and rushed the blockhouse. All were shooting as they went. As they charged the blockhouse, grenades were thrown at them, and as one exploded front of him Cousins fell forward, killed outright.*

*Madden received a severe head wound and Delap was concussed. The waiting group under Wilson heard bursts of fire, exploding grenades and a lot of shouting including* 'Kamerad'. *Wilson's group then ran forward as planned. Forty yards ahead Cousins was lying dead with Marine Madden beside him. Delap had recovered quickly and was continuing to fire his Bren gun Tomlinson and Howe were firing and throwing grenades. Wilson by this time had a German prisoner with him who was ordered to shout to the men in the blockhouse to surrender: a white flag appeared and they did so. Cousins had been killed but his sacrifice was not in vain. The bloc had not only been captured but its capture and the manner in wich it was achieved had weakened enemy morale.*

As aleady mentioned, Captain Vincent (B Troop) leading the right assault troop had taken his men to the east 'firing from the hip as they went' ignoring 'possible mines trip wires'. This determined attack helped break the will of the defenders. 'As Vincent's men turned to close with the enemy an officer and seven Germans surrendered'. These were soon joined by others including an *Oberleutnant*. Colonel Phillips sent his last reserve to clinch victory. Captain Forfar summed up the situation:

*The assault party of four officers and twenty-four other ranks, outnumbered four to one, without artillery or air support and attacking up a steep slope, with an enemy familiar with the terrain and enjoying much greater firepower, the benefit of concreted, entrenched, barbed-wire and mine-protected positions which looked down on their assailants, had succeeded against the odds.*

**Point 72- Mont Cavalier**

The garrison of Point 72 was originally designed to be strong enough to cover the Commando's rear from the inevitable German counter-attack but to feed the needs of 47's battle for the port and the Eastern Feature, the defenders were progressively sucked away from Mont Cavalier. This left a much reduced garrison, of Commando Rear HQ, holding this key feature.

While the fighting was going on in Port-en-Bessin, during the afternoon and evening of 7 June the group of fifteen Marines, of whom only half were armed thanks to loss of weapons during the landing, were subjected to a strong counter-attack from the south west, which Colonel Phillips had confidently expected.

The Marines were manning a pair of fire trenches near the top of the hill and at first were able to hold the enemy back but at 1930 the area was heavily mortared. At 2030 hours accurate rifle fire and further mortar fire from the area of the Château to the south west began 'and a little later fifteen of the enemy advanced towards them'. In the gathering evening gloom, waving to the Marines 'in a friendly Allied manner', the Germans were able to get close to the Marines but were beaten off. John Forfar wrote:

> *Around 2200 hours, back at Point 72, the Germans mounted yet another attack on the Rear HQ. By this time the occupants of the trench had destroyed all documents. Illuminating the position by firing star shells, thirty to forty Germans, closing in from the semi-darkness beyond the star shells, attacked. They got within ten yards of the trench when they were temporarily held up by two grenades and two smoke bombs thrown by Capt O'Connell. An attached corporal from the artillery regiment, Cpl. Jenkins, was killed and the FOB, Lt Irwin, and his sergeant wounded. In the confusion some of the HQ personnel managed to escape from the trench. Others, including Regimental Sergeant Major Dollery and Marine George Wood, together with the wounded and Marine Bryant, were captured.*

As a result of overrunning the position on Point 72 and

*A Commando observer takes a compass bearing prior to calling for mortar fire.*

capturing the Marines the Germans had not only released some of their own prisoners but threatened the Commando's rear at a crucial point in the battle. Most of the Marines taken prisoner, however, subsequently regained the Allied lines.

## 2 Devons Re-take Monte Cavalier

231 Brigade planned that 2 Devon would relieve 47 Commando in Port-en-Bessin as soon as possible, which was not originally expected to be before the morning of D+1. 2 Devon's war diary entry made in the early hours of D+2 records:

> *8 Jun 44. 0400 hours. Bn received orders to attack westwards to Port-en-Bessin, clearing up enemy strong points on the coast north of Le Mesnil and Bouffay. Port-en-Bessin was attacked yesterday by 47 RM Commando but they have failed to take it completely though they succeeded in entering the town.*

The entry concludes with the words so often heard in war 'The situation is rather obscure'. Lieutenant O'Brian with the remains of Y Troop having been separated from the rest of 47 by the German advance over Point 72 the previous evening made his way to Longues-sur-Mer, arriving at Lieutenant Colonel Nevill's HQ. With the situation only a little less obscure, as O'Brian knew nothing of the successful capture of the Port, the Devons quickly sent further men and transport west, while the remainder of the Battalion would follow on foot. The Colonel describes 2 Devon's advance:

> *The post of Le Mensil surrendered after an artillery and MG* [2 Cheshire] *bombardment. Two officers and thirty-six other ranks were captured. We suffered no casualties.*
>
> *The advance continued rapidly, and it was soon clear that there was no more opposition between us and Port-en-Bessin. We immediately decided to turn south and take over from 47 Commando the high feature known as Pt 72 two miles south of Port-en-Bessin. The hill had been the scene of heavy fighting the day before, and it had changed hands twice.*

With the Commandos now relieved, meanwhile, C Company and a squadron of Sherwood Rangers leading, the Devons had quickly cleared the Germans from Point 72 and set about digging in, with the tanks deployed in 'hull down' positions on the crest. Meanwhile, the commanding officer, Colonel Nevill, focused his binoculars on a château a thousand yards to the south east that had been pointed out to him as the source of all the trouble on Point 72. The Commanding Officer described the attack by his battalion:

> *C Company relieved the Commandos and preparations were made to attack a large chateau immediately south in full view of the hill. It was known to contain a strong enemy force who were responsible for the trouble with the Marines on the previous day. The top of the hill was subjected to spasmodic fire from the chateau, which made reconnaissance somewhat difficult. A request was made for artillery support* [from 8 Armoured Brigade]. *This was only granted after Div HQ were assured that we were in fact going to attack Germans and not Americans; the doubt had arisen as the chateau was actually within American territory. Twice we were asked, and twice we were able to assure them that there could be no mistake. It was at this point that we planned to link up with Lt Col Horner's Combat Team of the American 1st Division; however, they had not yet arrived owing to the very heavy fighting in which they had been involved on the beaches.*

*The Eastern Feature or* Stützpunkt *bassin from* WN57 *looking across the port.*

> *The attack on the Chateau proved to be a very tricky operation, because the battery in support* [from 147 Field Regiment] *could only be available until 1800 hours. As it was already 1700 hours, there was no time for detailed reconnaissance, and we knew there were two rivers between us and the objective. However, the risk had to be taken, as an attack without artillery fire on the enemy position well dug in amongst the buildings would have been asking for trouble.*

The attack was eventually a success but Colonel Nevill was well aware that if his companies had been halted, they would have been in an unenviable position, pinned down in an open valley. Continuing the attack, despite dwindling ammunition, was the only credible option open to him. Recognising that the inevitable German counter attack would destroy the companies before they could be resupplied with ammunition, the CO ordered the two companies back to stronger, less isolated, positions around Point 72.

At 2130 hours on 8 June, 2 Devon and 47 Commando's patrols finally made contact with the 1st US Division below Point 72 in the village of Escures. The Allies finally had a single, linked beachhead.

## Port Operations at Port-en-Bessin

Almost immediately after the strongpoints on the cliffs had been subdued, Royal Navy Beach Commandos arrived in the Port. Commander Cowley-Thomas RN, set up his Headquarters and began the work of bringing it into use for the landing of stores. Captain Hutchings RN also arrived shortly after the Port's capture and was quickly at work on PLUTO (Pipe-Line Under The Ocean). The pipeline was designed to deliver the majority of the vast quantity of fuel needed by modern armies, through a spreading network of shore based pipelines. The first 6-inch 'Tombola' line to deliver fuel from tankers moored at sea came ashore at Port-en-Bessin on D+19 (25 June) and was delivering 8,000 tons of fuel per day. It was also found that the port had a greater capacity for landing conventional stores than anticipated. By 14 June the port was handling 1,000 tons of supplies per day. It was to continue working with not only fuel but other stores once the US Mulberry A harbour had been

*The Western Feature or WN57 from* Stützpunkt *Bessin.*

destroyed by the storm of the 19-21 June. In fact, the port, fuel depot and pipelines continued to play a significant part in the North-west Europe campaign long after the battle had moved on to the very borders of Germany.

## Visiting the Battlefield

This tour assumes that the visitor is following the Route of 47 Commando from JIG Sector of Gold Beach to Port-en-Bessin.

From Arromanches head east through Le Hamel/Asnelles on the D514. At a cross roads, lookout for a sign advertising oysters. Turn left and follow the road to the beach and park in the car park next to the ramp. On the beach are the smashed remains of the *WN 36* strongpoint, which was taken by 1 Hampshire. It is astride this point that the various craft loads of 47 Commando landed having moved laterally from the area of the point to the east in a correction. They came under fire from *WN 37* in Le Hamel 800 yards to the west and assembled behind the dunes in the field that is now covered by the adjacent holiday homes.

Return to the D514 and head west through Le Hamel and fork left, following the D205 towards Ryes and le Carrefour. At the crossroads park in an open area by a farmyard and track to the left heading in a southerly direction. Walk a short way up this track. It is in this area that the Commando passed through 1 Dorset and on through the German positions on the ridges in a westerly direction across country.

Return to your car and drive to Arromanches. In the town pick up the D516 heading towards Bayeux. Do not take the D514 to Port-en-Bessin from the roundabout but head a further two miles inland to the la Rosière cross-roads. This was a significant point on the Commando's route west. Turn right onto the D127 signed towards Longues-sur-Mer. 47 Commando took a mainly cross-country route just to the south of the road over the Masse de Crodalle.

Rejoin the D514 and follow the road through Longues-sur-Mer towards Port-en-Bessin. This is the route along which the Commandos, Devons and RASC vehicles ran the gauntlet to resupply 47 Commando. At the sharp downward sloping bend in Commes take the D100 left to Escures. The Commandos followed the ridge of high ground to your left (south) to Point 72 (Point 69 on the modern IGN map), where they were to form their firm base for the attack on the port. It is possible to walk a part of the way up to Point 72 on a public right of way (a stony track) at a slightly offset cross road on the D100 just south of Escures. The hill itself is private land.

Return to your vehicle, drive through Escures and onto the D6 towards Port-en-Bessin. Go across the traffic lights, towards the centre of town. The church used by the Commandos as a rendezvous and aid post is a hundred yards further on. Parking can be difficult in Port-en-Bessin, which is busy most of the time. Park when the opportunity presents itself alongside the fishing boats in the inner basin or in the area surrounding the outer basin. Both parking areas are a short walk across the lock gate to the foot of the Port-en-Bessin East defences. Covering the small piece of beach to the east of the harbour is a casemate with a memorial plaque to 47 Commando mounted on it. Take the path up the slope past the seventeenth century tower. Reaching the plateau and the Port-en-Bessin East defences it is easy to follow the overgrown trench lines from position to position. This is one of the most extensive and best preserved *Widerstandnester* on the Invasion Coast and is well worth taking a good look around. The difficult task facing the Commandos is self-evident.

The Port-en-Bessin West defences can be seen from the edge of the plateau on which the Eastern defences were built. Those who wish to inspect the western defences more closely should be aware that most of the casemates have been incorporated in the post war development in this area. The best route up is via the lighthouse on Rue du Phare.

If heading east towards Arromanches, keep an eye out for another 47 Commando memorial (unveiled in 1997) on the left-hand side of the road in the modern outskirts of the town.

*If posting from outside of the UK please affix stamp here*

Pen & Sword Books
FREEPOST SF5
47 Church Street
BARNSLEY
South Yorkshire
S70 2BR

## Chapter Six

# St Aubin to Langrune-sur-Mer

Heading east along the invasion coast the next Commando action was in the very centre of the Second Army sector at JUNO Beach. One of the themes of Commando and Ranger operations was clearing coastal positions to facilitate the linking up of the various beachheads but as GOLD and JUNO Beaches were only separated by half a mile of marshes (LOVE Sector) a Commando was not necessary. Between JUNO's NAN Sector and QUEEN Sector of SWORD Beach there was a considerable gap: four miles with three sprawling holiday resort villages Langrune, Luc and Lion, each with the suffix 'sur-Mer' and each containing a strongpoint and other defences.

While their main effort was to get inland as far as the Caen – Bayeux Road, I Corps's plan for the Commandos was that they would land after the main force and clear the coastal strip. 48 Royal Marine Commando was to land on Nan Sector and make its way east, meeting 41 Commando who would be heading west from Queen Sector of SWORD, in Luc-sur-Mer. The story of 41 Royal Marine Commando's battles will be told in the following chapter.

48 Commando's task of landing behind 3rd Canadian Division and fighting an independent action, on a flank to link up the two beachheads, was never going to be easy, hence the commitment of Commandos to the task. In the coastal resort villages were a series of *Widerstandnester* held by the reinforced *9. Kompanie* of *Grenadier Regiment 736* and a part of *10. Kompanie* of the same regiment. The *Widerstandnester* at Langrune-sur-Mer, as forecast, proved to be well constructed and surprisingly determinedly held by the German coastal infantry and *Osttruppen*.

### The Commando Plan

Number 48 Commando was formed from elements of 7 Royal Marine Battalion and volunteers from the Mobile Naval Base

*Achnacarry Castle Commando Training Centre, by the banks of the river Arkaig in the heart of Lochaber. No volunteer could join a Commando unit, or wear the coveted Green Beret, without passing the six weeks course.*

Defence Organisation in March 1944, at the Royal Marine Barracks Deal in Kent. As an OVERLORD priority, Lieutenant Colonel Moulton took his new 'Commando' north to the Commando Training Centre at Achnacarry for an abbreviated conversion and training package. After six gruelling weeks in the Highlands, 48 returned south. They were the last Commando to be formed and had been born out of Montgomery's expansion of the invasion plan and, consequently, had none of the Commando raiding experience of the other new Commandos as a shakedown. That is not to say that the Marines of 7 RM Battalion were green. Many had fought in Crete but like most units in 4 Special Service Brigade, there was a high proportion of younger men.

*Training complete in Mid-April 48 Commando returned south to lodgings in Gravesend, where they would daily assemble to do such training as time allowed but they were conveniently close to areas of the bombed out East End that had been given over to urban warfare training.*

Lieutenant Colonel Moulton outlined the plan that had been developed by I Corps and Brigadier 'Jumbo' Leicester of 4 Special Service Brigade:

*Between the Canadian 3rd Division on Juno Beach and the British 3rd Division on Sword Beach, there was a gap of five miles, caused by a reef off the coast which prevented landings; No. 48 Commando was immediately behind the North Shore Regiment, the left battalion of the Canadians, wheel left, and clear the beach defences opposite the reef – until it met No. 41 Commando, who would be doing the same thing, coming the other way, after landing behind the right battalion of the British 3rd Division. We were to meet at a group of houses on the stream, which runs through a village, engagingly called Petit Enfer* [Small Hell]. ... *When we started off on our task, a squadron of*

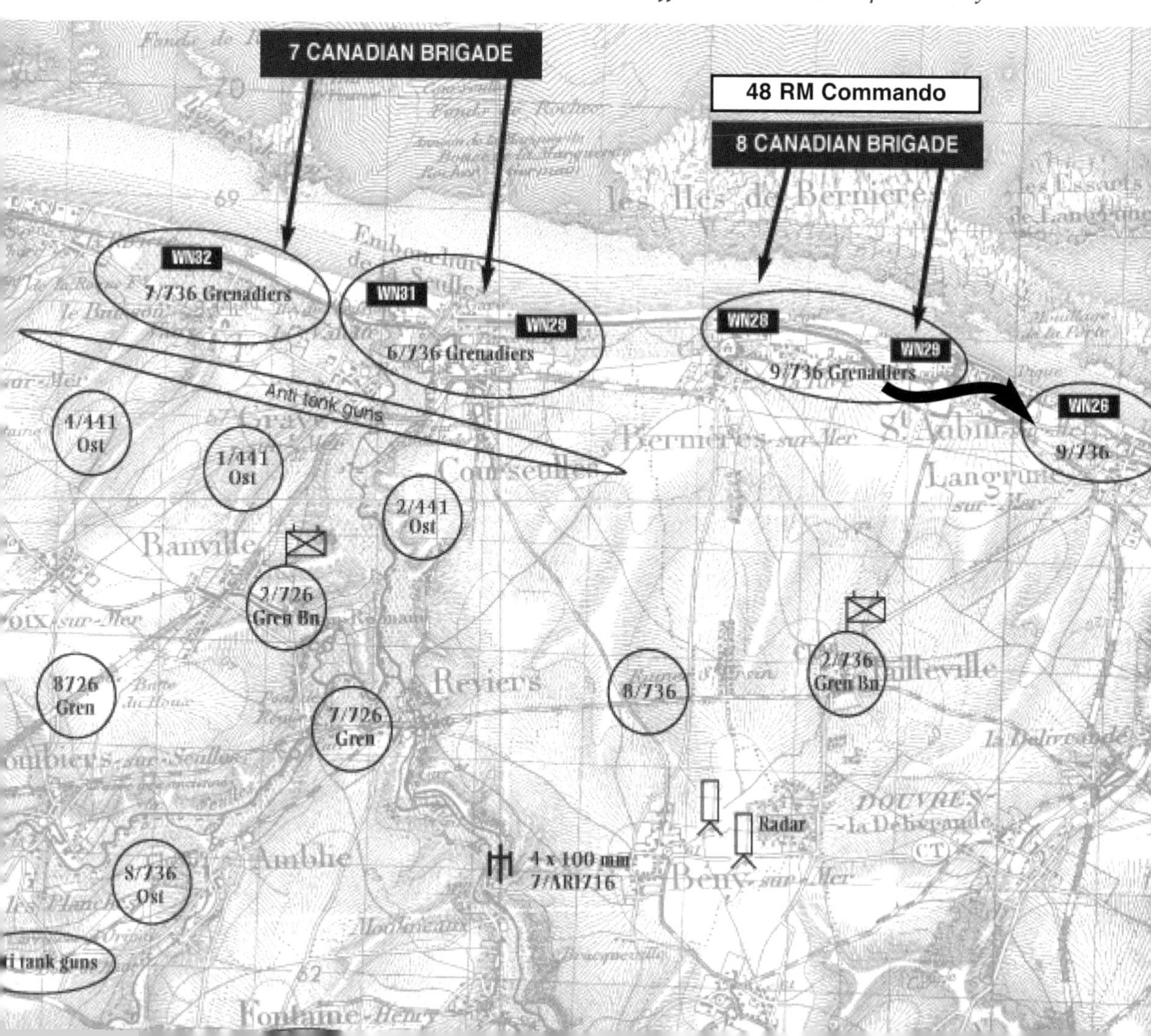

*light support craft would work along the shore to support us.*

*... As we should not be under fire when we landed, and as our transport would not be available for the first day, we would land carrying a fairly heavy load of ammunition and explosives. We would dump this at St Aubin and then lightly equipped, would move down a road parallel to the shore to Langrune. This would be our firm base, and from it we would tackle the coast defences from the rear.*

However, the elegant simplicity of this plan, in common with many D Day plans, did not survive contact with the enemy. The Royal Marines were to be committed to a difficult and bloody fight that tested their six weeks of Commando training in Scotland to the limits.

Planing to land behind 48 Commando was Headquarters 4 Special Service Brigade, presumably to organise support for its newest unit if necessary.

## The Crossing

48 Commando was sealed in their embarcation camp at Swaythling, near Southampton when news of the twenty-four hour postponement of D Day came on 4 June. But 24 hours later they were moving in a convoy of trucks which with dozens of others, was making its way to the embarkation point. As with other Commandos who were to cross in Landing Craft Infantry, 48 was heading on the carefully organised but circuitous traffic circuit to Warsash. Along with the rest of Force J they moved out from the River Hamble at 1700 hours into the Solent, aboard a landing craft flotilla of six LCI (Small) commanded by Lieutenant Timmins RN. Here they took their place amongst the myriad of ships waiting for dusk and the time to start heading south.

The journey across the Channel was uneventful but, as usual in an LCI, uncomfortable. Lieutenant Dan Flunder commented:

*As Adjutant I was OC troops on board and spent the night in a cramped little mess-deck; almost everyone was sick. I had the men up on the superstructure early because I thought that the fresh air would restore them and because men are always happier when they can see what is going on.*

Those who came up on deck early on 6 June could discern the coast ahead through the smoke and sea mist. With radio silence imposed they were unaware that the naval plan for the landing of 3rd Canadian Division had miscarried. The landing was already delayed in NAN Sector by fifteen minutes due to a dispute over 'rocks' off the coast between Bernières and St Aubin. The RAF air photo units had 'taken pictures of the beach with rocks clearly visible' at a time when, according to the Navy's charts and tide tables, they should have been covered by six feet of water. What the RAF had in fact photographed was long strands of seaweed that grew on the rocks.

In the event, the fifteen minute delay was exacerbated by landing craft bearing the Canadians getting into the wrong swept lanes between the Transit Area and the shore. Consequently, the leading craft of 8 Canadian Brigade touched down on NAN Sector at 0805 hours some additional twenty minutes late. Lieutenant Timmins's flotilla of landing craft was however on time and, getting no response when they hailed a Naval command ship for instructions; they went ahead and landed almost on schedule at H+45 or 0843 hours. This understandable decision was to pitch 48 into a cauldron of trouble, every bit as serious as that which had faced 47 Royal Marine Commando landing five miles to the west.

## The Landing of 48 RM Commando

*Widerstandnest 27*, in the village of St Aubin at the eastern end of NAN Red Sector, formed a part of the Canadian initial objective to be taken by assault immediately after H Hour. B Company North Shore Regiment, the left of the battalion's two assault companies, were to land and clear the area. It was essential that *WN 27* be taken and opposition cleared for an orderly landing of troops who would take the battle inland towards the Canadian's objective. For the Commandos it was equally important that *WN 27* be cleared so that 48 Commando could begin its clearance of the coastline to the east in good order. As on other beaches, they had been expecting the NAN Beach to be cleared and gaps through to their assembly area open and marked.

Landing late, the North Shore's B Company touched down

just as the Germans were recovering from the effects of the bombardment and the majority of Canadians had consequently been pinned down by machine gun fire from *WN 27*. To make matters worse the strongpoint's 50mm gun knocked out the first tanks coming up onto the beach and the Canadian Official Historian, in a masterly understatements recorded that 'An especially unlucky landing was experienced by 48 Commando'. The RM Commando D Day report goes on to explain that:

> *Even before touching down on Nan Red beach in six LCI (Small) at H plus 45 minutes, these troops were engaged by machine gun and mortar fire from the beach defenders, who chose at this moment to return to life. They had previously been subdued by the neutralizing fire from sea. The Commando therefore suffered heavy casualties before reaching the beach.*

Heading in on schedule with Commando HQ, was Lieutenant Flunder:

> *Soon we were running into the beach and I walked up and down the bows keeping an eye on the Navy people responsible for lowering the ramps. The sea was covered with craft as far as the eye could see. The shore was under bombardment, craft were sinking, and from where I stood it certainly didn't look as if the Canadians had secured the beach - things didn't look good at all.*
>
> *I didn't realize we were under fire until I saw two men collapse and fall over the starboard side. By then it was too late to beat a retreat and I later found three bullet holes in my map case, they must have passed between my arm and my body during that period.*

Lieutenant Colonel Moulton described his unit's run-in to the smoke shrouded beach, which at first was relatively uneventful:

> *As we closed the beach… I tried to pick up the beach signs and beach parties. The beach seemed confused and they were difficult to spot, but it was clear that there were a lot of people there, and we could see some signs of work on the beach exit to the right of the houses. Now we were very close. No one seemed to be shooting at us. It was probably all right. Our forward motion checked sharply and… we hung rolling on the beach obstacle we had fouled; then a wave caught our stern, swung us, and carried*

> *us forward to the beach at a bad angle and rolling. As we struck the obstacle, the enemy opened fire with mortars and machine guns from the esplanade, a little more than a hundred yards away* [to the left]. *The sailors replied with crashing bursts of Oerlikon fire.*
>
> *I looked around and saw the other landing craft of the squadron in confusion. Our craft and the three next to it on our left had got through to beach reasonably close in, further left the other two were hung up on beach obstacles, helpless and well out from the beach, in the noise and confusion, I realized that the enemy were firing at us and that men were being hit. No question now of our smoke upsetting the Canadians' battle or interfering with the work on the beach – that had all too clearly gone very wrong…*

Lieutenant Flunder recalled that 'The tide was high and we had craft hitting the beach obstacles and becoming fixed'. Two of the Commando's six LCIs, with Y and Z Troops aboard, became stuck on the cruciform hedgehog beach obstacles a hundred yards or so out to sea and were soon sinking. These craft were the two furthest to the left and as sitting targets they bore the brunt of the fire still coming from *WN 27*. Fortunately it would appear that on this particular sector there were fewer mines on the beach obstacles.

Colonel Moulton took prompt action:

> *I looked for the mortar men to fire the smoke. Thinking that they would not be wanted when we were first fired at on the way in, they had dismounted their mortars and gone forward ready to land. I shouted to them, realized that my voice was powerless against the noise. I jumped down from the bridge on the port side and ran forward a few paces to grab one of them by the arm. He looked around, saw me, said something I could not hear, then ran back to the sandbags and started to mount his* [2-inch] *mortar. Someone had done the same on the starboard side. Back on the bridge, I realized with a sinking heart that the Commando was meeting something like disaster. Then the mortars popped, and seconds later, hissing out of the sky on to the esplanade to windward, came the blessed smoke bombs. The other craft, seeing our smoke, joined in with theirs, and in a minute or two we were*

*in dense white smoke, and the Germans were firing blind.*

Lieutenant Flunder was amongst the first Commando ashore on Red Sector of NAN Beach, where 48 had been landed accurately in front of 'the Three Chimnied House with sea-wall':

*When we grounded we got the starboard ramp down, which wasn't easy with the waves thrashing the stern about. I was half-*

*way down when a big wave lifted the bow and somersaulted the ramp and myself into the sea. I saw the great bows coming over me and the next thing I remember is walking up the beach, soaking wet, with some of my equipment torn off, including my pistol, but still clutching my stout ash walking stick. When I got to the top of the beach, I was violently sick.*

*The beach was covered with casualties, some Canadian, some ours. The surf was incredible, with beached and half-sunken craft wallowing about in it. Offshore, other craft came steadily on. Some tanks struggled ashore and some bogged in the shingle. Those that were advancing had their turret lids shut and were heading for a large group of wounded. I was sickened to see one run over two of our wounded and it was heading for our good padre, John Armstrong, who had been badly wounded in the thigh. I had spoken to him on the way up the beach; typically, he had been vehement that I should not stop by him, exposed to enemy fire. I ran back down the beach and hammered on the turret of a tank, to get someone a put his head out. When this failed I stuck a Hawkins anti-tank grenade in the sprocket and blew the track off-that stopped it.*

Cases of the wounded being run over by armour on the beaches, sometimes through sheer necessity, were far from uncommon, particularly on JUNO, where the Sherman DD tanks landed behind the infantry and assault engineers, their landing craft having become disorientated during the run-in.

Chaos reigned on the beach. Most of the Commando's A, B and X Troops were landed in about three feet of water but, according to 4 Special Service Brigade's war diary:

*On reaching shore, troops made for the cover of the earth cliff and sea wall. Here they found a confused situation. The cliff and sea wall gave some protection from SA fire but any movement away from them was under MG fire. The whole area was under heavy mortar and shellfire. Under the sea wall was a jumble of men from other units including many wounded and dead. The beach was congested with tanks, SP guns and other vehicles, some out of action, others attempting to move from the beaches in the very confined space between the water's edge and the sea wall. LCTs were arriving all the time and attempting to land their loads, adding to the general confusion. A quick recce showed that the beach exit to the right of the isolated houses was free from SA fire, except for occasional shots, and that a gap had been cleared through the mines.*

'Some men from Y and Z Troops attempted to swim ashore heavily laden; a high proportion of these were lost, drowning in a strong undertow.' Others abandoned their equipment. Most survivors on the stricken craft and some of the wounded were, however, taken off the foundering wrecks of their landing craft ensnared on obstacles, by LCTs who braved the diminishing fire from *WN 27*. Most eventually made it ashore to join the Commando in its assembly area.

Even though the beach was still under fire and *WN 27* still active, sufficient Royal Engineers had survived the landing and got to work clearing barbed wire and mines to the west of the 'Three Chimnied House'. The exit that should have by now been wide enough to take tracked vehicles was but a narrow path marked by mine tape.

The root of the problem on the beach was that having missed the effect of the bombardment, the Canadian infantry had found it an exceedingly slow and costly business to break into *WN 27*. Colonel Moulton wrote that 'The time allowed for the Canadians

*48 RM Commando landing under the gun of WN 27.*

*The point at which 48 RM Commando landed east of* WN 27 *photographed at high water several hours after the landing.*

was very short, and in the circumstances quite impossible. We realised this from the start and never had any inclination to blame the Canadians for our bitter medicine'.

To get on with their own task the Commandos had to leave the Canadians to subdue *WN 27*. About forty-five minutes after the North Shore's landing, an AVRE 'cracked the concrete casemate with a "Dustbin" and took the sting out of the Germans.'

About an hour and a half later *Widerstandnest 27* had more or less fallen to the North Shore's B Company, however, resistance from German infantry in the houses along the esplanade and in the village was to persist until 1800 hours. These were principally men who had escaped from the strongpoint and fallen back into the village where, further to the east, some of the houses had been prepared for defence. It was not until the following morning that an isolated group of *Osttruppen* gunners finally surrendered. They had been told that they would be killed as traitors by the Allies. The brutality of their own Soviet society, their experience in the Red Army and the *Wehrmacht* led them to, understandably, believe that this may well have been true.

## Inland and the Advance East

Having made their way through the exit, which had been blown and was being bulldozed in a section of foreshore where there was a 160 yard gap in the sea wall, and made their way through the coastal minefield via the white mine taped exit, the leading elements of 48 Commando arrived at their assembly area. Here, behind the 'crust' of German defences, it was 'much quieter' but Colonel Moulton found that most of his unit was missing. Various estimates have been made as to 48's losses but it is clear that, initially, the Commando mustered only about fifty per cent of its strength and many men had lost equipment, weapons and ammunition, particularly support weapons. Leaving the troops to reorganize in the assembly area, the Colonel retraced his steps back to the beach. Here, according to the war diary:

> *A considerable number of men of mixed troops were found under the cliff and these were moved off to the right. He found Y Troop attempting to get ashore from an LCT to which they had transferred from their LCI. However, the landing of Y Troop was very slow and few men managed to get ashore before the LCT shoved off, taking with her about fifty men of the Commando to England despite their energetic protests. Z Troop was more fortunate and about forty men were eventually collected in the assembly area.*

With a much reduced strength but, as planned, 48 Commando moved east through the village and country east of St Aubin towards Langrune and SWORD Beach. After the noise, death and confusion of the beaches, once through the crust of defences, all seemed ominously quiet. While near the beach Colonel Moulton had been hit by splinters from a mortar bomb but he remained in command despite the pain and discomfort from his wound.

## Langrune-sur-Mer

**See map page 148**

Lieutenant Colonel Moulton directed A Troop across the half mile of relatively open country that separated St Aubin and Langrune. Taking an inland route, their mission was to head towards the walled farm (Manoir des Templiers) on the south-eastern outskirts of Langrune that had been chosen as the Commando's firm base for the clearance of the village and the *WN 26* strongpoint. Meanwhile, the depleted X Troop was moving to clear the seafront houses between the two villages. They were assisted in this by the fire of various converted landing craft whose crews used a variety of weapons and 'brassed up the seafront buildings as X Troop advanced'. At the same time B Troop was on a parallel route through the houses between the lateral roads and the light railway line.

*A pair of Ostruppen officers, the men that were told that the allies would kill them all if they were taken prisoner.*

Having set up his headquarters Colonel Moulton:

> *...ordered Z Troop to organize its defence and A Troop to start on their sector of house clearing. At some time about then, I sent an officer's patrol to our junction point with No. 41 (RM) Commando* [a small stream west of Petit Enfer, a half mile east].
>
> *B and X Troops had met nothing but snipers and patrols, which withdrew before their advance; a little later, B Troop rejoined us at the farm... X Troop reported that it was held up. Moving along the sea front, they had reached the west side of Langrune, but could make no further progress. I pressed him for more definite information about what was holding him up, but all he could say was that he was losing a lot of men to snipers. Feeling rather futile, I told... B Troop to work down the road leading to the seafront on the east side of the village, so getting behind whatever was holding up X Troop. I gave him our one* [3-inch] *mortar, under Lieutenant Mike Aldworth of S* [Support] *Troop, who had now reached us from the beach, in case he met opposition.*
>
> *Soon, B Troop reported that they were in contact with the enemy, ...I went down to have a look. We walked through the back gardens, scrambling over walls and pushing our way*

*Commandos assemble on the lateral road behind the beach. Note the handcart and dispatch riders' motorcycles.*

*Commandos advance inland. In the background, a Churchill AVRE carrying a Standard Box Girder (SBG) Bridge.*

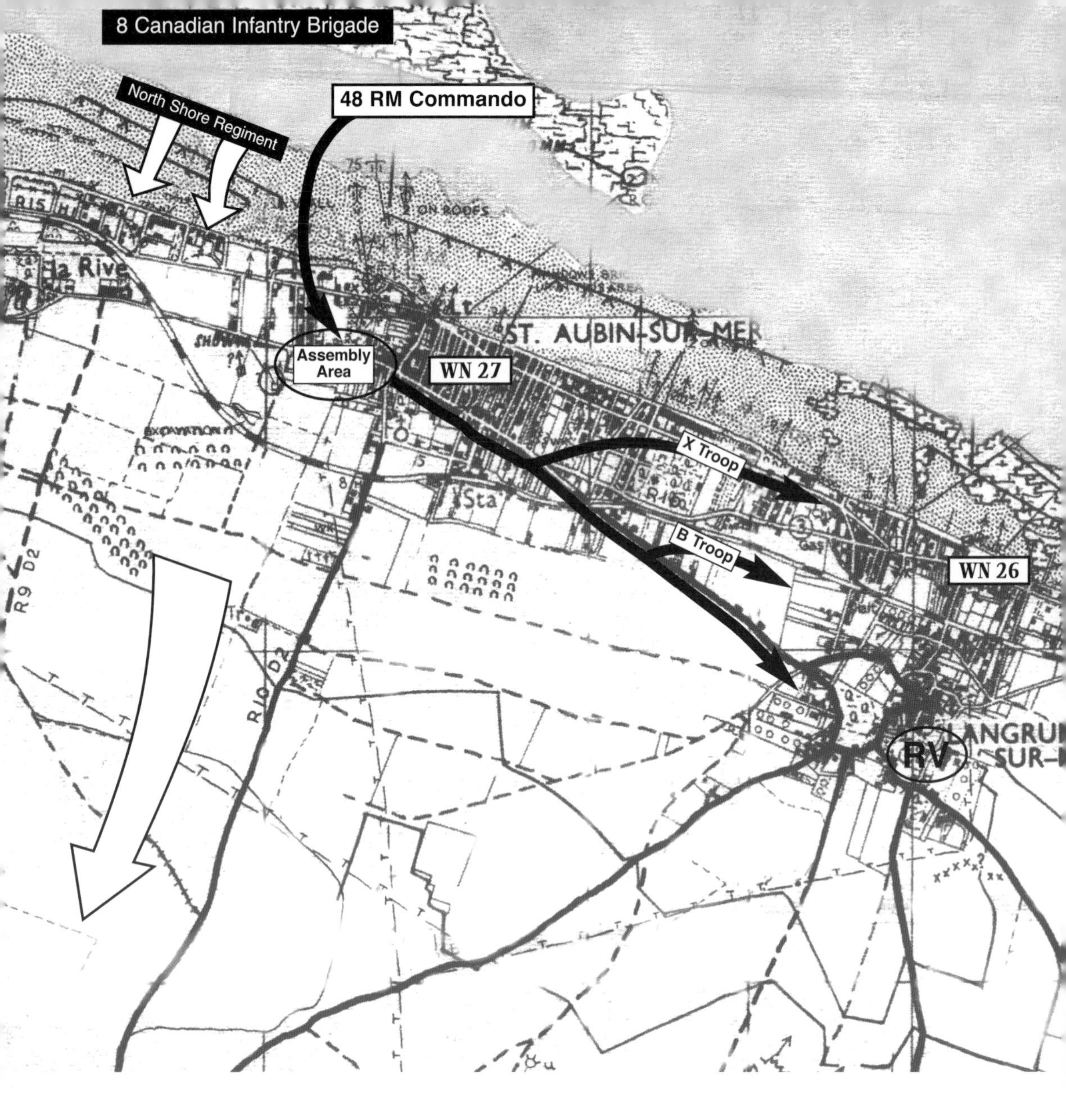


*through side doors; passed Aldworth who started to range his mortar, and came up with the men of B Troop. They were having a good many casualties from light mortar fire, we could see the tails of the bombs flying about, and I told them to keep inside the houses until they were wanted. At last, we reached a house …, and were directed upstairs to find the OC B Troop in the loft. I started to haul myself up through the hatch, but my arm and shoulder felt very sore from mortar bomb splinters, so I stood with my head and shoulders in the hatch, talking to the OC. He said he could see right into a German post, and was quite confident he could capture it as soon as he had a fire plan arranged.*

The 'strongpoint' (*WN 26*) defended by a reinforced platoon from *9 Kompanie 736 Grenadiers*, was centred on a group of fortified houses on the Langrune seafront and included a 75mm and a newly casemated 50mm anti-tank gun.

The Royal Navy's landing support craft continued to fire at *WN 26* but their weapons were too light to do more than chip the concrete. Captain Dye RA, the attached Forward Officer Bombardment (FOB) contacted HMS *Vigilant*, with her four 4.7-inch guns:

*We began ranging the destroyer that was assigned to support our attack. The strongpoint at Langrune was battered with accurate fire from the destroyer but showed little sign of giving up.*

The attack on *WN 26* began with the already below strength B Troop dashing across the lateral road to attempt to break into the

*Z Troop digging in on the outskirts of Langrune-sur-Mer.*

*Canadian Infantry shelter behind a typical WN barricade in St. Aubin.*

houses on the far side of the crossroads. However, the Germans had prepared the buildings for defence and according to Colonel Moulton, 'They [B Troop] seemed unable to get in. I watched them crouch under the ten-foot wall that blocked the street, and saw half a dozen stick grenades come over it to fall among them. Miraculously, it seemed, there were no casualties.' Despite the confidence of the company commander, the attack by B Troop had been halted.

The attack on *WN 26* was renewed, this time supported by a pair of Centaur tanks from 2nd Royal Marine Assault Regiment but this too failed. The Centaurs' main role had been to bridge the fire support time gap between the end of the amphibious bombardment and the deployment of the SP field artillery ashore. However, their landing craft were top-heavy and of the eighty Centaurs, only forty-eight made it to shore on the morning of D Day. Most of these, as planned, remained in the immediate beach area. In the attack on the Langrune strong point, the first Centaur attempted to destroy an anti-tank wall some ten feet high by four feet thick. It used up all its ammunition without seriously damaging the wall, exposing the limitations of the 95mm howitzer, though the wall would even have challenged the AVRE's Petard demolition mortar. The second Centaur ran over a mine amongst the rubble surrounding the defences. Despite the failure to breach the concrete wall, some of the Commandos had forced an entry into the strong point but had 'fallen foul of anti-personnel mines'. Colonel Moulton admits that he '…should have had more men close up, ready to back up their momentary success'. He continued his account:

> *We were nearly back where we had started, one Centaur less, and the road blocked to tanks. Worse, we now knew that the enemy had built and wired themselves into the block of houses they were holding. It seemed that, until we could knock something down, it was physically impossible to enter, while, by demolishing house on our side of the crossroads, they had given themselves a clear field of fire to prevent our close approach. While I was digesting these unpleasant facts, Jumbo Leicester came up and told me to call off further attempts on what we now began to call the Langrune strong point, and to organise the rest of the village for defence; German armour was moving up towards the coast, and Langrune was on its axis.*

This was the drive of *21. Panzerdivision* around Caen from the east into the gap between JUNO and SWORD and as the east-most troops in the coastal area, on the southern outskirts of Langrune, the Commandos were in a potentially important position.

As darkness fell, the officers' patrol returned from the junction point, reporting that they had seen nothing of 41 Commando but had met no enemy either. Isolated, the Commandos prepared their defences and went into their night-time routine. Overnight, Colonel Moulton considered the problem posed by *WN 26*. How were they going to force an entrance? 'The Germans had so arranged things that they could shoot at us while we were doing so, it was not going to be simple for us, and could be very costly'. With an uncertain situation inland, the Commandos were a low priority for support. However, *21. Panzerdivision* did not, as expected, push home their attack and at dawn:

> *The Brigadier came up and confirmed that... our job was to finish off the strong point. I realised our duty, both to the military world at large and to our own self-respect, to capture it ourselves and not to leave it to someone else; it would make a great deal of difference to the Commando's future morale to finish the job – and we all, by now, had a personal score to settle. But then weakness: the strong point was beginning to seem impregnable; and it would be nice to stop and lick our wounds, without the prospect of more casualties, more danger and perhaps another failure. Jumbo Leicester's matter-of-fact order was just what I needed, and I recognised not only its correctness, but the moral stiffening, which I needed, and which it gave me. I tried not to show all this, as I acknowledged his order in what I hoped was an imperturbable way.*
>
> *The Brigadier also gave me some tanks to replace the Centaurs: two Canadian M10s and a troop commander's Sherman from the Royal Marine Armoured Support Regiment.*

But the knocked out Centaur was blocking the route from the lateral road up to the strong point and the open, fire-covered, approaches were mined. However, amongst the ammunition that the Commandos had safely landed were some Bangalore Torpedoes. These were six foot long steel pipes packed with explosives, which when detonated would shred barbed wire defences through which they had been placed. They also caused sympathetic detonations to mines that were laid near the torpedoes. The following morning, having screwed several Bangalores together end to end, the Commandos used this effect to breach the minefield. Colonel Moulton described the operation:

> *We used some smoke; Lieutenant Mackenzie, with some of A Troop, rushed across the road behind the Centaur and into the field, placed the Bangalore Torpedo, checked its placing and lit its fuze, then rushed back into the cover of the houses, and the*

*Bangalore exploded with an almighty bang.*

*Covered against possible anti-tank weapons by our men in the houses, one of the M10s went forward, swung clear of the Centaur, followed the line of the Bangalore past it, then swung back into the road. I watched, heart in mouth, fearing to see another mine go up under it; but nothing happened, and now it could blow us a hole in the masonry, it started to fire at the wall across the street. Yesterday, the Centaurs' high-explosive shells had burst on the thick, concrete wall and hardly dented it; now, the M10s' solid, high-velocity anti-tank projectiles went right through it.*

The M10 used up most of its ammunition but the wall had plenty of small holes in it and one of the Royal Marine's Sherman command tanks was brought up 'to have a go with high-explosive. ... In a while, the wall and the house on one side of it began to crumble'. According to the Royal Marines' D Day report: 'An assault party then went in and seized the houses on either side of the gap. One of these was blown up by a demolition party and the resultant rubble used to fill in the anti-tank ditch inside the wall.' Colonel Moulton continued his account of the end of the battle:

*After a bit, I judged we could make it and gave the word, Lieutenant Mackenzie led the way with A Troop, and I followed with B, then... X Troop and a working party from Headquarters with shovels and explosives. While A and B Troops worked through the houses along the sea-front, the working party blew down what was left of the wall, and shovelled the debris into the trenches and fire positions around it, so that a tank could pass. Germans were firing down the open promenade, but Mac seemed to be getting along well through the houses. The Sherman ground its noisy way across the debris of the wall onto the promenade, slewed to fire along it, and as it did so put a track into a trench on the promenade and wrenched it off. Hell! Were we going to fail now? The tilted Sherman fired as well as it could down the promenade, and I tried to follow Mac down the houses to see if I could do anything to help him. Then, suddenly, grey figures began to emerge with their hands up. RSM Travers fell them in and checked to see that they were unarmed, and the officer in*

*Colonel Moulton watching the M10 at work on the enemy defences.*

> *charge was brought to me, but we had no language in common. As we looked at each other, I saw one of 48 kick a German bottom, and shouted to him to shut up being a fool. Mac came along and reported no further opposition; the prisoners were marched off; and that was that.*

Meanwhile, 41 Commando, who had been landed on Sword Beach the day before, had been fighting westward through the coastal villages of Lion towards Luc-sur-Mer to meet up with 48 Commando and link the two beachheads. 41 Commando found the strong point in Petit Enfer strongly held and, as we will see, it was only finally overcome on 8 June.

On 8 June, 48 Commando was directed inland to occupy Luc-sur-Mer. This did not involve serious fighting, 'just some mopping-up'.

### Petit Enfer – 46 RM Commando

With 41 Commando held up in Lion, 46 Commando Royal Marines, who had been kept afloat as 4 Special Service Brigade's reserve, were landed and effected the link up on the coast by clearing the coastal strong point at Petit Enfer (*WN 24*) and the infantry position on the southern outskirts of the village; *WN 25*.

Realizing that 48, having suffered 50 per cent casualties, were not in any shape to take on an assault on another *Widerstandnest*, Brigadier Jumbo Leicester, 4 Special Service Brigade, sought agreement to bring his so far uncommitted reserve ashore to complete the link-up. Overnight authority was granted and orders dispatched to Lieutenant Colonel Hardy. The war diary records:

> *0600 hrs Received a signal that 46 (RM) Commando to come under the command of I Corps, and to land at Bernieres-sur-Mer* [NAN Green]. *The C/O went to HQ of the 4th SS Brigade at St Aubin-sur-Mer where he was ordered to capture the German strongpoint at Petit Enfer with one troop of RM Armoured Support Regiment who would be under his command. This strongpoint occupied a built up area 400 yards in length and 150 yards in depth and sited at the eastern edge of the town.*

Having marched from Bernières via St Aubin, the two leading 46

*German prisoners being marched to the beach for transport to England.*

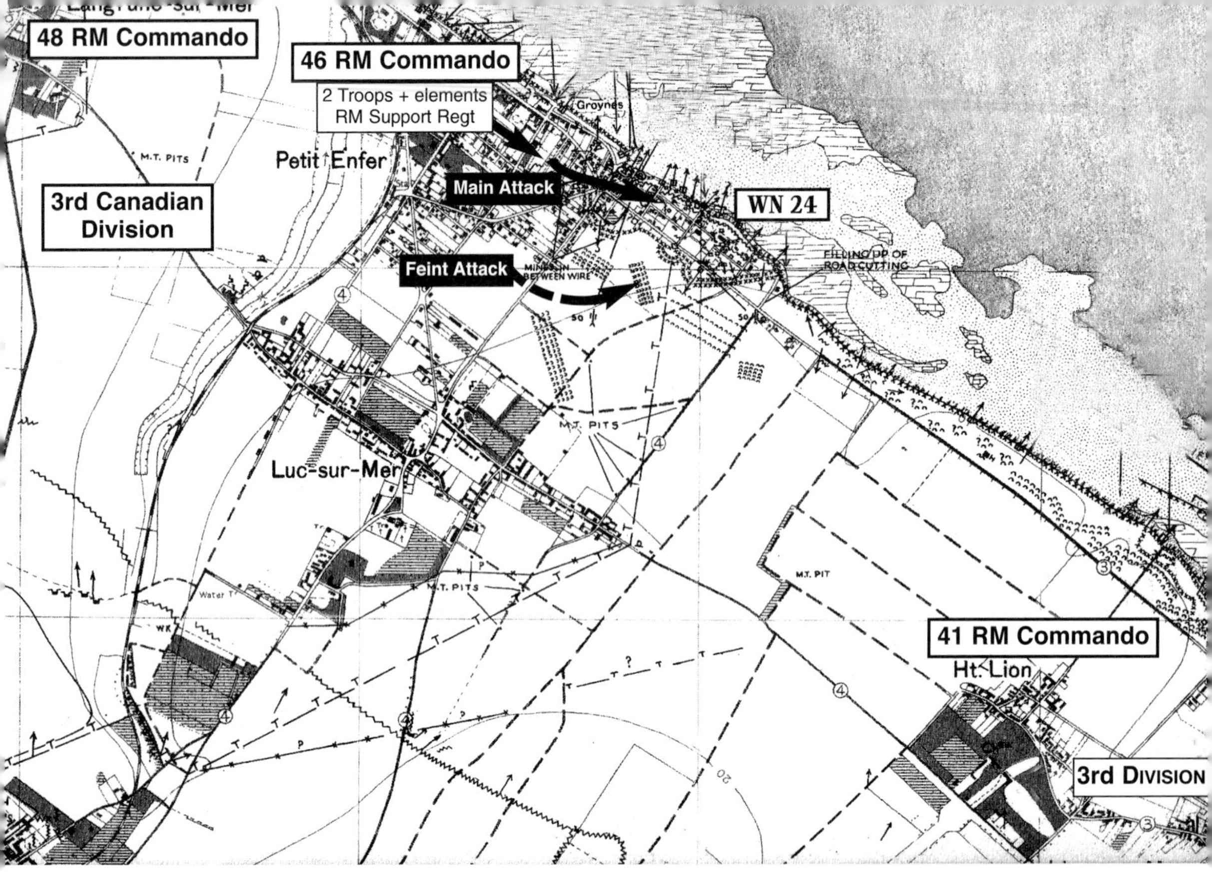


troops secured the road on the western edge of the Petit Enfer without casualties but 'there were shots from snipers', which slowed down their advance but phase one of Colonel Hardy's plan was complete.

> *The attack commenced at 1330 hrs from Langrune-sur-Mer in three phases. When the naval bombardment was over, tanks of the RM Armoured Support Regiment moved forward to make contact with the enemy on the west side of the strongpoint, with the remainder of the Commandos following up closely. These two troops were to secure suitable OPs so as to plan the attack.*

In position to observe the extensive *WN 24* position, the Commandos could see that the western defences of the *Widerstandnest* were centred on an anti-tank gun at the crossroads on the edge of the town and that as expected, there were belts of mines and wire covering an extensive trench system. 'The remainder of the strongpoint consisted of pillboxes and a reinforced house.'

With the plan confirmed and orders given, the attack proper

(phase 2) began with a diversionary attack from the south by a troop supported by two of the Centaurs. As Colonel Hardy hoped, with the enemy's attention focused to the rear of the position, the attack from the west on the anti-tank gun by the other two troops supported by the second Centaur was successful and they destroyed the gun and cleared the enemy's trenches and bunkers. The Commandos had a foothold in *WN 24* and the final phase of the attack could begin.

> *During further attacks on the strongpoint, one troop engaged enemy from the south, enabling the other troop to cross the wire and the minefield. After a brief encounter one troop entered the strongpoint and the enemy surrendered.*

By 1800 hours, enemy resistance ceased and some sixty prisoners from *716th Division* were rounded-up along with a number of weapons and equipment; no casualties. The Commandos went on to clear and occupy the remainder of the town by nightfall on 8 June.

At 2000 hours, two troops were ordered to occupy the town of Douvres-la-Délivrande two miles inland passing 41 (RM) Commando who had been in Luc-sur-Mer for most of the day. Douvres had been heavily shelled with naval gunfire and consequently badly damaged. They reached Douvres with its distinctive double-spired cathedral at 2200 hours and occupied it without opposition although a counter-attack was expected during the night. At some stage communications with the two troops in Douvres failed, and a patrol from the remainder of the Commando went forward to clarify the position but returned at before first light without finding the two Troops. They were in fact fine and there had been no counter-attack on Douvres. Brigade HQ, however, gave orders to send another patrol to Douvres after first light.

On this more extensively built up stretch of coast, the Royal Marine Commandos had been committed to fighting along the coastline, with little support, while I Corps's main effort lay in getting as far inland as possible. The result was some serious fighting for the newest Commando unit.

*A recently completed 50mm anti-tank gun casemate. A standard construction found in most costal strong points.*

*German defenders killed at Langrune by Commandos attacking their position.*

*A 50mm anti-tank gun enfilades 8 Brigade landing beach at St Aubin where the North Shore Regiment landed. Note the crash-landed P47 Thunderbolt.*

## Visiting the Battlefield

From the D514 coast road, drive into St Aubin and make you way to the seafront and park just to the west of the casemate and the collection of memorials.

This is *Widerstandnest 27* complete with a 50mm anti-tank gun and a sizeable group of flags and memorials, chief amongst which are The North Shore's and the Fort Garry Horse's memorials, the first units to land here, and of course 48 RM Commando. Most of the strong point has been lost to coastal erosion or lies under the car park and cliff area to the left of the memorial. Below is NAN RED Sector of JUNO Beach and 48 Commando landed here just to the west around the prominent building.

Four Eight made their way to their objective in Langrune through the streets of St Aubin avoiding the area of the strongpoint. By vehicle, follow the one way system inland from the seafront, turning left onto Rue Maréchal Foch and following the road past the crucifix to the roundabout. Follow the sign to Lagune-sur-Mer – on the D7 Route Langrune-sur-Mer. Follow the D7 until you reach the church. After 150 yards turn left on to the D84 Rue de l'Abbé Rolland. Stop. To the right of the D84

*Men of 48 RM Commando moving inland.*

Rue des Chasses is the Manoir des Templiers, which was the HQ of 48 Commando during the attack on *WN 26*.

To reach *Wiederstandnest 26* follow Rue de l'Abbé Rolland and after 150 yards, turn left and then right onto Rue de la Mer, follow this road to the seafront square and park.

The strong point, based on a 50mm anti-tank guns and several *Tobruk* machine gun positions, was one of the smaller coastal defensive positions, as the bluffs flanking Langrune made this an unlikely spot for a major landing. There is little to be seen of the German defences except for the rebuilt houses at the rear of the square. The square contains an NTL totem, a US army truck crushed into a cube to represent 'the destruction of war' and, more conventionally, another memorial to 48 Commando Royal Marines.

To reach le Petit Enfer/Luc-sur-Mer and the scene of 41 RM Commando follow the D514 east from the square.

## Chapter Seven

# SWORD Beach and West

So far the Rangers and Royal Marine Commandos employed on the western D Day beaches were, as units, new to action, though many experienced commanders had been cross-posted. 41 Royal Marine Commando, as a battle-experienced unit, was one of the donors of such experienced leaders. Men who went to the new units from 41 had fought for six months in the Mediterranean, taking part in the Operation HUSKY landings in Sicily and those at Salerno, the latter as a part of General Mark Clark's Fifth US Army.

Having been 'selected for the Second Front', 41 Commando left the Mediterranean aboard the SS *Otranto* on Boxing Day 1943 in a convoy that made its circuitous route to the port of Gourock in Scotland, arriving on 4 January 1944. Corporal Mitchell recalled:

> *Despite the very early hour of arrival, a dozen or more smiling WVS ladies were waiting beside a long line of trestle tables piled high with packets of sandwiches and morning newspapers hot off the press.*
>
> *The train moved off, eventually, to round after round of spontaneous cheers and throughout the hours of daylight, as the journey continued ever southward, the exuberance persisted. Anyone within range was given enthusiastic waves, and a barrage of wolf whistles was directed at anything in a skirt.*

After a journey of twenty-four hours the train pulled into Deal on the south coast, where at the Royal Marines Depot the travel stained and bleary eyed Commandos, still clad in khaki drill, promptly felt the full weight of Corps's tradition and standards: 'a highly polished adjutant was very quickly seen heading across the square to sort us out'. Issues of heavy battledress more suitable to English winter weather followed breakfast. A threatened formal inspection was cancelled and the Commandos dispersed across the UK on fourteen days of disembarkation leave.

On return from leave the Commando, as usual, left the Royal Marines Barracks for billets in the seaside towns of Ramsgate and Margate. From here the Commando, now a part of 4 Special Service Brigade, mounted a series of training exercises, culminating in participation in the D Day rehearsal Exercise FABIUS; assaulting Hayling Island.

**The Commando Plan**

The D Day task of 41 Commando was to land behind 8 Brigade of 3rd British Division on QUEEN WHITE Sector of SWORD Beach, turn west and clear the coastal village of Lion-sur-Mer, while 3rd Division concentrated on getting to objectives inland. Once Lion was secured 41 was to advance west to meet 48 Commando at le Petit Enfer. The Commando's detailed tasks were in Lion to subdue Strongpoint TROUT (*WN 21*) on the western extremity of SWORD and to take the enemy position in the area of the 'Château' – *WN* 22.

The houses of the Lion-sur-Mer coastal strip had virtually all been incorporated into the defensive scheme of 9 *Kompanie* 736 *Grenadier Regiment*; Most had been bricked-up and a few had been converted into pillboxes by pouring a thick layer of concrete inside the domestic shell. But the main defensive position was *WN-21*. This position, TROUT was an anti-tank strong point with a 75mm gun and a pair of 50mm cannon; the latter obsolescent tank guns. As usual the concrete casemates and shelters, as well as their interconnecting trenches, were surrounded by belts of barbed wire and mines.

Lieutenant Colonel T M Gray's plan was to split the Commando into two: Force I, which he would command and Force II that his Second-in-Command, Major Barclay, would command. Having assembled behind the beach in their cleared and designated area, the two sub-units would take an inland route to their objectives entering Lion from the south east. This would leave the intermediate coastal defences amongst the bricked up villas strung out from La Brèche westwards to Lion to be neutralised by the Royal Navy. In this case the Fleet Class destroyer HMS *Verulam* mounting four 4.7-inch guns would be in support. In simultaneous independent actions, it was intended that Force I would take TROUT, while Force II would subdue enemy in the area of the Château. Colonel Gray was supported by his own heavy weapons, Royal Artillery Forward Observation Officers (FOOs) and Naval Forward Officer Bombardment (FOB) Party who would direct the fire of a second Fleet Class destroyer HMS *Virago*, who would support the attack on Objective TROUT and the Château. *Virago* was a considerable asset, her four-gun broadside alone equivalent to an entire field regiment of twenty-four 25-pounder guns.

## Deployment

Having arrived in concentration Camp 19 from Kent, 41 Commando were allowed out under close supervision in order to maintain their peak of fitness and 'to prevent staleness as a result of incarceration setting in'. Corporal Mitchell recalled:

> *By Whit Sunday 28 May, Britain was under heat wave conditions ... Possibly as a holiday treat, the Unit was permitted a brief escape into the civilian world for a keep-fit march. The dress was 'shirt sleeve order, without arms or equipment', and no one seeing that column of unshaven men in collar-less khaki shirts with sleeves rolled up above the elbow and braces showing, could ever have imagined that they were Royal Marines.*

The D Day plans started to be revealed down the unit's chain of command on 29 May but unlike many less well trusted men who had been let into the extremely closely guarded invasion secret, 41 had an opportunity to be indiscrete:

> *When all briefings had been finalised, a last taste of Olde England was granted in the form of a brief 'run ashore'. It was organised on a Troop basis and given the unofficial codename of Operation Pub. Those who elected to take part – i.e. to partake – were marched to a secluded hostelry with a beer garden, to ensure that the men were segregated from any possible civilian contact. There they were allowed to buy two pints of beer (no more!), with SNCOs acting as waiters, taking the orders and delivering the goods.*

If the Army security authorities had been aware of the true meaning of 'a run ashore', Operation Pub would certainly not

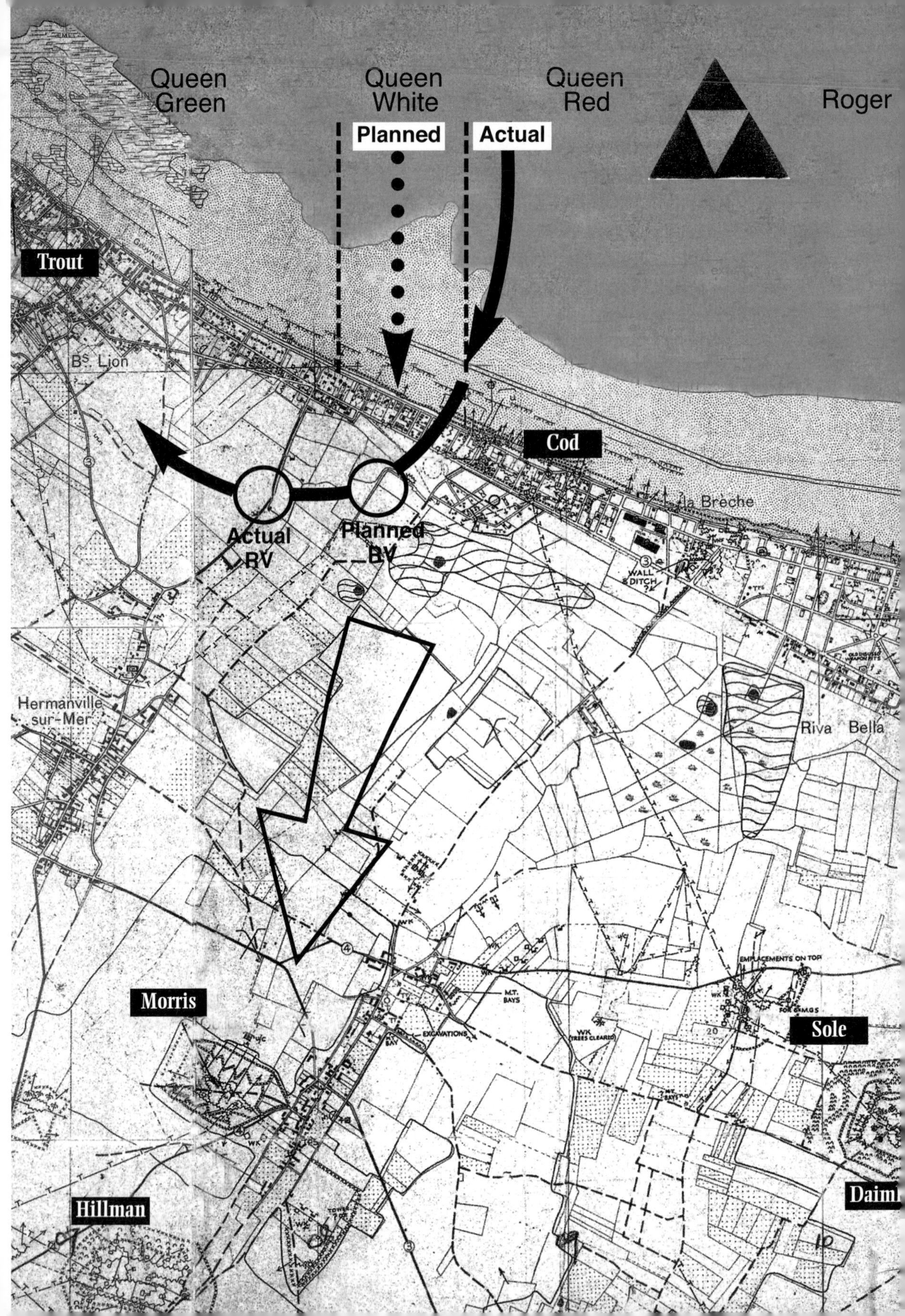
Queen Green
Queen White
Queen Red
Roger
Planned
Actual
Trout
Bs Lion
Cod
la Breche
Actual RV
Planned RV
WALL DITCH
Hermanville sur-Mer
Riva Bella
Morris
M.T. BAYS
EXCAVATIONS
EMPLACEMENTS ON TOP
Sole
Daiml
Hillman

have been allowed!

After a day's delay because of poor weather, under leaden skies, 41's ten mile drive in trucks through the throngs of vehicles moving, waiting or hidden in long lines under trees at the side of the road, left the Commandos in no doubt that they were just one small part of a very large undertaking. Arriving at HMS *Tormentor* on schedule on the afternoon of 5 June, they were marched to the pier and loaded aboard five LCI (Small) and were soon out in the Solent.

Despite the cramped and uncomfortable conditions, sleeping on bare boards, fully dressed and booted, with a single blanket, most had a good nights sleep as the great armada headed south from St Catherine's Point to Normandy.

**The Landing**

H Hour for 3rd Division's first assault wave had been at 0725 hours and an hour later the Commandos could clearly see and hear the battle as they approached the coast. Their war diary noted that SWORD:

> *... appeared to be a bit of a shambles. It was littered with dead and wounded and burned out tanks and with flails flailing through wire and*

*mines, bulldozers clearing gaps, etc., mortar bombs and shells were crashing down fairly plentifully. It appeared that RED Beach was getting a better share of this than WHITE.*

Five minutes later at 0830, the LCAs were under shell and mortar fire as they made their run-in to the beach. Damage to the craft from near misses was slight but significant; landing ramps damaged by the enemy fire further affected the orderly disembarkation of the Unit.

Landing at 0845 hours, 41 touched down not on QUEEN WHITE Sector as planned but 300 yards to the east on fire-swept QUEEN RED, thanks largely to a strong easterly current. As with the case of the other Commandos, SWORD Beach was far from clear and none of the expected signs, marshals or even the 'military policemen that had stood, white gloved, directing us off the beach during [Exercise] FABIUS'. The problem was that the extensive strongpoint at the back of the centre left of QUEEN WHITE, *WN-20* or COD, was still not taken. Even though under attack, *Hauptmann* Kuhtz's soldiers of *10 Kompanie* were still able to put some fire down on the beach, which was supplemented by well-directed artillery and mortar fire from *916. Division* further inland.

*Still under fire with obstacles not cleared Sword Beach was a challange for the Commandos.*

*Wrecks of 79th Armoured Division's assault armour litter the beach.*

*Royal Marines Commandos experiencing difficulties getting ashore.*

Middle East veteran Cyril Ellis was amongst the first Commandos ashore:

> *It was horrific. First we were making our approach; then we were 50 yards away; then 10; then the doors went down and we were moving. We were making for the seawall – there were people falling on either side of me. We lost quite a few that day.*

To make a difficult opposed landing worse, the grounded flat-bottomed LCIs swung in the surf, some ended broadside-on in conditions that inexperienced crews could not master, especially as the craft lightened with the disembarkation of the Commandos. In the worst cases men had to queue under fire to use the only viable ramp, others fell or jumped off into three or four feet of water. On the beach there was 'an indescribable chaos of noise, movement, smells and smoke'. Marine John Venables wrote:

> *As our craft touched the shingle the bullets were zipping all round us and into the ship. We jumped out and waddled up the beach just as a tank came by. I called out to our lads to get behind it and run forward. As I did so I sort of overbalanced as we were all carrying heavy loads. I fell over next to the front left track of the tank and in that split second I thought I'd go right under it and be squashed flat. The next second I was grabbed from behind and thrown aside by very strong arms. I was amazed as the Sherman missed me by inches and as it went past I got a face full of exhaust fumes. I saw one of our other NCOs rushing up the beach, a chap I never really knew, and he had saved my life. By the afternoon he was dead.*

Corporal Mitchell, a dispatch rider in Headquarters Troop left his LCI carrying a 'Parascooter', a diminutive motorbike.

> *There was time for no more than a glance at the beach, a shambles of burning tanks, shattered landing craft and bodies floating in the shallows, as we queued to use the one usable ramp. It was bucking about like a cake-walk, so I had no option but to sit down, cradling the bike in my arms to stop it ending up in the drink. I needn't have worried about it because in trying to keep up with my troop, I found the machine too heavy to carry for very long, and its small wheels simply gouged a furrow in the soft*

*QUEEN Sector, junction of White and Red Beaches at 8.45 am.*

*sand when I tried to push it. Some tank men were crouching against their knocked-out Churchill tank. 'Here mate!' I gasped to one of them. 'Want a motorbike?' Then I abandoned it and ran on.*

The Commando mantra to 'get of the beach' served Four One well but even so, numerous bodies bearing the distinctive Combined Arms patch were soon washing around in the surf and rising tide amongst those of the assault battalions of 3rd Division. Casualties to the already slim Commando establishment had a disproportionate effect when it is considered that an ordinary assault infantry battalion landed with almost double the strength.

Even though the troops encountered a variety of challenges ranging from uncut wire and uncleared minefields to active enemy in the dunes and houses, 41 Commando were across and off the beach in five minutes. The designated assembly area was, however, also under fire and on arrival with elements of his HQ, Lieutenant Colonel Gray moved the still assembling unit to a quieter spot further inland. This undesirable move meant that stragglers from the beach would have difficulty in locating the Commando but staying at the 'RV' planned was not an option. It was now 0920 hours, some thirty-five minutes after 41 Commando's landing.

Lying in the cover of the trees and walls around the first houses he had reached, Marine Tim Holdsworth was surprised to find himself apparently alone as his mates were either lying dead or wounded or invisible in cover.

*I was a bit surprised to be in one piece. The shock of going into action had hit me quite hard and I'd seen chaps I knew falling all over the place. The trouble was we couldn't see the enemy who had run back and set up new positions, and being Jerries they knew what they were doing and you never had it easy with them. The bullets were smashing about everywhere and I could see that none of us still alive felt like moving. Two DD tanks came along and the bullets were pinging off their armour. When they came closer some of the lads jumped up and got behind them, so I waited my chance and did the same. This way we managed to get along a little lane and seemed to be missing most of the fire until we reached a curve in the road when our tank got hit by an 88 and brewed up. So we all had to hit the deck again. I hid behind a wall with other lads as the Sherman started exploding, like rockets going off. I felt very sorry for the poor beggars inside the tank, but there was nothing we could do for them. The thing was blazing and bullets were still hitting it and the road and trees around us.*

*After a few minutes an officer appeared and showed us how to get behind the wall and into some undergrowth, so we followed him in fear, but he seemed to know what he was doing and the enemy fire was now missing us completely. We went on through a copse and saw houses across a field and a few Jerries stupidly*

*An infantry signaller from a 3rd Division unit and a Commando complete with toggle rope and bergen rucksack seeking to communicate from the shelter of coastal rubble.*

*showing themselves. They seemed to be arguing as to what to do next and had no idea we were near. We let them have it and I think bagged the lot. The officer then led us over to them in a rush and we found all but one dead. He was in a bad way so we left him and ran down a little street until more Jerry fire forced us into one of the houses where we were pinned down. Every time we tried to leave we were fired at. Then at last another Sherman waddled up and started shelling all the houses including ours, so we dived out the back into a little garden and our officer was able to signal the tank crew. By then the Jerries had had it or run off, so we were able to get over the gardens at the back of the house and enter the village.*

**See map page 176**

*The SWORD Beach air photograph from 3rd Division's war diary, annotated with details of 41 RM Commando's operations.*

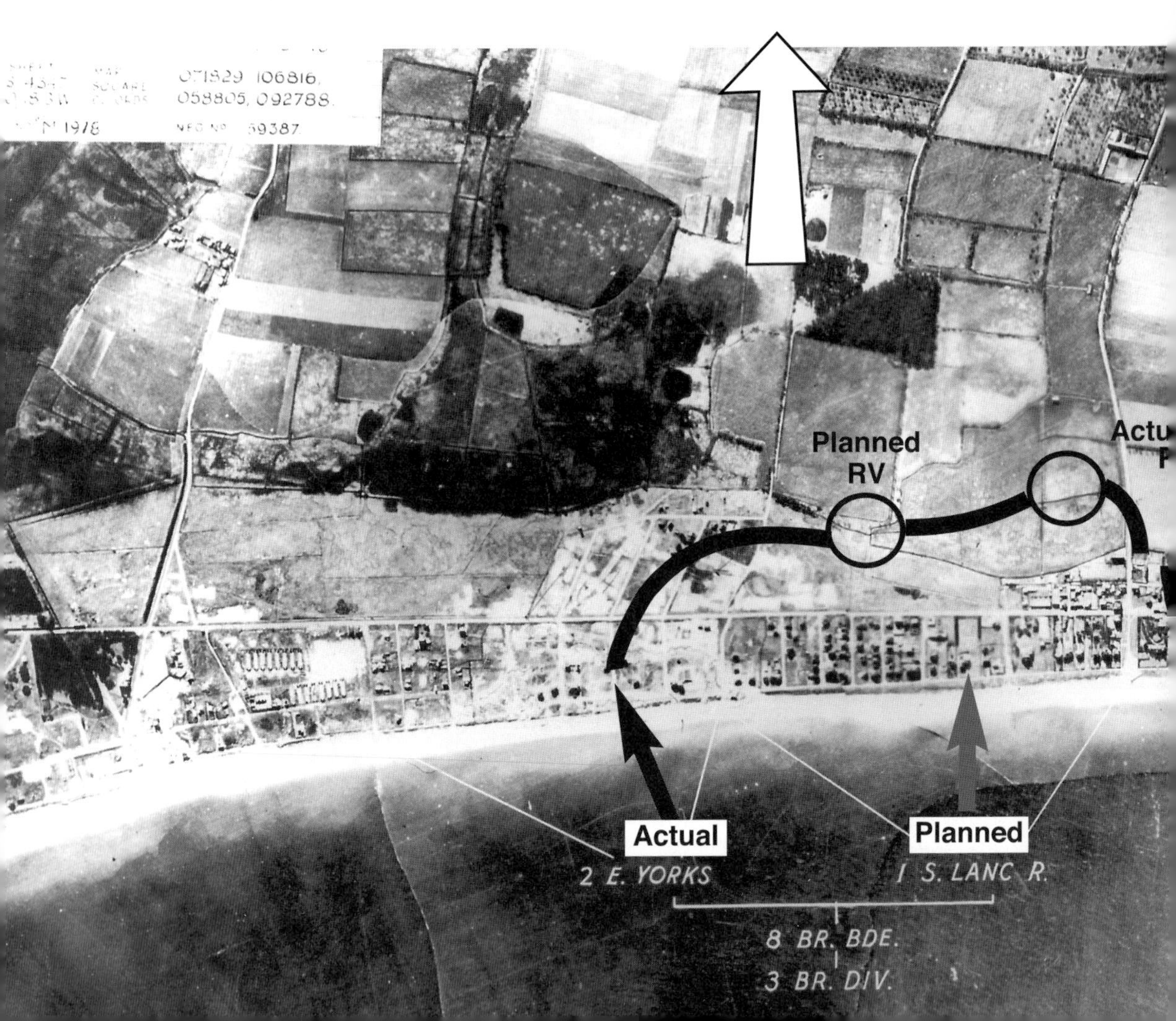

At 0940 hours, a review of the situation by Colonel Gray led to a change of plan. Casualties in the troops reaching the RV had been between 30 and 50 per cent and to make matters worse they had been particularly heavy amongst the unit's leadership. Amongst the losses were key personnel, including his Second-in-Command who was to lead Force II, his signal officer, Regimental Sergeant Major and several troop commanders. Consequently, Colonel Gray amalgamated the two forces under his command but to save 'order, counter order and disorder' he preserved the principles of his original plan.

**The Lion-sur-Mer Objectives**

At about 1000 hours, first away to their objective in Lion were P and Y Troops who were to take TROUT. A Troop followed, heading for the Château, with elements of HQ Troop behind them. Other individuals, sections and troops were directed to their respetive objectives as they arrived from the beach. Corporal Mitchell with HQ Troop followed the main advance:

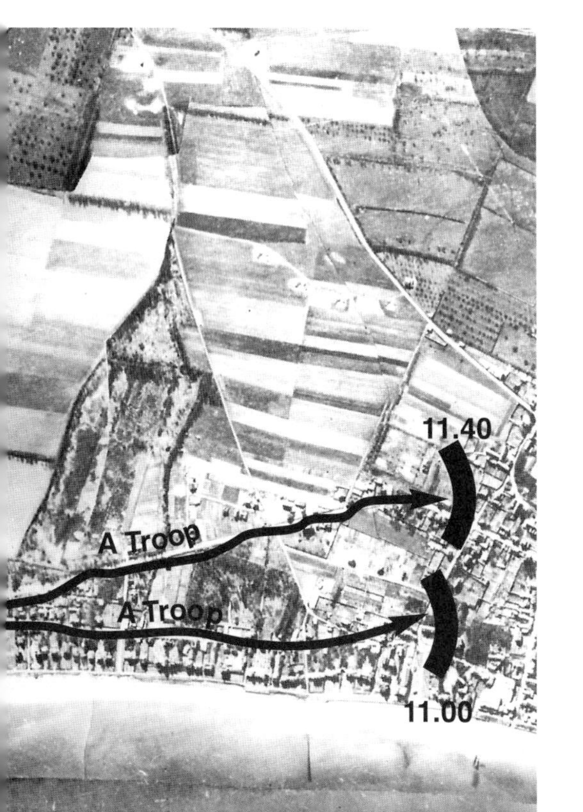


*We doubled into Lion-sur-Mer, making very little noise in our rubber-soled 'brothel creepers'. Curious faces peered at us from the windows as we passed, until we stopped on the pavement in front of a small newsagent's shop, where I spent what was probably the very first 'Invasion Money' used in France. I was persuaded to go inside to buy some matches for one of our number who had his soaked in the landing.*

By 1020 hours messages were brought in by runners who reported to Tactical HQ, at the Church, that P

Troop's advance was held up in Lion at a cross roads near the strongpoint and that the majority of the village and coastal strip had been abandoned by the enemy. The naval gunfire had clearly done its job. This fire had been by direct observation from HMS *Verulam* and to coordinate fire from HMS *Virago* against TROUT the FOB party was needed but Lieutenant Miller RN's signallers had all been killed or wounded on the beach and his radios damaged by shot, shell or seawater. The FOO for the supporting Royal Artillery 25-pounder battery was similarly unable to provide support and to compound matters the link with the 95mm guns of the Royal Marines Support Regiment was not working. Colonel Gray and 41 Commando would have to tackle their objectives, not only with seriously reduced manpower, but with only lightest of supporting fire.

In an entry timed at 1040 hours, the war diary makes it plain that the overall situation had not improved and that enemy were reappearing in cleared parts of the village. It is also recorded that the 1st South Lancs who had been advancing to Hermanville on 41 Commando's inland flank were similarly now pinned down by heavy mortar fire. At 1100 hours, 8 Brigade's reaction to 41 Commando's problems was to dispatch a troop of three AVREs from 5 Assault Regiment Royal Engineers to help subdue TROUT. However, with their short range Petard mortars they had to manoeuvre, under covering fire of their BESA machine guns, to within 100 yards range and this meant advancing into the cleared field of fire of the enemy's anti-tank guns. All three were knocked out by the German's casemated 50mm guns in short order and with the Commandos being too few, out of mortar ammunition and lacking artillery support the stalemate at TROUT was confirmed.

See map page 176

By 1140 hours the stalemate was complete. It was apparent that B Troop heading towards the Château had also been driven to cover near the crossroads by fire from both the Château and from crossfire from TROUT, as well as fire from an assault gun. The Germans not only had crossfire between the two positions in Lion but also mutually supporting positions on the hillside between Hermanville and Cresserons, which were giving 3rd Division's infantry their own problems. 41 Commando's history records that:

> *... 4 Special Service Brigade Liaison Officer, Lieutenant Pat Kay, was dispatched to 8 Brigade HQ to stress the critical situation being engendered by the continuing lack of artillery support.*

41 Commando was now in a perilously extended position, nerve and drive alone had not been enough to overcome the enemy and Colonel Gray withdrew his men from TROUT to his HQ by the church. B Troop, however, remained in distant contact with the Château and A Troop in the centre of Lion, well short of TROUT. With the village under increasing fire Commando HQ had been forced to go firm and to dig-in. The church with its stout surrounding walls was an obvious point, conspicuously marked on the map.

And so the situation remained until 1310 hours, when A Troop in the central area of Lion reported that they were under heavy mortar and small arms fire and that their Troop Commander had been wounded. 'Almost simultaneously, B Troop reported that enemy infantry, about sixty strong, were counter-attacking on their left flank with mortar and infantry gun support.' This group was almost certainly *III Battalion Grenedierregiment 736*, supported by the self-propelled 155mm guns of *10 Battery Artillerieregiment 1716*. With the support of these heavy guns firing into the flank of the Commando's positions around the

*Commandos laden with bergen rucksacks move inland through a minefield gap. Note the minefield lane marker in the foreground. It would have been coloured red and white.*

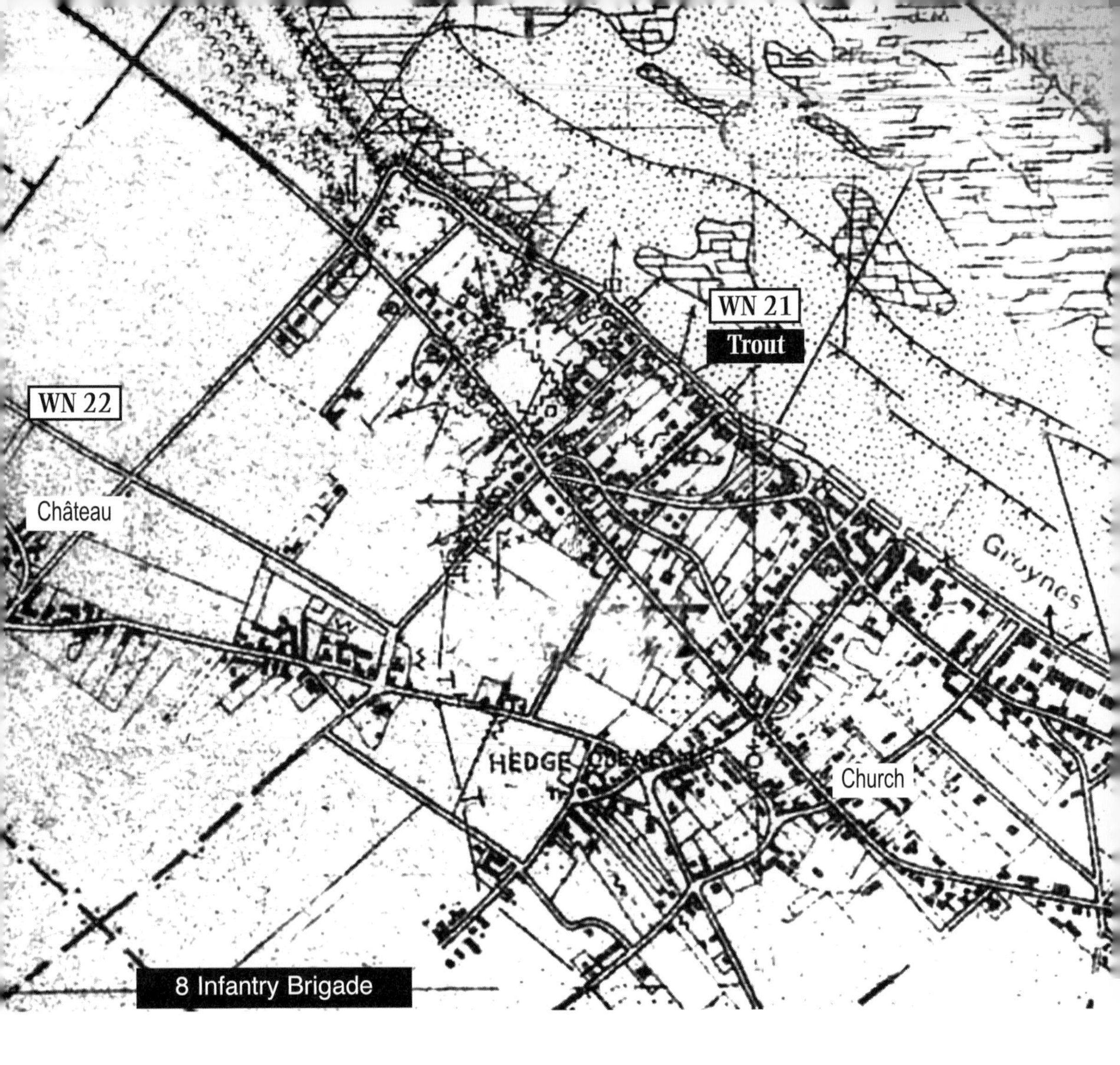


Château, the counter-attack down the open inland slopes made good progress but was eventually halted by concentrated British artillery fire, presumably directed by observers in the Hermanville area.

As far as he was concerned, with the situation deteriorating Colonel Gray had to make a decision. The unit historian recorded:

> *... appreciating that this determined counter-attack on his greatly reduced strength Commando could become general,* [Colonel Gray] *decided to pull back to the more easily defensible line from the Rue du Vivier/Rue du Château du Eau road junction to the beach. This re-grouping was accomplished by*

> *1330 hrs, when it was found that one section of 'A' was missing. 'X' Troop, being so greatly reduced in numbers, was amalgamated with 'Y' at this time.*

Meanwhile, dispatch rider (temporarily without any motorised transport) Corporal Mitchell was in the eastern outskirts of Lion-sur-Mer:

> *We were left there while the fighting troops of the Commando went about their business, and my smattering of French enabled me to understand some French ladies who came to tell us that they had wounded men in their homes; I sent two of our Sick Berth attendants back with them. Later, when mortar fire became intense, we moved into the church grounds to dig in. I was given a pushbike and did a few local trips, then was sent back on it to the beach to find some of our Jeeps. There was also a "Famous James" 125cc motorbike on the LCT, so I rode it back to HQ leading the Jeeps, which were put to immediate use, evacuating wounded.*

Corporal Mitchell and the Jeeps arrived at Commando HQ as the unit was beginning to execute Colonel Gray's order to withdraw and 'so were able to expedite the move to the new location in an apple orchard near the junction of Rue de Ouistreham and the Chemin du Moulin. With that accomplished, the Jeeps proceeded to do invaluable work in evacuating wounded'.

By mid afternoon 9 Infantry Brigade had made its much delayed and 41 Commando was transferred to its command. Appraised of the seriousness of the situation here and reports of the arrival of leading elements of *21. Panzerdivision* west of Caen who were heading to the coast, the Brigadier deployed 2nd Royal Ulster Rifles (2 RUR) and 2nd Lincolns:

> *... to extend Colonel Gray's partly-formed perimeter being held by 41, and they were in position by 1600 hrs, with 2 Lincs to the immediate left of 41.*

Fortunately, one of the Jeeps brought forward by Corporal Mitchell belonged to the FOB and at last they had a workable radio. Lieutenant Miller established contact with HMS *Virago* who had been lying off shore all day 'able to do very little.'

Again the old Gunner adage 'No Comms, no bombs' applied here. Shoots were called for on both 'The Strongpoint' and 'The Château', and these were carried out between 1700 and 1800 hours.

At about 1730 hours, with *Virago's* 4.7-inch naval shells smashing into their targets, the missing section of A Troop, which had been cut off when the Commando withdrew, was able to escape and rejoin the remainder of the unit. Lieutenant Stevenson report that, on his way back through the village, he had knocked out a German armoured car, with a grenade.

The attack on 41's objectives was not to be renewed on the evening of D Day, as 3rd Division were standing on the defensive, in preparation for the counter-attack, which in the event bore-down into the gap between them and the Canadians coming ashore at JUNO Beach. Consequently, once dug-in, the Commando had a relatively peaceful night disturbed by sporadic mortar fire and a bomb dropped by 'a sneak raider' that fell 'rather close' to Colonel Gray's HQ.

Thus D Day ended without a link up on the coast between JUNO and SWORD Beaches, with both 41 and 48 RM Commandos failing to take their primary objectives. This of course was by no means unique for 6 June 1944: very few units of formations reached their objectives and 41's significant early casualties had a knock-on effect throughout the day.

## D Plus One

After a rest and reorganisation, 41 Commando's depleted ranks were placed on immediate notice to move and were awaiting instructions to resume their attacks on TROUT and the Château, when there was the sound of aero engines above:

> *Although initially confined to 'noises off' – racing aero engines and bursts of cannon and machine-gun fire – three Heinkels with Spitfires in hot pursuit suddenly broke through the low cloud cover. They were watched with little more than passing interest until a large cylindrical object was seen to fall from the belly of one of the enemy aircraft; the container opened to disgorge a cascade of small, silvery, fish-like objects. Urgent shouts of 'Anti-personnel!' rang out and men flung themselves to the ground or*

*into slit trenches if near enough. Within seconds, hundreds of SD-1 bombs – about seven inches long, weighing 2 pounds – were bursting like vicious firecrackers over a wide area.*

The orchard in which Commando HQ was established bore the brunt of the bombing in 41's area, killing four men including the FOO and wounding nine others, including the CO and the Padre. Now that both the CO and the second in command had become casualties, command of the unit devolved upon the Adjutant, Major Taplin. While the Commando was again reorganising and evacuating wounded, at:

*... 1130 hours, the Commanding Officer of 2 Lincolns called upon him with the information that 9 Brigade had put 41 Commando under his command for the duration of the action around Lion-sur-Mer.*

*An early version of the cluster bomb which was effective against infantry and 'soft-skin' vehicles in the open.*

At 1415 hours, the Brigadier gave his orders. The Lincolns were to attack the Château. He placed most of the remains of 41 in reserve but deployed a troop to the south of the objective to cover the left flank. A combination of their previous day's casualties and the bombing had rendered the Commando less than fully effective, hence an unaccustomed subsidiary role. The attack duly went in at 1536 hours and 'was completely successful, with only one man being wounded'. It would appear, however, that the majority of the *9 Kompanie* garrison had withdrawn; only two prisoners were taken. 41 Commando came forward and occupied houses at the north east end of the Château to protect the open flank of 2 Lincolns as they moved into Lion to attack TROUT. In covering the Lincolns the Commando dispatched patrols south and west towards Luc-sur-Mer and what appeared to be abandoned positions on the inland ridge. The patrols were:

*... probing forward in the general direction of Luc-sur-Mer along a minor road parallel to and about a mile inland from the coast,*

> *searching large country houses* en route. *After an hour or two it became clear to that force that there were no enemy in the area and, by late afternoon the French country people were greeting the marching column with waves, cheers and red roses thrust into pockets and webbing equipment.*

With the success of the Lincoln's attack on TROUT, at 1730 hours, the remainder of the troops supporting 2nd Lincolns from the area of the Château were ordered to advance on the coastal route to Luc-sur-Mer. The town was reached by early evening without meeting any resistance but there were still plenty of welcoming French civilians. Here 41 finally made contact not with 48 Commando as planned but with 46, the reserve Commando, which had been landed that morning to complete the link up from the west.

Remaining in Luc-sur-Mer overnight, the following day 41 became responsible for the defence of the Luc and Petit Enfer area once 46 had moved inland to Douvres-la-Délivrende, some two miles inland.

## Visiting the Battlefield

This short tour starts at la Brèche d'Hermanville look out for the large ochre painted building, a former hotel which was used by Admiral Ramsey as his first HQ ashore. Park near the 3rd Division Memorial square (Place du Cuirassé Courbet) and walk down to the beach. This is QUEEN WHITE SECTOR. Look right (east) onto Red Sector. About 300 yards in this direction is the area where 41 RM Commando touched down from where they made their way through the villas to their RV/assembly point in the area beyond Ramsey's HQ and a little to the west.

Return to your car and follow the D514 west through the village of Luc-sur-Mer. Reaching the end of the village is a roundabout with an AVRE and sundial memorial to the Commandos and the village's liberation. Turning right at the roundabout it is a very short drive or walk to the site of *WN 21* (Objective TROUT) most of which has been built over.

To reach the Château objective, return to the roundabout. Go straight across, heading inland on Rue Henri de Blagny (D221). At the second cross roads, a junction with the D60 Rue Morel du Than/Route du Luc. The Château and its grounds are behind the trees to the right. Rue Morel du Than is the axis taken by the Commando and subsequent attackers. A better view of the Château itself can be had by turning right at the next junction south.

Chapter Eight

# Douvres Radar Station

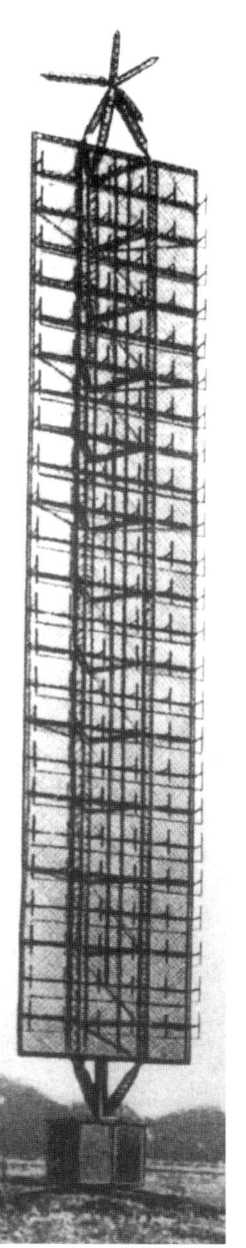
*Freya radar antenna.*

The British developed the Chain Home Radar (Radio Direction and Ranging) network in time to make a significant contribution to the victory in the skies over Southern England in 1940. However, the Germans had been independently developing their own version of radio wave technology, which famously included the direction finding equipment for their bombers. However, by 1941, the Germans were deploying radar along the Channel coast. The technological battle led to Britain's first airborne raid at Bruneval. At this site on the coat, east of le Havre, an RAF technician dropped in with a company of 2 Para to seize radar components. Little did Flight Sergeant Cox know that the Paras were under orders to kill him if he was in danger of falling into enemy hands! Such was the value of the secret radar technology.

By 1944, the *Luftwaffe* had deployed a dense pattern of radar sites (the *Kammhuber* Line) designed to 'vector' night fighter aircraft against British bombers that were ranging across mainland Europe. German radar provided considerable help in ensuring that night RAF bombing raids could only be carried out at a tremendous cost in both men and aircraft. In the strategic bombing campaign the percentage of casualties suffered by Bomber Command aircrew almost equalled that of the infantry fighting in North-west Europe campaign.

The Douvres-la-Délivrande radar site, manned by *8 Kompanie 53 Luftnachrichten* [Air Signals] *Regiment*, had become fully operational in August 1943. The four radars were located in two linked sites, in what was to become 3rd Canadian Division's D Day beachhead. In the smaller, northern, site a single *Wasserman* (Allied code name 'Chimney') long-range early warning radar, was surrounded by mines and wire and was defended by

*Luftwaffe* personnel manning trenches with 20mm guns and twin *Spandau* in concrete Tobruks. A short distance south across the Bény-Douvres road was a larger site containing two *Freya* radar, for general air defence, including the direction of anti- aircraft fire, and a single, shorter range (forty miles) but more accurate Giant *Würzburg* radar that was capable of directing night fighters to intercept individual targets. Five 50mm anti-tank guns, a 75mm field gun and mortars, defended the main site, along with dual purpose ground/anti-aircraft machine-guns in bunkers, Tobruks and open emplacements. The Douvres site was well constructed, with heavy concrete casemates, some of which extended four storeys below ground, sheltering most of the equipment and two hundred men. The position was proof against the heaviest bombardment but, while the men and equipment were safe, the radar antenna in the open were vulnerable to Allied attack.

As the German coastal radar sites could provide timely information that would deny the Allies vital tactical surprise on D Day, the *Kammhuber* Line posed a significant threat to Operation OVERLORD. Consequently, most radar sites were hit during precision attacks by fighter-bombers. Those that were left operational were bent to Allied purposes, as a part of the D Day deception plan, which included exploitation of the electromagnetic spectrum, by the use of strips of radar reflecting metal foil, code named 'Window'. These metal strips were dropped by aircraft to distract the Germans by producing a signature of a mass attack at the *Pas de Calais*. Douvres, along with all other sites in Normandy received the constant attention of the Allied air forces. However, despite this attention, the radar antennae were active to some extent until the Germans destroyed the sets just before they were captured on D+11.

The village of Douvres-la-Délivrande and the radar site were towards the left flank of the 3rd Canadian Division's D Day area. 8 Canadian Brigade were scheduled to capture the site with the support of 30 Commando's technical specialists, whose task was to secure items of intelligence interest such as radar equipment. The Canadian infantary of the North Shore Regiment had been held up by stronger opposition than anticipated at the hamlet of Tailleville. Consequently, 8 Brigade ordered the radar site to be

Northern site
Douvres-la-Délivrande
Main site

by-passed, the Queen's Own and the Chaudière were to continue their advance inland on a more westerly route via Bény-sur-Mer. Tailleville was only occupied during the course of the evening. Here the Canadians reorganized overnight after twelve hours in action and very little sleep during the previous thirty-six hours. General Keller's orders for the night were sent out by dispatch rider. 8 Cdn Brigade were 'to contain Douvres-la-Deliverande with a view to clearing it at first light in the morning'.

### The First Attack

The North Shores resumed their advance in a southerly direction from Tailleville and they promptly bumped into an enemy position in the woods south west of the village. The battalion's A Company, as recorded in the war diary, overcame enemy resistance, 'With the co-operation of the tanks, the position was taken and two officers and thirty-six other ranks were taken prisoner of war'. The war diarist goes on to recount a bitty and frustratingly slow advance to their objective, the radar station.

> *Considerable sniping in Tailleville and forward of A Company is very annoying and slowing up the advance. Progress is slow and the ammunition dump in the woods blew up, which temporarily halted the advance.*
>
> *C Company who had been sweeping the woods and scrub on the left, moved over and cleared through the HQ dug-out in the Wood* [Alternative HQ II/736 Grenadiers]. *Only four prisoners of war were taken from this area but it was found later that they had escaped to the rear and surrendered to 9 Cdn Brigade's HQ. This HQ position was well dug in with underground offices, trenches, cookhouse and so on.*

In this position, C Company reorganized for the attack on the radar station.

I Corps intelligence estimate prior to D Day was that the *Luftwaffe* specialists would not have the stomach for a fight and that the site as a whole would have been severely damaged by the bombardment. In the event they were proved to be wrong on both counts.

The North Shores had a squadron of the Fort Garry Horse's Shermans under command and, in support, the twenty-four 25-pounders of 19 Canadian Field Regiment, which complemented its own machine guns, mortars and anti-tank guns. However, Lieutenant Day complained, with justification, that

> *... the central area of the objective was huge and we were not permitted to bring fire down on the central sector for fear of destroying the radar equipment which the Commandos particularly wanted to capture intact.*

With restricted fire support, C Company attacked the radar site but, according to the Official Historian, they 'produced little results and eventually even a battalion effort met with no more success'. An entry in the North Shore's war diary summarized the situation.

*The short range and more accurate Würzburg was used to vector night fighters to their target.*
*Reconstructed radar hut and dish, now part of a museum.*

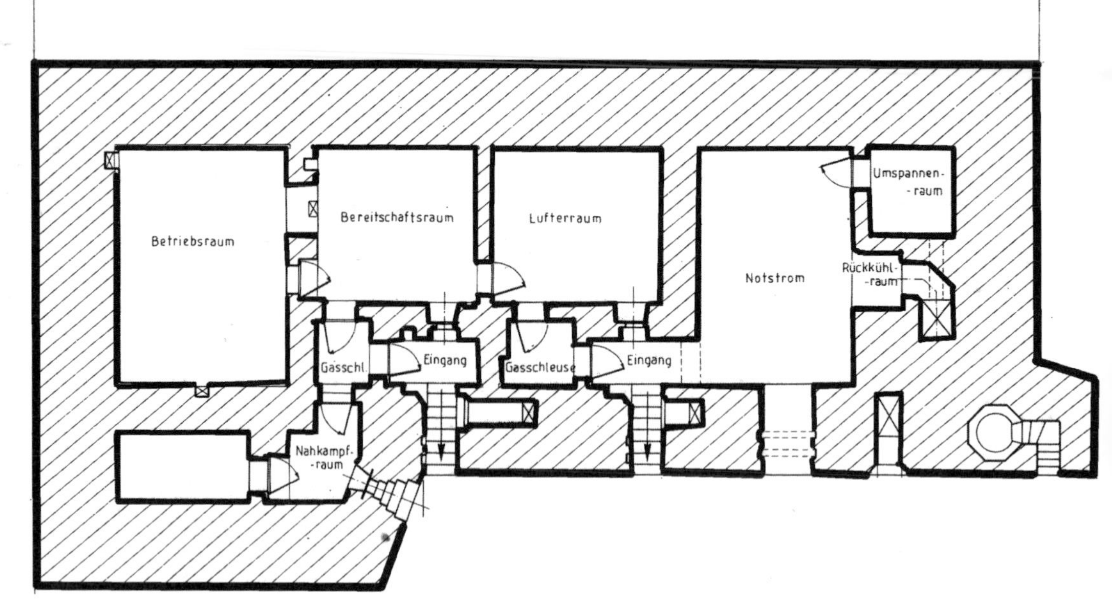


*A Plan of one of the bunkers in the complex.*

> *The Radar Station was found to be stronger than had been anticipated and was engaged by 19 Cdn Fd Regt, which was in support of us. Our mortars also took on the Station but as the concrete works were rather thick and well dug-in, little or no damage was done. The day was fast drawing to a close and a decision was finally made and Bde permission obtained to by-pass the Station and move on to the Bde RV.*

The Douvres position was the only significant part of their initial D Day objective that the Canadians were unable to take. To enable them to move inland, 51st Highland Division, I Corps's follow-up infantry formation, was tasked to deal with the radar site.

Lieutenant Colonel Thompson's orders were to take 5 Black Watch forward to the radar station but he set off with scant information other than 'there were a pocket of Germans holding out' and other limited detail gleaned from the overprinted intelligence map. 5 Black Watch were allocated two AVREs to help deal with the concrete defences. As the Scottish infantry moved forward, they were assured that the Canadians had moved on inland. Their route to the radar station took them through a wood:

> *It was very thick and movement very difficult in it. Troops were encountered, who were taken for Germans. They were in fact Canadians. But after that little trouble had been sorted out,*

> *Thompson got ahead. There was a wide open space beyond the wood and between it and the radar station. This was being swept by a murderous enemy fire, and it was evident that the station was much more strongly held than had been supposed. An 88mm gun, firing somewhere from Douvres village itself, accounted for the two RE vehicles.*

It was clear that the Black Watch would need greater support but Lieutenant Colonel Thompson was ordered to disengage his battalion and pull back 'although he planned a new form of attack from the rear of the objective, orders came that he was to bypass the radar station, which was left to be shelled by the Navy'. *Oberleutenant* Ingle and 238 men of *8 Kompanie 53 Luftnachrichten Regiment* and others were to hold out and provide a valuable observation and reporting service to the enemy.

Eventually, 4 Special Service Brigade took over the task of containing the enemy. 48 Commando and 46 Commando took over the responsibility for the Radar Site. On 10 June, the radar site and the positions surrounding it came under control of 41 Commando.

During this period, the Douvres radar site was considered to be 'More of a hindrance than a nuisance'. However, from the casemates, the Germans could not only operate their radar but , as mentioned, they could also pass back information on Allied activities in the centre of Second Army's area, as well as target information. The site also represented a valuable pivot for the German's planned attempt to drive the Allies back into the sea. The commander of the radar site was exhorted via the surviving telephone line to hold his position. The radar site's garrison was now made up of about 160 surviving *Luftwaffe* technicians and a mixed bag of soldiers from *716 Division* who had been ousted from their own positions on the beaches on D Day. Secure underground and being within three or four miles of promised relief, the Germans had little reason to surrender.

By 11 June, 41 Commando had been left on their own to contain the largely inactive German garrison in their underground casemates. However, with Commando units marching to more active parts of the front, 41 Commando's

Mortar Platoon was detached, as the Germans in the Douvres radar site 'wouldn't have even heard their 3-inch bombs explode'. In order to let the enemy know that they hadn't been forgotten about, they were regularly attacked by rocket firing Typhoons. In addition, two Centaur tanks were placed under command of 41 Commando. The task of these two AFVs was to provide close support and to join in the harassing fire programme that was laid down by the Commando's PIATs, 2-inch mortars, Bren guns and snipers.

> *This was designed largely but also to deter movement between their various "safe havens" during the hours of daylight. 'F' Troop came across a German anti-tank gun with a supply of ammunition and were delighted to fire it off at the slightest provocation.*

This programme also prevented the German technicians from coming out of their casemates and repairing cables to the radar antenna. In true Commando style, 41 were not content to dominate the ground with fire alone.

> *Reconnaissance patrols during the hours of darkness were a major factor in keeping up to date with the situation of the surrounded Germans. Of great value in this task were the handful of attached German speaking men of 10 (Inter-Allied) Commando who were at times able to assess conditions in the bunkers by overhearing German conversations. Their senior rank was CSM O'Neill although he was neither Irish nor even British but a Czechoslovakian by birth who, like all other Commandos who had family in their home countries, had adopted an 'English' name for the duration of the war.*

A recce patrol on 12 June reported that the northern radar station had been abandoned by the Germans. Therefore, it was decided that, once it was dark, a twenty man fighting patrol provided by A Troop would enter the northern radar site and 'verify the situation [but] if the station was found to be occupied, it should withdraw'. The patrol was to be supported by six AVREs of 5 Assault Squadron RE. Raymond Mitchell wrote:

> *At 0100 hours on 13 June, CSM O'Neill led a party forward to blow a gap in the outer wire using bangalore torpedoes… By*

*0200 the AVREs had approached to the northern edge of the minefield and were engaged in hurling their Flying Dustbins at the bunkers: in view of their short range... they had to get in close. This provoked no response from the enemy, so the patrol moved through the outer wire and Lt Stevens led two men forward to blow the inner wire. On the explosion of the bangalore torpedo, the Germans opened up with MGs and machine-carbines from four separate locations, but were firing very wildly and obviously did not know the exact position of their attackers. A firefight ensued for about fifteen minutes then, as instructed, the patrol withdrew at about 0300 without casualties. For some time thereafter, the Germans vented their spleen by subjecting the Commando positions to heavy shell and mortar fire.*

This proved that the Germans were still in communication with their fellow countrymen whose artillery positions were by now south of the Caen-Bayeux road.

On the night of 14 June, a German aircraft attempted a supply drop to their beleaguered comrades. However, as recorded by the Commando's historian:

*In the event, P Troop were quicker off the mark than the Germans and their men reached the containers first. Instead of the food or water, however, which had been assumed to be the enemy's major requirements, the delivery comprised breech blocks for PAKs, small arms ammunition, booby traps and instruments.*

The Commandos continued to penetrate the two sites' defences and it is recorded that some patrols:

*... worked their way through the wire and mines right up to the casemates and on one such incursion, Sgt Hazelhurst of 'A' Troop banged on the steel door of one of the bunkers with the butt of his Tommy gun, yelling, "Come out, you silly bastards!" but to no avail.*

The Germans holding out at Douvres were becoming notorious and with numerous reporters now in Normandy, it was only a matter of time before they attracted their attention. BBC reporter Robert Barr recorded a description at the scene at the radar station on the morning of 17 June 1944.

*There is still one German strong point which is holding out*

> *within six miles of the Normandy coast and many miles behind our front line. The Navy have had a try at smashing it. The Air Force had a try. But still the German garrison held out. We've called off all big-scale attempts to clear it up because the commander in the area has ruled that no heavy casualties must be risked in smashing it. But the point is that this strong point of the West Wall, which the Canadians swept past in the first day is still intact. All you can see of it is ordinary fields, with a few grass mounds here and there indicating defence points. You can see a concrete tower hidden amongst trees, and through binoculars you can see the signs: "Achtung. Minen". Beware of mines. This is a sample of what the Germans hoped to prepare for us along the coast. We've surrounded it, we've shelled it, we've bombed it, and it's still unopened.*

The Allies had been happy to simply contain the enemy but, but by 14 June the German *Luftwaffe* technicians sheltering in the Douvres radar site were effectively denying a large area of valuable terrain in the restricted beachhead. In particular, the Germans were hindering the use of an airstrip constructed for RAF rocket firing Typhoon aircraft, 'whose pilots were not greatly enamoured to have to brave machine-gun fire as they took-off and landed!' Also, as the Beachhead became increasingly congested, every square mile was increasingly important. Finally, 41 Commando's casualties from German fire were mounting and the Royal Marines were ordered to 'Get them out!'

## The Capture of the Radar Site

On 16 June 1944, 41 Commando prepared its plan of attack. Lieutenant Colonel Palmer had assembled forty four armoured vehicles to assist with the task, including flails of B Squadron 22 Dragoons, reinforced by troops from C Squadron, and four troops of AVREs from 5 Assault Squadron RE. The 7.2-inch guns of a Royal Artillery heavy regiment were to supplement the normal support of the field artillery regiments..

The attack was to be preceded by a thirty minute bombardment. However, as the Royal Marines commented, 'even their 202-pound shells did little more than chip the massive concrete bunkers, and perhaps giving the inmates a slight headache'. Meanwhle the AVREs of 77 Squadron were to mount a noisy and obvious diversionary attack on the southerly radar site, just before H Hour. The importance of planning input by officers from 79th Armoured Division was now becoming clear as they had quickly learned that:

> *Crabs or AVREs placed under command of the infantry would be mishandled and suffer heavy casualties. Particularly did they not allow for the short range of the Petard and consequent vulnerability of AVREs.* [As was demonstrated at TROUT on D Day.]

The Commando's lack of cross training with 79th Armoured Division's various equipments was telling. There had been too little time in the run up to D Day, as the divisional staff resettled with the latest technical challenges and the vale of secrecy was only reluctantly lifted to key personnel. However, after two weeks in action, lessons had been learned and the 41's plan conceived with input of assault engineer officers, was effective in its execution.

The bombardment began at 1630 hours and, as planned, at 1700, the armour advanced. Half of B Squadron's Sherman flails, two vehicles each attached to the four troops of AVREs, started to beat their way through the wire and across the minefields that surrounded the two radar sites. The remainder of the Squadron gave covering fire with particular attention to the five anti-tank guns. The 22nd Dragoon's history records that:

*Sherman flails or as they were known Crabs*

> *In clouds of dust, and with a shattering clanking of chains, the flails moved into the minefield. German machine guns stuttered away here and there, swishing around them apparently at random. From a patch of dead ground, a group of supporting flails, hull down, loosed off machine guns and 75mm shell to keep the German heads down.*

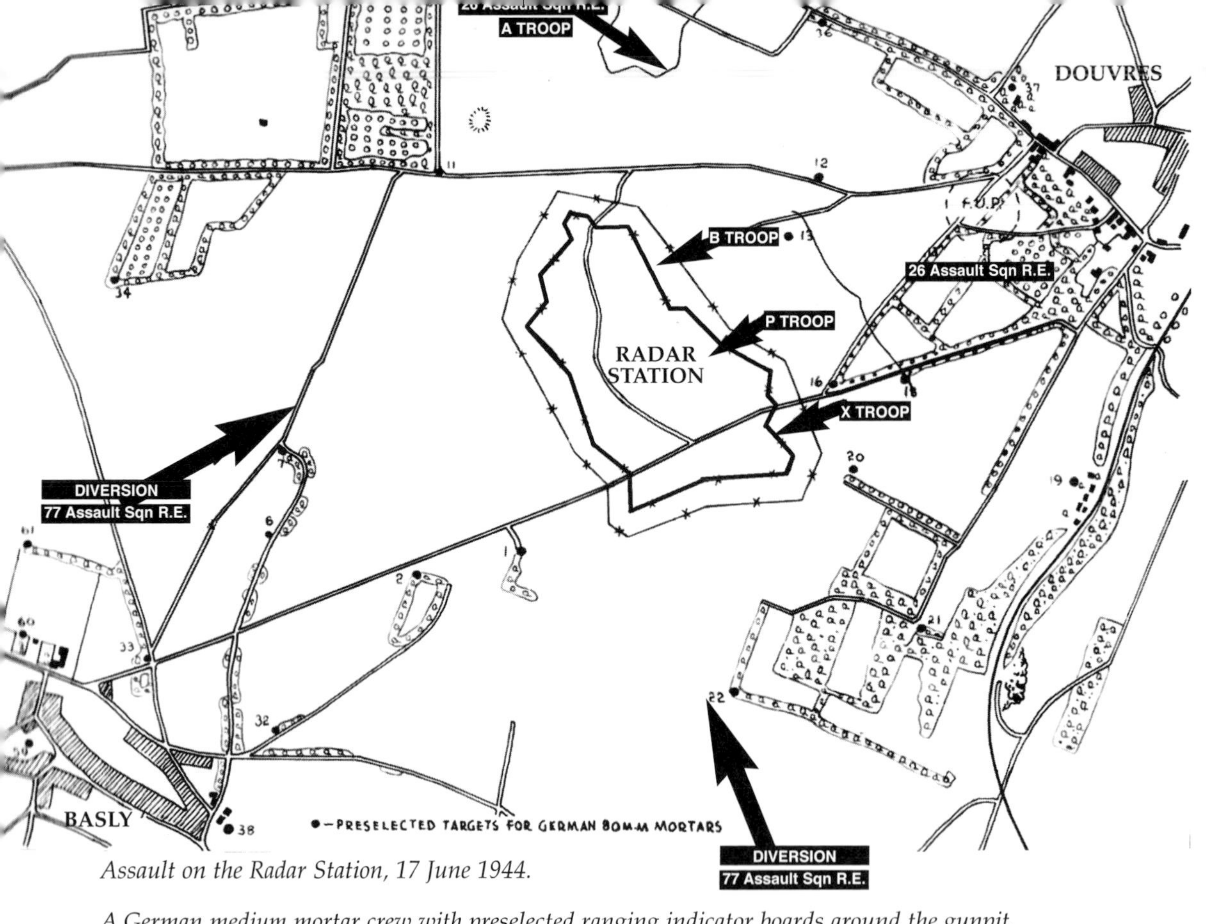


*Assault on the Radar Station, 17 June 1944.*

*A German medium mortar crew with preselected ranging indicator boards around the gunpit.*

*For half an hour and more, the flails moved smoothly on, biting through the minefield and touching off mines that sent up tall pillars of heavy black smoke. Then they were through, and in the most leisurely manner the AVREs rolled up the lanes to the mouths of the fortresses, ...But there was little opposition; there could not be, for the whole area was swept by fire from the flails.*

With the enemy subdued, the AVREs drove through the breaches and engaged the casemates with their Petards. Lance Corporal Sorensen, an AVRE driver described how:

*...the* [AVRE] *Squadron moved up to the forward start line, which was about half a mile from the radar station and concealed from it by trees and a farm. ...At about 1700 hours, we moved forward.*

*We penetrated about one-third of the minefield before anything happened. But then we came under heavy anti-tank fire. ...I could see a column of dust and smoke go up as a shell landed and the flashes from the75mm guns of the Crabs as they replied.*

*The AVRE in front of me succeeded in getting its offside track in a deep trench and it was stuck there immovable. My commander gave me the order to overtake on the left. As I did so, there was a terrific concussion and my vehicle gave a lurch. My instrument panel lights went out as well as all the interior lights. My first impression was that we had hit a mine and I tried the steering to see if the tracks were intact. As I did so, I saw my co-driver lying with a terrible wound in his head. He was unmistakably dead, and I then realized we had been hit by a shell. The next moment, the whole compartment caught fire. I was almost suffocated by flame, but managed to open the hatch over my head enough to scramble through. As I was climbing out, the ammunition in the hull Besa was exploding and a piece of shrapnel hit me in the right leg. I jumped clear and ran for a bomb crater about fifteen yards away. I was joined by my wireless operator and my gunner. Hardly had we dropped into it when my tank blew up. The force of the explosion blew the turret, which weighs about ten tons, fifty yard away.*

*...On my, way back out of the position, I saw the other tank crews place their 70-pound charges on top of the underground emplacements and lie doggo until they were blown... The white*

*A 50mm Pak 38 anti-tank gun being inspected by men of 41 Commando on the afternoon of 17 June 1944.*

Inset: *One of the AVREs blown apart during the battle to clear the radar site.*

*flag appeared and the job was done.*

The job was not however, completely 'done' until the position had been thoroughly cleared and prisoners rounded up. Following through the three gaps at 1720 hours were B, P and X Troops, while A Troop attacked the smaller northern site. Y troop remained in reserve. However, by this time, the Commando's war diarist wrote '...the enemy had been dazed, shocked or frightened into surrender and came out with their hands up.' Once their protective concrete had been breached, the *Luftwaffe* technicians gave up. The battle was over by 1830 hours, with 227 Germans being taken prisoner, including five officers. In 22nd Dragoon's history the prisoners were described as, 'for the most part badly shaken and dispirited men, glad to be out of it all'.

41 Commando suffered one casualty during the attacks, while the Dragoons had four Crabs disabled due to mine damaged tracks but all four were repairable. Closing with the enemy, the Royal Engineers lost four AVREs knocked out and three damaged, with three Spapers killed and seven wounded.

The following morning, having just walked around the radar site, Frank Gillard returned to the BBC studio five miles away in Creully town and recorded a short report that was broadcast later that day:

*You have heard of that colossal strong-point just along the coast at Douvres where getting on for 200 Germans held out till last night. That's a place to see. Somebody this morning called it an inverted skyscraper. That's not an unreasonable description. Fifty feet and more into the ground it goes – four stories deep. On the surface you barely notice it. The top's almost flush with the ground. But going down those narrow concrete stairways you think of going into the vaults of the Bank of England. And the Germans did themselves well down below there – central heating, electric light, hot water, air conditioning, radios, telephones, comfortable well-furnished rooms and offices, well-equipped workshops and ample supplies of food and ammunition. The Germans who were standing here on this ground fourteen days ago certainly must have thought that they had little to fear, and yet what a change now!*

*Entrance to one of the bunkers at the radar station after the fighting.*

CHAPTER NINE

# 1st Special Service Brigade

As befits the account of a formation's operations, that of Lord Lovat's 1st Special Service Brigade will be divided up into a number of short chapters to reflect the geography of the battle and the diversity of tasking within the Brigade. It will, however, still be an easy matter to follow the chronology of the action as a whole from SWORD Beach to the hedgerows and orchards of the Amfreville Ridge from D Day and into the first few days of the campaign.

The Commandos had been formed as a loose alliance of raiders under the ultimate control of HQ Combined Operations but as the war progressed the independence of the Commandos was eroded and now with a move towards the more conventional infantry role it was inevitable that a brigade structure would need to be put in place. 4th Special Service Brigade, as we have seen, however, fought on D Day as independent units, fighting largely independent actions but 1st Special Service Brigade was destined to fight much more as a formation.

The title 'Special Service' was by this stage in the war not particularly popular; one and all in the Brigade preferred the name Commando, which more accurately described them. But it took a realisation that the abbreviation 'SS' handed the enemy a PR opportunity, for the request to make the change in title stick. The catalyst for change was the growing body of allegations and evidence of war crimes and atrocities being committed by the *Waffen SS* in Normandy, particularly by *I SS Panzer Korps* that made the SS initials undesirable, especially amongst liberated peoples.

The three Army Commandos of Brigadier Lord Lovat's four units were experienced. No 3 had taken part in early raiding, the Dieppe Raid and then fought in Sicily and Italy. They were arguably the most widely experienced Commando unit. No 4 also had a fine raiding pedigree but had suffered heavy casualties in the Dieppe raid and remained in the UK. No 6

Commando had fought in North Africa before returning to the UK for the 'Second Front'. The Brigade's 'new boys' were 45 Royal Marine Commando, which had been formed in Portsmouth in August 1943 from 5th Royal Marines Battalion. Brigadier Durnford-Slater's opinion after a visit was that they had 'a long to go to catch up with the others [in the Brigade], but I thought that under Lord Lovat and in such good company they would be able to make the grade'. Events proved that this was a correct assessment. The final element of the Brigade was the two troops of French Commandos attached to No.4 Commando, with Commandant Philippe Kieffer acting as a hybrid liaison officer/sub-unit commander

*Commandant Pillippe Kieffer*

**On the Home Front**

Like other bemedaled Middle East veterans, the suntanned members of the Army Commandos enjoyed near-celebrity status on their return to the grey and austere Home Front and were consequently much in demand, not least No. 6 Commando. They had brought home with them a fine collection of captured German uniforms, equipment and weapons to make training more realistic. The aftermath of a demonstration of German infiltration tactics, where 6 Commando played the enemy, 'looking the part' in the captured enemy uniforms had a slightly unusual aftermath. Lord Lovat recalled:

> *After the actors had been dismissed they returned, as was customary, to various lodgings in the town. One man was surprised to see his landlady rush in from the garden and bolt the door against him. Two others entered a pub and ordered a pint of beer; the taproom emptied rapidly, except for a determined-looking character behind the bar, obviously resolved to sell his life dearly to the enemy. Other soldiers waited at the bus stop, when, to their dismay, the double-decker put on speed and went past, with anxious faces peering from the windows. After several*

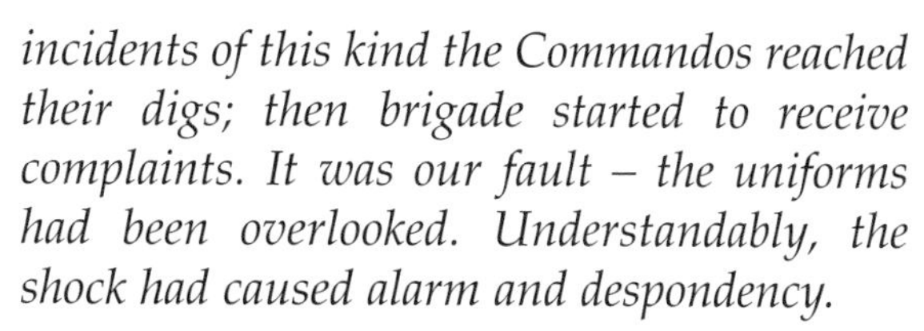

*incidents of this kind the Commandos reached their digs; then brigade started to receive complaints. It was our fault – the uniforms had been overlooked. Understandably, the shock had caused alarm and despondency.*

In between demonstrations of enemy and own forces' tactics and capabilities, the Commandos undertook the usual rigorous pattern of training that progressively became more focused as the D Day tasks that the Brigade was to undertake were gradually revealed.

Another incident that amused the Commandos but infuriated the more conventional officers of Southern Command who came to watch a Commando demonstration is again recorded by Lord Lovat with a degree of relish.

*Lord Lovat and Lovat Scouts badge*

*All the top brass came down from London and I advised Generals Morgan, Bob Laycock and Freddy de Guingand, along with Dempsey's Chief of Staff, to stand clear of the beach and not to part with the keys of their cars! I provided the running commentary on a loud-hailer… The craft carrying No. 6 Commando ran in, well controlled, in line abreast, hitting the sandy beach… two-inch mortars to thickened up the smoke. The little bombs rained down just wide of the spectators, obliterating the landing. There were lucky escapes, but not one got hurt. Some of the higher staff, fearful of mishap, shouted for a cease-fire, but I continued the commentary as No. 6 swept inland through the crowd. 'Rude but high-ranking' was Bill Coade's comment as he cannoned into a furious G1* [senior staff officer] *from Southern Command. He was coughing in the fog, trying to find me. 'Lovat, call off your bloodhounds – somebody is going to get killed.' …Section leaders became pirates as they crossed the sea wall and doubled inland …staff cars, Jeeps, motorcycles – everything in sight was commandeered; protesting drivers were tipped out of their seats or relieved of keys. No umpires caught up to interfere, and fully thirty vehicles (one belonging to a high-up in the Military Police, handling traffic control) roared out of the car park and headed across country for our objective at Arundel.*

*The whole Commando had reached the Arundel gap in the Downs beyond the river when I called a halt. Generals Morgan and Freddy, and John Durnford-Slater, were delighted. The planners were impressed. Everybody else was extremely angry: Southern Command asked for my head and put in a claim for damaged vehicles.*

There was of course plenty of serious training designed to maintain standards and incorporate the replacements that in some cases numbered almost fifty per cent of the units.

**Brigade Tasks and Plans**

1st Special Service Brigade's D Day plan was summarised by its commander in his memoirs:

***The intention***

*The 6th Airborne Division and 1st Commando Brigade* [sic] *would be responsible for holding the left flank of the Allied bridgehead.*

***The method***

*The brigade, consisting of four Commandos, to land on the extreme left of BEF on Queen Beach (Sword) and cut inland to join forces with two brigades dropped inland overnight by glider and parachute. No. 4 Commando to destroy a battery and garrison in Ouistreham then later rejoin. The rest of the brigade, landing thirty minutes after No. 4, to fight through enemy defences to reach and reinforce brigades of 6th Airborne Division, meeting astride bridges spanning the River Orne and Caen Canal at Bénouville. Glider regiments of the Air Landing Brigade would arrive late the same evening descending in country cleared of the enemy.*

Lord Lovat accurately commented 'We had been assigned a formidable task'.

1st SS Brigade would be under command of 3rd Division for landing but once across the Orne Bridges they would come under Major General 'Windy' Gale's 6th Airborne Division, joining the two parachute brigades who were to drop overnight on 5/6 June.

In more detail, the Brigade's main body, landing behind 3rd Division, would strike five miles across country to the canal bridge at Bénouville, at the time codenamed RUGGER but now known as Pegasus Bridge, and a further two miles to Le Plain on the Amfreville ridge. Avoiding tangling with the enemy *en route*, the seven mile march from the beach was to be completed in three hours from touching down and was considered by many outside Commando circles to be 'over ambitious'. Lord Lovat was himself aware of the difficulties:

*Spearheaded by No.6 Commando, the Brigade would pass through the demoralised enemy positions. The momentum of the advance inland must be kept at the double to reach the Airborne Division. Dropped overnight, the Paras would be holding high ground across the canal and river bridges north east of Caen: we were not going to let good men down.*

*The break-out meant fierce fighting by direct assault on a narrow front, without getting involved on exposed flanks or being stopped by hold-ups. Each Commando would leapfrog through one in contact with the enemy, and there would be no pause to halt the speed of our thrusting attack.*

Lieutenant Colonel Peter Young

With the Brigade Major (Lovat's senior staff officer) in front, No. 6 Commando was to lead the march, followed in order by No. 3 and 45 RM Commando. The cycle troops of the three Commando units would make best speed independently to RUGGER. No. 6 Commando was to secure positions on the Ridge around Le Plain, while Lieutenant Colonel Peter Young's no. 3 would clear the ground on the Brigade's left or seaward flank. 45 Commando had additional tasks: firstly, to capture destroy the coastal artillery battery at Merville (if not already completed by 9 Para); secondly, to capture Franceville Plage.

**See map on page 202**

**See map on page 253**

The first unit of the Brigade to land at H Hour plus 75 minutes would be No. 4 Commando; the tasks allocated to them in Ouistreham will be covered in detail in a separate chapter. Once the Commando rejoined the Brigade they were to dig in on the left flank.

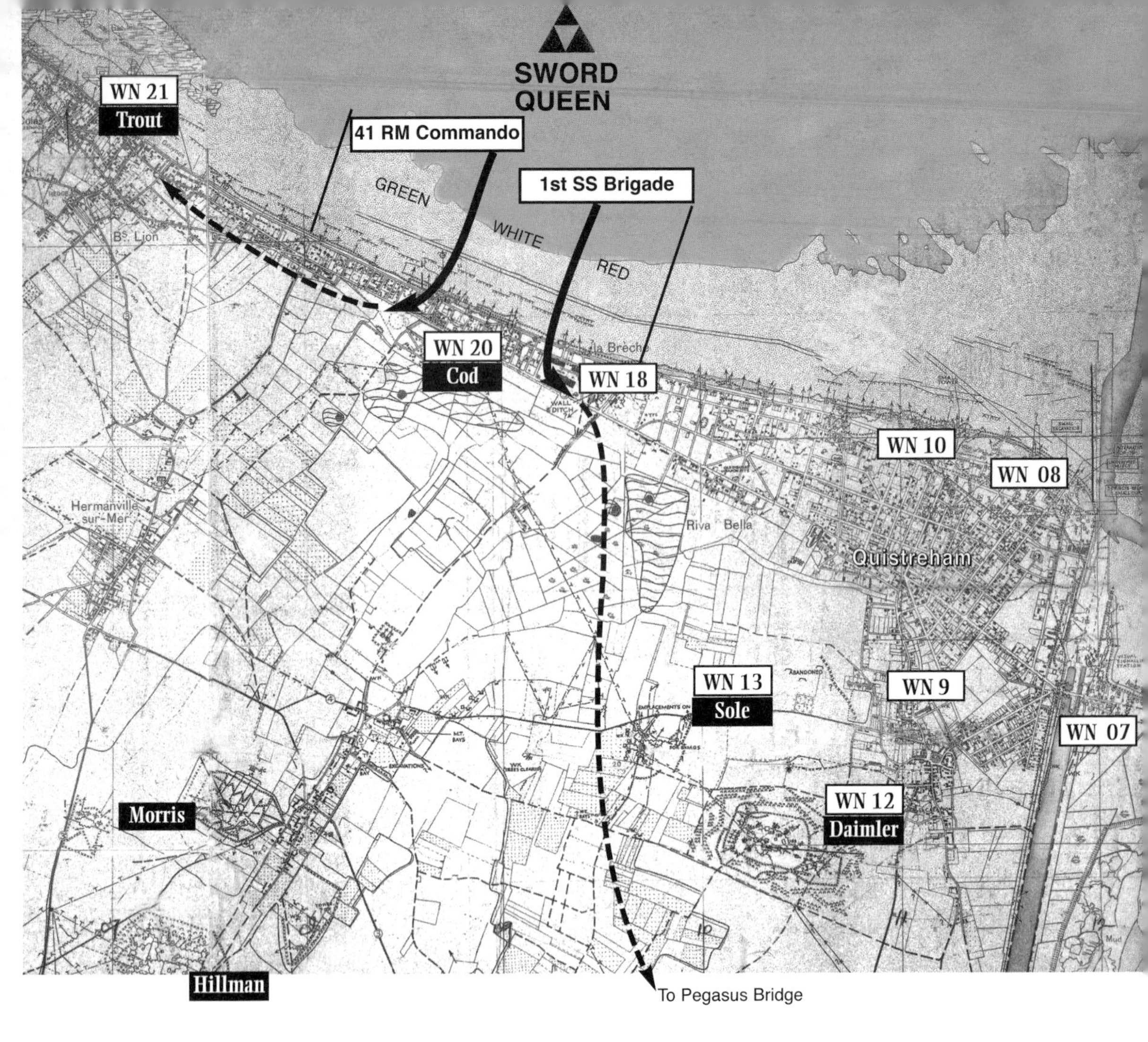


## Embarkation and Landing

1st SS Brigade's experience of briefing, embarkation and crossing was similar to that of the other Commando units except that the Brigade was concentrated in Camp C 18 just north of Southampton alongside fellow Commandos in 4 SS Brigade.

Brigadier Lord Lovat remarked to another veteran Commando officer that he felt 'uncomfortably exposed making an approach to a hostile enemy coast in broad daylight'; he said that he 'much preferred the cloak of darkness' as in a raid.

The Brigade less 4 Commando was scheduled to land on SWORD Beach at 0840 hours in a variety of landing craft types and, as they drew closer to the beach, details of the action ashore became visible:

*Sword Beach QUEEN RED and east to the outskirts of Ouistreham where 1 SS Brigade landed.*

*...small craft were battering their way through the heavy seas, ferrying troops ashore and returning to their parent ships. Spouts of water all around them indicated that the enemy were not idly looking on. Closer still, a line of battered, roofless buildings could be seen on the seafront, testimony to the accuracy of the pre-H-hour bombardment. A few tanks could be seen on the beach, their guns occasionally spouting flame. Their targets were invisible but this caused much speculation as to the degree of opposition the enemy were putting up.*

*When about a thousand yards from the shore, the craft came under fire. Airbursts appeared overhead and shell splinters smacked into the water. Accounts at this time are varied. One*

*Often forgotten, casualties were heavy amongst Royal Navy and Royal Marines landing craft crews.*

*Chaos on the beach! Knocked out and bogged down vehicles everywhere as the landing craft come in under fire.*

*man's impression was that the enemy were laying a curtain of fire along a line about two hundred yards from the beach.*

This is quite likely, as interdicting and causing attrition to follow-on waves, in theory, left the front line defenders to deal with the leading attackers. This is a standard artillery tactic, indeed one that would have been familiar to the Commandos' fathers fighting on the Somme. For No. 3 Commando:

*This enemy fire by now was far too accurate to be pleasant, and the small craft were rocked by the explosions from near misses while shell splinters rattled on the decks. Away to the left a tank landing craft was burning fiercely and the crew were seen scrambling off as the ammunition exploded. Three of the Commando's craft received direct hits from high-velocity shells. No. 6 Troop's boat was badly holed and all the three-inch mortar ammunition exploded. The Troop sustained at least twenty casualties before the craft beached. Nevertheless, in view of the sustained and accurate enemy fire, overall casualties during the landing were much less than was expected.*

*Most of the troops were still below decks during the run-in, but some were crouched behind the ramps, prepared to rush ashore as they were lowered.*

Amidst the exploding shells veteran Commandos indulged in an admirable show of bravado that did much to buoy-up the confidence of new members of the unit:

> *Corporal Jennings and Sergeant Osborne of No. 3 Troop could be seen sitting fully exposed in the stern, criticising each shot from the German battery and encouraging the enemy with such instructions as 'Put your sights up, Jerry'. 'Down little and give her more wind gauge,' as the shells came over and missed the craft. With each miss they cheered anew and offered the Germans further advice.*

Casualties were suffered across the Brigade before the craft touched down and when they did come to rest the craft had grounded on a false beach some distance from the water's edge. Presenting the Commandos a problem even for the fittest men weighed down by their heavy bergen rucksacks. They had touched down more or less accurately on their respective parts of QUEEN RED. 'Consequently the heavily-laden men, having plunged into about five feet of water, experienced some difficulty in reaching dry land.' Equipment including a number of bicycles was lost in reaching the beach.

The Brigade's post operational report records that:

> *At 0840 hours, exactly as planned, the first flight of 10 LCI(S) in line abreast carrying Bde HQ and 6 Cdo touched down on Queen Red Beach. The shipping and beaches were under heavy gun and mortar fire, and the second Bde HQ craft received a direct hit as it was coming in, causing it to crash into the stern of the leading craft. Two of 6 Cdo's craft were also hit and sustained casualties.*

Lord Lovat's personal piper, the sea-sick Bill Millin recalled the landing:

> *Lord Lovat was in the next ramp. There were two ramps I was on one and he was up on the other one. He jumped into the water but I waited because he was over six feet tall, to see what depth it was. While waiting someone came up on to his empty ramp and was immediately shot; he fell and sank. I jumped in pretty smart and my kilt floated to the surface; the shock of the freezing cold water knocked all feelings of sickness from me and I felt great. I was so relieved of getting off that boat after all night being violently sick. I struck up the Pipes and paddled through the surf playing "Hieland Laddie", and Lord Lovat turned round and looked at*

*Piper Bill Millin, Lord Lovat's Piper, waits to go down the ramp. This photo was taken less than a minute after that on preceding pages.*

> *me and gestured approvingly.*

Millin goes on to record an incongruous exchange with his commander:

> *When I finished, Lovat asked for another tune. I looked round and with the noise, people lying about, the shouting, the smoke and the crump of mortars, I said to myself 'You must be joking'. He said 'What was that? And repeated 'Would you mind giving us a tune? I asked 'Well, what tune would you like, Sir? 'How about The Road to the Isles?' 'Now, would you want me to walk up and down, Sir? He replied 'Yes. That would be nice. Yes, walk up and down.'*

Millin duly played as he walked up the beach and noted,

> *... people lying face down in the water going back and forwards with the surf. Others to my left were trying to dig in just off the beach. ... Yet when they heard the pipes, some of them stopped what they were doing and waved their arms, cheering. But one came along, he wasn't very pleased, and he called me 'A mad*

*bastard!' Well, we usually referred to Lovat as 'mad bastard'. This was the first time I had heard it referred to me.*

The men of 45 were luckier than their Army counterparts with some even managing to step ashore from the shell-damaged ramps of their LCIs barely getting their feet wet. Others landing just a few yards away had to struggle through deep water with 'enormous loads on their backs and holding weapons up to keep them dry'.

The Brigade's report records that once ashore:

*Contact was made with the Advance Bde HQ and the beaches cleared at good speed. …The gaunt and gutted buildings among a maze of tangled wire and shell craters made up a kind of Martian landscape.*

Once ashore the state of the beach shocked even experienced Commandos, who were of course, used to being the first ashore. Private Mason recalled running through 'bodies stacked like cord wood. They had been knocked down like nine pins'. Corporal Fred Mears said he 'was aghast to see the East Yorks lying in bunches. It would have never happened if they had spread out'. Those Commandos who had been forced to swim ashore were able to rearm themselves from the dead and wounded on the beach.

Amidst all the chaos and death, Piper Bill Millin now struck up *Blue Bonnets*, keeping the pipes going as he played the Commandos up the beach. One suspects that this was not the

*Barbed wire at the back of the beach. 45 Commando at the back of the beach start to assemble before heading inland to the Brigade RV.*

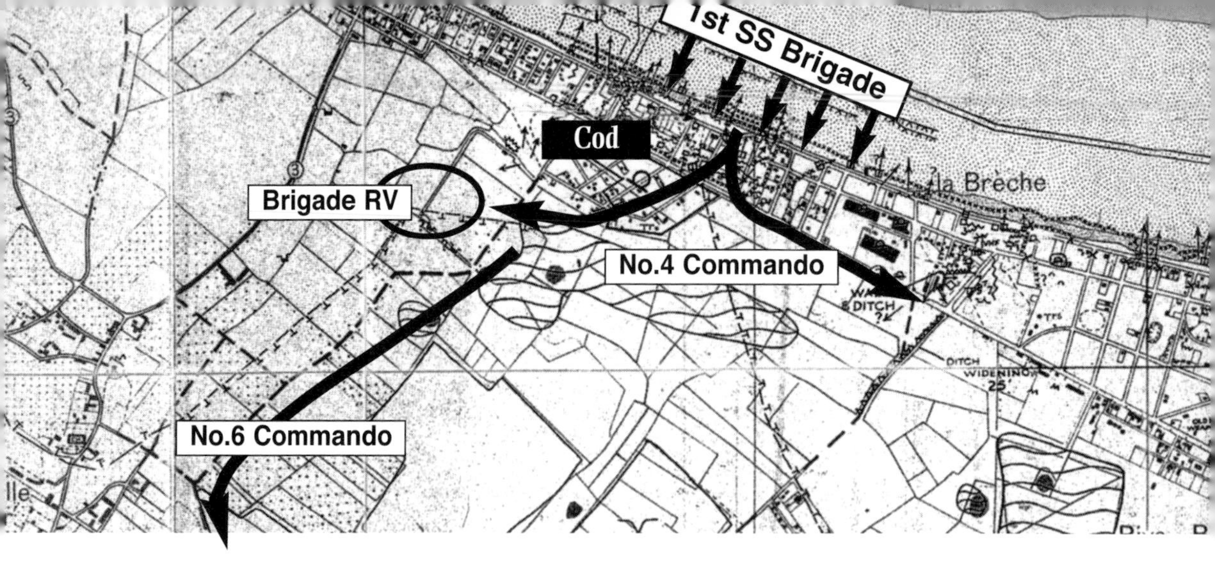


most tuneful rendition.

The Commando brigadier was uncomplimentary about 3rd Division. His comments could of course be regarded as distain of lesser mortals by a lofty Commando but there is more than a glimmer of truth in his words:

> *... 8 Brigade's poor showing in the last* [D Day] *rehearsal was faithfully repeated on the battlefield.*
>
> *The 3rd Division, in spite of the good record before Dunkirk under Monty, proved sticky throughout the landing. They had become muscle-bound mentally and physically, after four years of training in the United Kingdom.*

The Commandos with their accustomed speed raced across the beach and in spite of machine-gun fire, wire and other obstacles, were soon gathering under cover of the houses between the sand dunes and the road. 'It was a scene of confusion. Large numbers of troops were lying about in the dunes and very little appeared to be happening, although the enemy were maintaining sporadic mortar fire.'

Lord Lovat recalled a scene here that affected him deeply:

> *David Wellesy Colley ...lay against the pack of a sergeant who pulled him into shelter. He was shot through the heart. Tears were running down the NCO's face. 'Mr Colley's dead, sir. He's dead. Don't you understand? A bloody fine officer,' he repeated in shock as he wrapped a field dressing around the dead man's broken arm.*

The pause in the dunes was only long enough to gather as much as possible of the units together before they headed inland. Lord Lovat commented that 'There was no time to catch the breath'. Leaving the dunes via the same route that 4 Commando had previously taken, the leading file of No. 6 Commando came under fire from nearby:

> *Throwing down rucksacks, the leading troop moved fast, mopping up pill-boxes and the immediate strong-points with hand grenades and portable flame throwers; supporting Bren guns sprayed lead at every loophole and casemate aperture. Houses not destroyed by bombardment were occupied by a few Germans; firing small arms they sniped from roof and windows. These pockets of resistance were wiped out by selected marksmen.*

It was not the Commandos' job to secure the dunes but only to clear the enemy from the area of their exit. The report continued:

> *Once on to the first lateral* [road] *6 Cdo took the lead and the advance towards the bridges began. The country beyond the road was marshy and intersected by deep ditches up to six ft deep with a thick mud bottom which made progress extremely slow for such heavily laden men who sank into the mud and found great difficulty in climbing out of the ditches. Scaling ladders were used effectively as hand rails across the ditches, but the area was also being mortared and it was about 25 minutes before the leading troops reached the pre-arranged forming up point.*

*Commandos take cover as they move through the houses immedeatley behind the trench. An AVRE of the Assault Regiment RE moves up to support them.*

*Commandos linking six-foot sections of Bangalore torpedos.*

Following behind, No. 3 Commando were attempting to get off the beach; 'Bangalore torpedoes blasting through wire. A dash across a road, and then a tram line; we were through'.

> *3 Commando moved off to the forming-up point* [FUP], *a large clump of bushes about a thousand yards inland. The route lay across flat, marshy ground, intersected by deep ditches. Patches of reeds afforded the only cover. Naturally, progress slow, for men frequently floundered waist-deep in slime. The enemy were bringing down artillery fire but fortunately the soft nature of the ground greatly minimised its effect and casualties were few.*

Reaching the FUP Lieutenant Colonel Peter Young described finding '... a company commander of one of the assault battalions sitting under a hedge with his CSM [Company Sergeant Major] and two others, waiting for his men whom we last saw digging-in on the beach a thousand yards behind him.'

> *Suddenly there comes an un-earthly, blood-chilling, bellowing noise like a gigantic cow in agony and six bombs land in the next field in a cloud of black smoke-our first meeting with 'Moaning Minnie', the German six-barrelled mortar, the* Nebelwerfer.

*German six-barrelled mortar, the* Nebelwerfer.

Landing at 0910 hours, 45 Commando had headed directly inland towards a small wooded hillock which was to be the Brigade's RV. This was just north of the outskirts of Colleville, which was supposedly being cleared by 1 Suffolk and the tanks of 13/18 Hussars. There had been some alarm in the days before D Day when the copse that was to be the RV started to be cut down, presumably for anti-glider, poles – 'Rommel's Asparagus' – or used to thicken up the beach obstacles.

Heading across the marshy pasture, the Royal Marines, amidst the sound of battle, soon heard the 45 Commando rallying call 'Gone Away' being played by the Adjutant on his hunting horn. It was 1000 hours and only half a mile had been covered by the Brigade in forty-five minutes!

As an example of the tenacity and commitment of the Commandos in the early stage of the operation it is worth recording in full the citation of Signalman Angus McKenzie McGregor's Military Medal. He landed with in the first wave of Commandos.

*During the landing of Advance Headquarters of the Brigade, all signallers were wounded by mortar and machine-gun fire, fifty percent being incapacitated. Signalman McGregor received two shrapnel wounds in the head, three bullet wounds in the arm, and a shrapnel wound in the leg. In spite of his wounds he continued to operate his set, and enabled essential information to be passed to the main body of the Brigade which was still afloat. He refused all assistance, denying that he was seriously hurt, and continued to operate his set during the initial stages of the advance until he was unable to rise after taking cover from further mortar fire. It was only then that the seriousness of his wounds became apparent. His devotion to duty was largely responsible for communications being maintained at an extremely critical period of the operation.*

### The Advance Inland

*If you wish to live to a ripe old age – keep moving.*
Brigadier The Lord Lovat

Arriving at the FUP one of the few radio messages permitted was received from Lieutenant Colonel Derek Mills-Robert's No.

6 Commando. 'Sunray [Mills-Roberts] calling Sunshine [Lovat]. First task accomplished [through the German coastal positions]. Regrouping [in the FUP] for the second bound.'

Unlike the Ranger and Commando operations covered previously in this book, 1st SS Brigade's Commando units were more or less intact, perhaps because of the relatively late hour of landing They had, however, been spotted by the enemy and were subjected to *Nebelwerfer* fire. Consequently, after the shortest possible delay in the FUP Lord Lovat ordered the advance to begin. The Commandos set off on foot on two main routes. The first was directly across country towards Bénouville and the second was a route to the east to be taken by the cycle troops on their 'Parabikes' who would 'dash' to the bridges as fast as was consistent with avoiding the enemy. The problem for both groups was of course fratricide with friendly forces who were dealing with identified enemy positions as they made their way inland (HILLMAN/MORRIS and SOLE/DAIMLER).

No.6 Commando was leading and soon reported to Brigade HQ that they were 'Moving left up the fairway on Plan A for Apple. Still on time.' This particular pre-planned route was to take the Brigade in a south easterly direction passing north of Colleville and 'into a patch of well grown woodland beyond', which was north of St-Aubin-d'Arquenay. Colonel Mills-Roberts wrote:

> *When attempting to infiltrate one's way through a strongly defended position, it is absolutely essential to avoid roads and tracks as far as possible and to use the most unlikely routes. The route we had chosen was possible only to foot soldiers and the idea was that it would by-pass most of the strong enemy positions which were concentrated on tracks and roads.*

Almost immediately the Brigade became ensnared in minefields, many of which had not been located by recce aircraft, and were consequently not marked on the maps. This naturally caused a delay while a route through them was found; a narrow track which the Commandos followed in single-file! At this stage the Allies had not worked out that those marked with white paint on a black background were real while those marked with yellow writing were the numerous dummy minefields.

The Commanding Officer of No. 6 Commando had no illusions:

*Men of the 1st SS Brigade heading inland. The Commandos were given the option of wearing their green berets or steel helmets for landing.*

*We had to get on … our orders were to blaze a trail to the bridges and not get involved with any enemy who were not directly barring our way, but there were inevitably encounters with the enemy.*

Captain Pyeman, commanding the leading troop, was expecting to have to deal with an enemy position on the outskirts of Colleville and according to Colonel Mills-Roberts,

*I got a message… he had destroyed his enemy position and had given the occupants of the pill-box a taste of his portable flame throwing apparatus. I knew that they were bursting to use it!*

If the main advance by 8 Brigade had been on time, this enemy position directly north of Colleveille should already have been dealt with by 1 Suffolk but as we have seen they were struggling to get through the remainder of 8 Brigade who were all but stalled in the area of the dunes and beach villas. The Suffolk's accounts state that as C Company arrived in the northern outskirts of the village they encountered members of No. 6 Commando heading east.

The next bound took the Commandos into the woods and orchards north east of Colleville, led by Captain Hardy's Troop. Immediately behind them was Commando HQ and the CO commented of this phase in the advance:

> *Now that we were committed... movement to either flank was sometimes virtually impossible, at other times bypassing would mean jumping out of the frying pan into the fire. Perhaps the greatest difficulty was that we were trying to beat not only the Germans but also the clock.*

The next action on the route was not long in coming and the column came to a halt. Major Bill Coad, the Commando's Second-in-Command, had been wounded by a grenade. Colonel Mills-Roberts went forward and was warned that a sniper was covering the gap he was just about to lead the way through. He explained:

> *There was no possibility of an alternative approach without running into more trouble. A wireless message came from Shinii Lovat: "Why are you halted" The rest of the brigade, it must be remembered, was following in our tracks. It was our job to blaze the trail.*
>
> *About seventy yards away on the right I saw a British DD tank, which had come straight up a track from the beach—these tanks had special flotation gear and had landed with the first wave of troops. I cut back to the tank and asked for fire. It lumbered forward and fired two rounds: the first one did no damage, but the second one split the pill-box like a rotten apple.*

Although the hold-up had only been a short one, the Brigade had no time to lose and by mid-morning a grey dawn had given

*Heavily laden Commandos following the light railway that ran inland from the beach.*

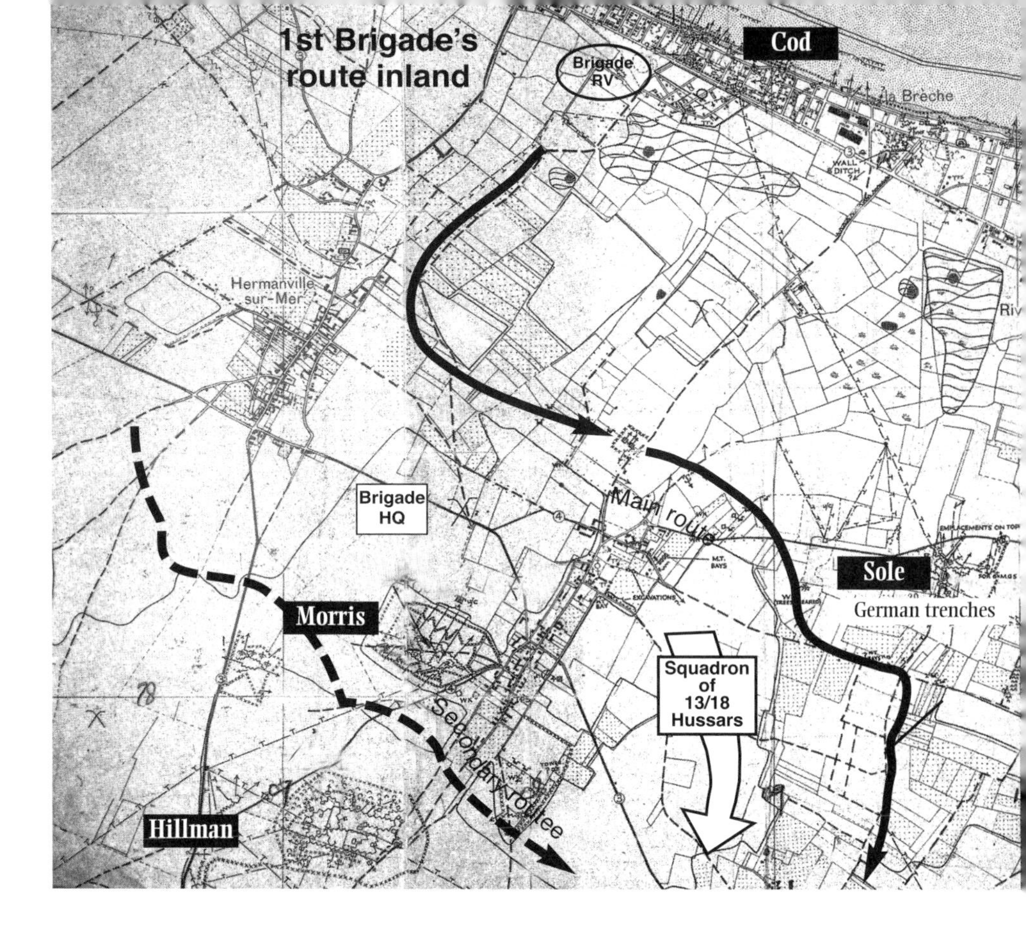


way to hot sun and virtually all the Commandos were sweating profusely in their wet battledress and full equipment.

> *The job of the leading troop was to lead the route to the bridges as fast as possible and to ignore their flanks. If Germans on the flanks 'were causing trouble, one of the following fighting troops would be detached to deal with it' and even then orders were clear that 'if it is only passive interference, then we will blind the enemy post with smoke from 2-inch mortars'.*

The Brigade's report makes it clear that there was some friendly help around:

> *Still covered by 6 Cdo, who fought their way across country as the spearhead, sweeping the high ground to the North East through the scrub, the Bde advanced through COLLEVILLE S/ORNE and ST AUBIN D'ARQUENAY. A squadron of tanks from 13/18 Hussars came up between COLLEVILLE and ST AUBIN and gave invaluable assistance in silencing pillboxes. Snipers lurking in the cornfields beyond ST AUBIN slowed up the advance slightly, . . .*

The planned route turned inland through the scrub, woods,

plantations and orchards taking the Commandos with in 500 yards of enemy artillery positions on their left codenamed SOLE and DAIMLER, both described as being 'bristling with trouble':

> *'and this we intended to by-pass. In front of us was a minefield surrounded by barbed wire, with a notice Achtung Minen. We did not know about the minefield, but in any case it had to be crossed: the only alternative was to get mixed up with the German strong-point to our left. Out came the cutters and bang went two over-tight strands of wire. It was strong wire and took one of the blades clean off a brand-new pair of cutters. I breathed a sigh of relief when I saw that the minefield was not as lethal as it sounded – this would save a lot of time and trouble; convenient-looking tufts of grass showed where some German working party had deposited the mines without levelling the ground properly. Nevertheless, care was needed as we pushed quickly across.*

Once through the minefield, the next problem was a small German position covering a road the Commandos would have to cross. This was the end of the next bound and the leading troop got down ready to cover the second troop, which was to go across the road into the lead. As they started to move forward:

> *A rifle cracked, and then came the high-pitched whine of German light automatic fire as the leading troop was fired on and pinned to the ground. The support troop was ready for this, and soon the enemy themselves were under a hail of small-arms fire. Round their left flank came a third troop into the assault and raced for the German position. This was not a pill-box but a small trench system which was quickly overwhelmed.*

Had the Commandos blundered on at speed and been ambushed without a proper plan, as the CO said 'it could have made a nasty mess of our column'.

Having safely crossed the minor road, they entered another belt of scrub the odd shot was fired and casualties suffered but the march continued south but not so fast that Colonel Mills-Roberts who was now leading failed to notice movement in the bushes.

> *The column halted and flattened itself on the track. We fired into the scrub on our right: after the second burst a small knot of Germans came out and surrendered. They were quickly interrogated, but appeared to know little of value. There was no time to waste now and we pushed on as hard as we could down the track, bustling our German friends along with us. Their movements became more and more reluctant. Eventually one of them – no doubt unwilling to make the 'supreme sacrifice' drew his interpreter's attention to the next bend in the track where an enemy post was situated.*

This post on the outskirts of St-Aubin-d'Arquenay was thoroughly dealt with '...more quickly and economically than would otherwise have been possible'.

> *No. 6 Commando was now on schedule after a quick half mile bash through the woods but close by, in a field to our right, was the noise of field guns firing. These were a battery of four Italian guns marked on the map as being in field positions rather than casemated and they were firing on to the beach.*
>
> *One troop peeled off and attacked them in the rear. The battery was manned by Italians, who surrendered without much fuss; to be honest, they were well and truly taken aback and had not much option. ...We left a wrecking party to spike their guns, whilst they joined our motley column of prisoners.*

Although few post-war Commando accounts mention the tanks, the Brigade's after action report makes it quite clear that a squadron of 13/18 Hussars was also advancing through the area and did much to neutralise German defences.

The Commandos were now about two miles from the bridges from where they could ominously hear the sounds of battle. Meanwhile, to the rear 45 Commando were being attacked, unsuccessfully by flanking enemy troops but it caused a delay; Lieutenant Colonel Peter Young's Commando had simply bypassed the action and headed onwards.

## Pegasus Bridge

Waiting in anticipation near Pegasus Bridge on the west bank of the Canal de Caen along with the Commander of 3 Para Brigade was Lieutenant Colonel Pine-Coffin. Over five miles from

SWORD Beach, 6th Airborne Division had been isolated since their drop just after midnight and a link-up with the Commandos would represent the establishment of the first tenuous lifeline.

First to arrive at the bridges were the Cycle Troop of No. 6 Commando but the chief concern was the approach of Lord Lovat's men to the embattled 7 Para, where the danger of fratricide was considerable. The solution was simple, Lord Lovat's piper, Bill Millin, would play a distinctively Scottish tune to announce their approach to the Paras. If the way into the airborne defensive position around the bridges was clear, Colonel Pine-Coffin would answer with a bugle call. This was of course in addition to radio communications if possible.

Lord Lovat while 'broadly following 6 Commando's route' was making his own way to the bridges, with 'Scouts out in front of the Headquarters (a motley crew – all armed to the teeth)'. They had captured, with the help of a stray DD tank some horse-drawn German transport, crewed by Russians, which was promptly pressed into use to carry the HQ's heavy radios, etc.

Piper Millin recalled that last leg of the route across open fields towards le Port:

> *We were walking in aircraft formation. That is single file on either side of the road, and I am Piping. It was a raised road, so we were very vulnerable and were being shot at by snipers from the other side of the canal and from the cornfields on the right side of the road. I could see this sniper about a hundred yards or so away ahead of me in a tree and spotted the flash when he fired. I glanced round, stopped playing and saw they were all down on their faces and even Lovat was on his knee. Then the next thing this man comes scrambling down the tree and Lovat and our group dashed forward. I went with them and had stopped playing by this time. We could see the man's head bobbing about in the cornfield, and Lovat shot at him. He fell and two men went into the cornfield to see what had happened and they brought back the dead body. Then Lovat said to me, "Right, Piper, start the pipes again".*

As the head of the column reached the road between le Port and the road running down to the bridges, Lord Lovat ran to the

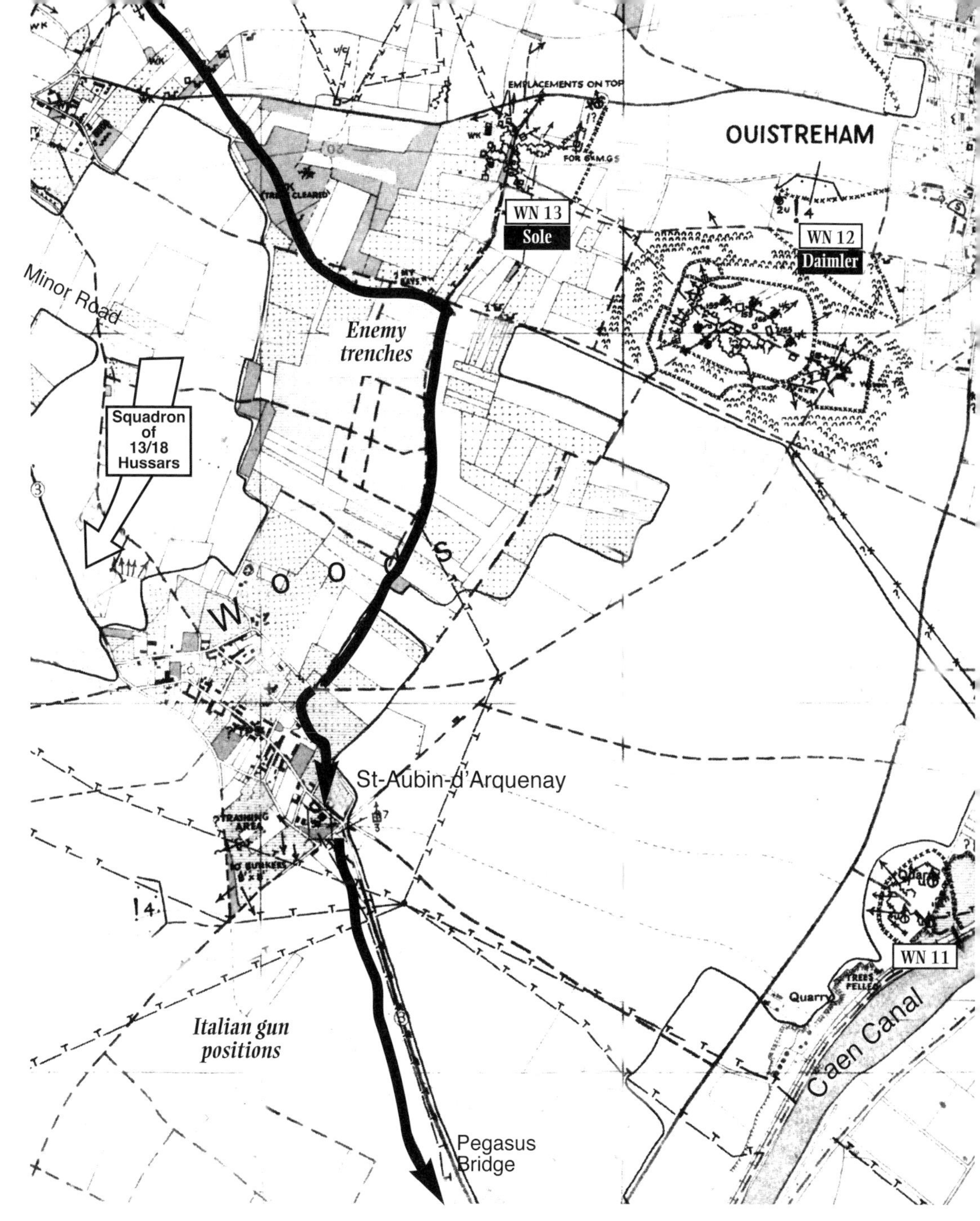


front of the Column accompanied by Piper Bill Millin. The pipes were again played (Blue Bonnets Over the Border) but Colonel Pine-Coffin wrote in his diary:

> *The temptation to reply by bugle was strong but had to be resisted because the way was not clear. Attacks were still being*

> *launched on the Battalion position and there were also snipers in le Port… Private Chambers* [7 Para's Bugler] *was forbidden to sound off and the Commandos made a slower and more cautious entry into le Port than they otherwise would have done.*

Reaching the junction he came across one of his men guarding the Italian gunners that No. 6 Commando had captured. The sentry explained that getting no signal [audible or by radio from 7 Para] Colonel Mills-Roberts had taken his unit down to the canal bank via a scrubby area north of the canal bridge. Here he temporarily drove away snipers who had been bothering 7 Para all morning.

The Brigade report records that '…by 1230 contact had been made with the Airborne troops holding the bridgehead at BENOUVILLE, and the two forces joined hands'. Lord Lovat himself arrived at the bridge shortly after 1300 hours.

At 1330 hours the Special Service Brigade started crossing Pegasus Bridge. While Piper Bill Millin did play his pipes in the area of the bridges, he did *not* at Pegasus Bridge. Lord Lovat explained:

> *I ran across* [the Bridge] *with Piper Millin, Salsbury and a handful of fighting men. There was a fair amount of mortaring, and a machine-gun up the water pinged bullets off the steel struts, but no one noticed and brave fellows from the gliders were cheering from their fox-holes at the other end. Soon I was hailing John Howard... He advised me to keep moving: it was no place to hang about.*

Lord Lovat in a footnote to his memoirs makes it plain '… no piper played on the first occasion while crossing the canal' but it was here that he apologised for being two and a half minutes late! He was now in fact an hour and two minutes late!

This is at variance with the claim by Colonel Pine-Coffin that the first crossings were made 'Without a single shot being fired'. Considerable effort had, however, been made to suppress the enemy in the area, including deploying virtually all the Commandos who had arrived at the canal into positions from where they could help keep the enemies' heads down and screen them with smoke.

It was at the Orne River (Horsa) Bridge where the enemy were

*HQ 1st SS Brigade complete with captured transport.*

less active that Millin played his pipes. When it was Lord Lovat's turn to cross, as he explained, 'good music drowned the shooting and we managed to stride over in step – almost with pomp and circumstance'.

*Lieutenant Colonel Pine-Coffin.*

As the Commandos further down the column took their turn to cross the bridge the enemy snipers returned and those not at the rear recall 'no stately march across the bridge' but 'more a mad dash with bullets ricocheting off the steelwork'.

At 1400 No. 6 and No. 3 Commandos were across and Lieutenant Colonel Raie, the CO of 45 RM Commando was amongst those Commandos hit while crossing the bridge around 1430 hours.

The landing on SWORD Beach by Lord Lovat's 1st SS Brigade and its subsequent advance almost six miles across enemy held territory was, when first proposed, regarded as being impossible if not 'totally fanciful'! The Commandos though, had not only reached 6th Airborne Division but had done so almost on time. A measure of the degree of their success is afforded by remembering that few other units of any nationality reached their D Day objective and even fewer managed it anything like on time. When one reflects on the fact that 3rd Division was not to reach Pegasus Bridge until well into the evening of D Day, the Brigade's achievements were remarkable.

## Visiting the Battlefield

Just inland of the D514 in the Village of Collville-Montgomery Plage locate the statue of Montgomery (twin of the one that stands on the seafront at Southsea near Portsmouth). From the nearby traffic lights take the Avenue de Bruxelles down to the sea front. This is the eastern end of Queen Red Sector. Looking out to sea, to the left is *WN-20* Objective COD and to the right the smaller *WN-18*. It is between these two *Widerstandnester* that the craft of 1st SS Brigade landed.

Return to the traffic lights and go straight across on the D60a to Colleville-Montgomery. Leaving the houses and into an open area, you are crossing the marshy ground behind the dunes and coast road. The Brigade's assembly area/forming up point was in the trees to the right a little further on, also to the right, in a field are the remains of some concrete structures. These were those captured by No. 6 Commando.

Drive on into Colleville. For those wishing to walk the scene of the Commando's action in Colleville, St-Aubin-d'Arquenay and the intervening woods should park by the church/Marie, retrace the route 100 yards and turn right onto Chemin des Perlins, on the walking route through Bois du Caprice into St Aubin and back to Colleville on the D35.

For those staying mounted drive through Colleville turning left on the D35 to St Aubin, making diversions if required to find the *WN-15* and 15a locations.

Follow the D35 road through St Aubin towards le Port. Go under the main road and drive into le Port turning right into the village centre. It is in this area that the Commandos made contact with elements of B Company 7 Para, cleared the ground between village and Canal and set of to Bénouville.

Drive on through the village to the roundabout turn left and park near the Café or across the bridge in one of the car parks there. Café Gondrée is an essential stop in any tour of the area, as it is heavy and central to the history of the area. The museum opposite is also worth a visit where the original Pegasus Bridge is preserved and can be seen without actually going into the Museum, whose focus is understandably 6th Airborne Division.

The tour from this point is continued at the end of Chapter 10.

## CHAPTER TEN

# No. 4 Commando Ouistreham

Lord Lovat had reluctantly given up his beloved No. 4 Commando on promotion following their success in destroying the heavy guns of the Hess Battery during the Dieppe Raid, one of the few bright spots amidst the general disaster on the beaches. On taking over command, Lieutenant Robert Dawson maintained Lord Lovat's training style and for the next eighteen months it was hard and varied exercises, but with the frustration of raids being repeatedly cancelled. Three troops were, however, lucky and were involved the MANACLE and HARDTACK programme of raids on the coast of occupied Europe. But for a variety of reasons, weather, navigation and the enemy not turning up to be ambushed, they were less than successful. As the weather improved greater success was anticipated but,

> *The … pin prick raids were finally abandoned on the orders of* [Brigadier] *Laycock because they encouraged the enemy to reinforce their positions which, in the longer term, could be disadvantageous to the Allies.*

*Brigadier Durnford- Slater*

No. 4 Commando, despite supplying its fair share of officers and NCOs to other Commando units, developed a depth of character and knowledge that more than weighed in the balanced against those Commando units who had fought in the Mediterranean but who had suffered significant casualties.

One of the many exercises in early 1944 was designed to demonstrate the Commando's capability to land from small boats on a hostile coast. The Cornish coast was hostile in both terms of physical geography and enemy; there were steep cliffs to scale a before delivering a raid on some poor unsuspecting enemy, played by the Home Guard. Brigadier Durnford-Slater had invited an audience of senior commanders and a film crew to the demonstration. Preliminary rehearsals went well, a number of options were tried, and an agreed method selected. The day of the final rehearsal dawned overcast with a stiff wind and a heavy sea swell but with 'the Brass' assembling from far afield for the following day's demonstration, C and D Troops went ahead. In the rough conditions at the base of the cliffs one of the boats foundered in the swell and two men were lost. Despite Colonel Dawson's misgivings, the demonstration went ahead the following day in marginally better conditions and was a great success for the Commandos.

Because of demonstrations such as the one in Cornwall and the Commandos' previous operational experience, it was initially proposed that No. 4 Commando should attack the massive Houlgate battery, whose six 170mm guns could cover SWORD Beach and most of JUNO. In fact these guns were potentially a far more serious problem to the invasion than the Merville battery, intended to be destroyed by 9 Para in the early hours of D Day. A shortage of Commandos for tasks in the immediate invasion area and the RAF and Royal Navy's confidence that they could neutralise the Houlgate Battery, led to this option being retained only as an on-call task (Operation FROG) for the floating reserve, 46 RM Commando. Another task similarly relegated was Operation DEER, an attack on the Berneville Battery (four French 155 mm guns).

As already mentioned, instead of independent raiding, as a part of 1st Special Service Brigade, on D Day No. 4 Commando would come under the command of 3rd Division for both landing and the capture of the little port of Ouistreham just over a mile east of SWORD Beach. This flank clearance task was essentially similar to the operations being conducted further west by 47, 48 and 41 RM Commandos. With their initial task in Ouistreham complete, Colonel Dawson would speed-march his men to Pegasus Bridge from where they rejoin their Brigade east of the River Orne.

## The Defences of Ouistreham

While the Allies had learned the lesson of Dieppe not to simply hurl flesh and blood against the concrete and steel of fixed defences, the Germans took the lesson that concrete worked. They set about building defences to deny the Allies a port large

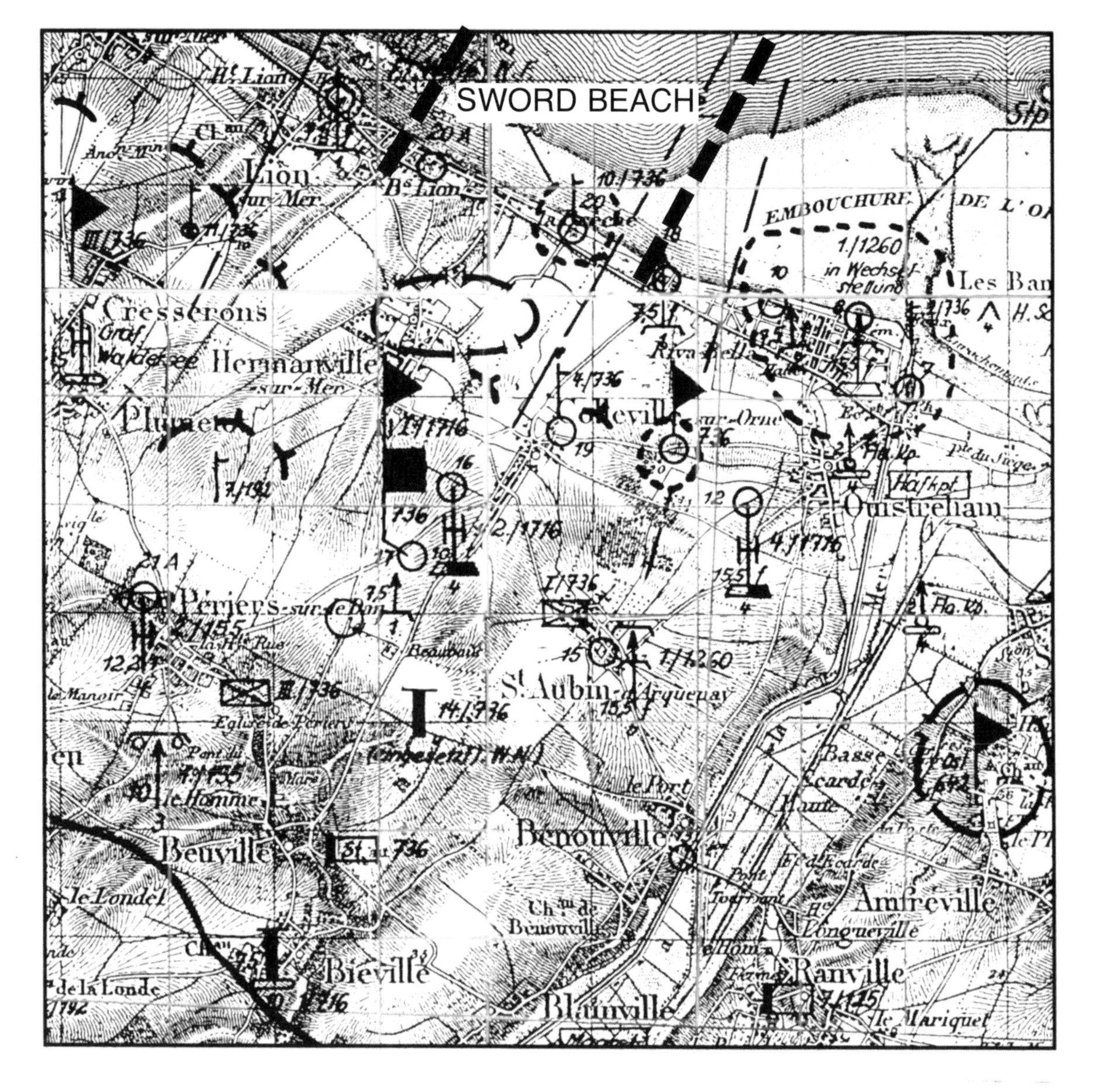

*German defenders of the Normandy coast. Manning Hitler's Atlantic Wall was a 'soft' posting, but that was about to change. Above: German map showing the defences in the Sword/Ouistreham area.*

or small and Ouistreham fell in the latter category. Deny a port and the invasion would fail calculated the German high command, who did not believe that the Allies could sustain a force as large as that being assembled for the invasion over the open Channel beaches.

Long before the Atlantic Wall became a reality, Ouistreham became a *Stützpunkt*: pill boxes, bunkers and cupolas were built, while gun batteries that would dominate the sea approaches were sited in concrete gun pits in the sand dunes. As D Day approached and work progressed on *Widerstandnester* all along the Normandy coast, the port's defences were progressively thickened up. More mines were laid, a fire control tower was built and an anti-tank ditch was dug; the work of a defender is never done!

Ouistreham was the responsibility of *Oberst* Krug's *Infanterieregiment 736*. From his command post on the northern slopes of the Périers/Beauville Ridge, codenamed Objective HILLMAN by the Allies: he could overlook the port and its defences. In immediate support, in the form of counter-attacks by infantry and a handful of *Sturmgeschütze*, was *716. Division's* slim reserve. The Ouistreham defences were based on two strong points, manned by coastal infantrymen of *2 Kompanie, I Bataillon* of the *736*, one (*WN-08*, two 50mm anti-tank guns) covering the entrance to the port and the second (*WN 10*, two 75mm anti-tank guns) was near the casino in the eastern outskirts of the town. Between them were the open guns pits of 4 Battery *Artillerieregiment 1716*, but by D Day they had been abandoned due to persistent Allied bombing, with the battery's four 155mm guns having been moved to the casemates of *WN 12* (codenamed Objective DAIMLER) a mile inland. This was not far from the HQ of *I Bataillon* and an infantry company at Objective SOLE (*WN 13*). Across the river mouth was a third platoon position in the port's defences, *WN 07*. This position mounted a captured 47mm gun and three obsolescent 50mm guns. Inland in the southern part of Ouistreham was a fourth infantry platoon

Generalmajor *Wilhelm Richter, commander of* 716. Infantriedivision

*Oberst Krug, commander of* 736. Infanterieregiment, *inspecting his defences in the SWORD/Ouistreham sector a few weeks before the invasion.*

position (*WN 09*); it had no anti-tank guns but could call on the fire of mortars.

### Commando Plans

As the intelligence picture developed in the weeks before D Day, it was more than apparent that the number of enemy manning the port's defences would be too much for the slim establishment of an unreinforced Army Commando. The solution, as explained in Chapter 2, was for Lord Lovat to negotiate the attachment of two additional troops from No. 10 Inter-Allied Commando, commanded by Captains Kieffer (No. 1 Troop) and Lofi (No. 2 Troop). As a fluent French speaker and Francophile, Colonel Dawson was able to make a potentially difficult relationship work throughout his unit. The two French troops although still officially a part of 10 (Inter-Allied) Commando, were permitted to wear 4 Commando flashes. Promoted *Commandant,* Philippe Kieffer became the senior French officer and effectively Dawson's second-in-command, his place as troop commander being taken by Vourch. French Commando Leon Gautier recalled that 'Colonel Dawson said, "We give the French the honour of being first ashore". That was a great honour and we thanked him very much for giving us the opportunity. '

Colonel Dawson wrote of his French troops:

*They were tough, self reliant soldiers, quick in action and very brave indeed. Even before D Day a measure of mutual respect had developed ... but after the initial phase the Commando became so firmly welded together at every level that it seemed entirely natural that we should fight and live side-by-side until the end of the war, as indeed we did.*

The plan for the Commando HQ, seven assault troops and one support troop was to land behind 2 East Yorks, with the French Troops supported by the Commando's K-gun Sections, due to touch down at 0755 hours on Queen Red just east of strongpoint COD. As already indicated the two French Commandos would land direct from LCIs (*527* and *523*) which they would embark at Warsash, while the remainder of the Commando would disembark into LCAs from their two Landing Ships, HMS *Astrid* and SS *Maid of Orleans*. Once ashore on a supposedly well ordered beach, they would cross the mined dunes on the cleared routes to their assembly area near a set of largely demolished holiday villas alongside the main coast road little more than two hundred metres inland.

Having assembled, they would move east along the coastal road towards Ouistreham. The French troops were to attack *WN-10* at the western end of the town while the five British assault troops would clear the main part of the town including *WN 08*

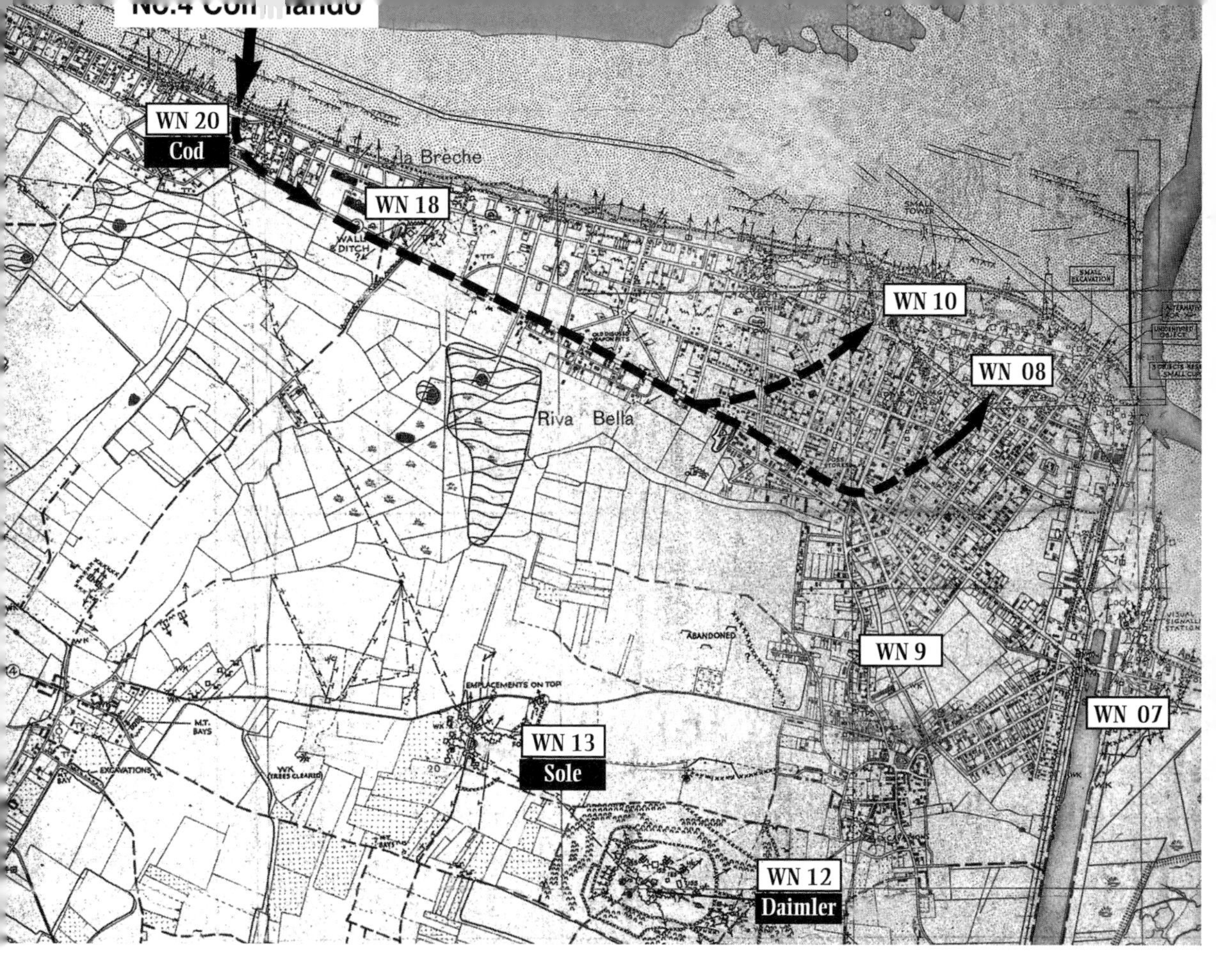


and the fire control tower. The area around the sea locks was the objective of 5th Assault Regiment RE along with the infantry position of *WN 07* at the southern end of the town. In addition to sundry destroyers and other gun-armed landing craft, fire support on the Ouistreham defences would be provided by the seven 7.5-inch guns of the cruiser HMS *Frobisher*, while HMS *Danae* (five 6-inch guns) would engage the DAIMLER/SOLE positions.

It is worth explaining Colonel Dawson's rationale for the roles given to the French in his plan.

> *It gave them the opportunity of getting to grips with something within their own competence, and under their own steam, whereas the battery No 4 Commando had to attack was so complicated in its layout that it could have been difficult to integrate the French into an attack on it when they spoke a different language and so on. You see, we'd never all been together in action before, and although subsequently we never*

*had any problems, on this first operation I thought it better to give the French their own targets.*

**Landing and Assembly**

*O Lord, though knowest how busy I must be this day. If I forget thee, do not thou forget me.*
Prayer of Sir Jacob Astley before Edgehill.

With the words of this prayer on his lips, Philippe Kieffer was one of the lucky Frenchmen to get some sleep aboard the flat bottomed LCI *527*. It was a rough crossing. No. 4 Commando's doctor described the conditions:

*The wind howled and it rained vicious scuds. The skipper said in his talk, 'The Allied High Command must be heavily counting on surprise, for the Germans must surely think that not even Englishmen could be fools enough to start an invasion on a night like this'.*

At 0330 hours, with the invasion fleet in the shelter of the broad Baie de Seine, the Commandos were roused from a fitful sleep and those who could face breakfast went to the ship's galley. At nautical twilight the flotilla bearing the Commandos passed the naval gun line. Lord Lovat wrote;

*The cruiser* Frobisher *joined the battleships on our port quarter* [Warspite and Ramillies]. *Muzzle blasts from the turrets of the ironclads lit the dawn with a yellow glare as their massive guns hurled shells of up to a ton into the enemy's batteries.*

*Tasked with laying down fire to suppress the Ouistreham defences: HMS* Frobisher, *and below HMS* Danae.

Leading the flotillas of the landing craft bearing 1st SS Brigade were No. 4 Commando coming in at more or less the same time as 41 Commando. Aboard LCI 523 was French Commando Leon Gautier who later wrote 'At 6 a.m., we could see France. Seeing my country after four years away was very emotional.'

As elsewhere on SWORD Beach the obstacles had not been cleared by the time the second wave approached the beach. Sub-Lieutenant Berry, commander of LCI *523* recalled, 'I saw about six rows of stakes and tripods in the water which had some converted captured shells on top of them acting as mines. Bits of wire and chain hung between them'. Bouncing off the obstacles and going in at full speed LCI *523* ran well up the beach; Lieutenant Berry had already decided that this was likely to be a one way trip for *523*. LCI *527* was not so lucky, as her propellers fouled one of the obstacles and a shell damaged her ramp. Consequently, her load of French Commandos had to disembark over the side using scrambling nets and race to catch up with those who had a dry landing from *523*.

Ashore at around 0755 were 171 men of the two French Troops along with six British Commando radio operators and medics. The heavily laden Commandos stepped out onto the beach to find virtually all the enemy positions unsuppressed and active, spitting fire. The random explosion of enemy artillery shells and mortar bombs was cut by the cracking of high velocity bullets from rifle and *Spandau*. Through this the Commandos ran in a desperate race for survival.

According to the Brigade's post operational report matters were little better when the main body of the Commando landed:

> *... when 4 Commando came in at 0820 hours they found the assault troops pinned down by intense machine gun and mortar fire from a strong point at the back of the beach* [COD]. *Some had not got beyond the waters edge and were still in two feet of water.*
>
> *Mortar bombs were falling in and around the LCAs as they*

HMS *Warspite with her* forward 15-inch guns delivering a broadside in support of the landings.

*SWORD beach photographed around the same time of 4 Commando's landing.*

> *touched down and the Commando suffered forty casualties including the Commanding Officer, Lieutenant Colonel R.W.P. Dawson, who was wounded in the leg.*
>
> *It was immediately apparent that the Commando could not count on the hoped for support from 8 Infantry Brigade troops, and pushing past the troops lying at the waters edge, C Troop No 4 Commando engaged the slit trenches and pill boxes at the back of the beach and broke their way out on to the main road.*

As was the case with 1st SS Brigade, it was quite a shock for the Commandos who were used to landing on deserted beaches to find themselves wading through the bodies of 2nd East Yorkshire soldiers who had been killed during the initial landing. Although it is clear that elements of the Yorks were pushing on inland and fighting in strong point COD, the Commandos all recall seeing infantry desperately scraping holes in the sand of the beach and dunes as they sprinted across the fire-swept beach. Heavily laden this can not have been a very fast 'sprint'. Leon Gautier recalled, 'I was carrying four days of food and ammunition – pack weighing 30-35 kilograms, which we left on the beach [*sic* assembly area], to pick up later.

Of the 177 French and British Commandos who had landed first, 114 reached the assembly area approximately where the statue of Montgomery now stands. The remainder of the Commando started to arrive and Colonel Dawson took the opportunity presented by the pause in events to recce the route towards Ouistreham and to attempt to locate the HQ of 2 E Yorks. Ian Dear tells of the Commanding Officer's return to the assembly area:

*... when he came back his face was a mask of blood and he was not in a good mood. "What the hell are you doing" he yelled at his adjutant, Donald Gilchrist. "Get moving." Gilchrist opened his mouth to protest that Dawson had not given any orders to push on. "Move!" shouted Dawson, and Gilchrist did. He ran to the Frenchmen, "Allez! Allez!" he screamed at them. "Vite, vite! Sacrebleu!" The French looked at him in utter amazement obediently began to move off to their objectives, and it wasn't until after the war that Gilchrist was told by the French that they thought he had been shouting 'Allah!'*

As the French Troops moved off, they passed the wounded Dawson who told them, 'Go ahead-we're counting on you'.

It was eventually established that a bill of some forty casualties to the British Commandos was the price for landing and getting across the beach. Colonel Dawson who now had a head wound as well as a serious wound to his leg. He was temporarily forced to hand over to his second-in-command, Major Menday, while his wounds were dressed. Returning to his unit to carry on Dawson was only evacuated when ordered into the medical evacuation chain.

As was often the case the artillery Forward Observation Officers and the naval Forward Officer Bombardment attached to No. 4 Commando had become casualties during the landing

*Commandos disembarking onto SWORD beach.*

*German machine gun teams sited on higher ground inland were able to cover the area immediately behind the beach.*

or getting off the beach. Consequently, once the prearranged part of the fire plan had run its course, they would be on their own.

### The Attack on the Casino Strong Point

Leading the advance down the coastal road to Ouistreham was the French 8 Troop and half a section of the Vickers K-guns all commanded by Alex Lofi. His objective was *WN 18*, which was only seven hundred yards east. This was an outlying position that had appeared late in the development of the Atlantic Wall to improve coverage of the beach between the Casino (*WN 10*) and COD (*WN 20*) strong points. Lieutenant Lofi wrote:

> *I gave the order to move off with Hulot's section at the head. We had already been bracketed by some mortar bombs and we had to cross another minefield before we reached the grounds of a large house. Hulot arrived and went in …with the task of clearing it. Just then we were caught in a heavy artillery barrage and the house was hit by shells.*

According to Lofi, 'Progress was now rapid'. The Frenchmen found several *Tobrukstände* abandoned by enemy machine gunners, a testimony to the effect of the naval bombardment. Closer to the town the greater was the enemy resistance. The Brigade report says that they were:

> *... coming up against heavy harassing fire from snipers and machine guns in houses. Invaluable assistance was given by a gendarme, a member of the Resistance Movement, who helped the leading troops to by-pass enemy strong points.*

Getting into the outskirts of Ouistreham, Lofi recorded that:

> *We skirted round the obstacles set up by the Germans at the entrance to Riva Bella. Notices saying '*Achtung Minnen*' were fixed on the walls of villas. As we closed in on the strongpoint a mortar, which must have been biding its time, dropped a bomb on Hulot's section and there were a number of wounded including Hulot himself. I helped get the wounded under cover and then ordered Bagot's section to take over the advance. As we approached our objective we came under heavy machine-gun fire and four scouts were wounded, though only lightly. We took up our positions in surrounding houses from which we could command the complex of very well hidden trenches in the middle of which a large blockhouse stood still absolutely intact.*

8 Troop's attack on *WN 18* began with a fire fight. With 'a few lucky shots' from their fire positions in the wrecked buildings around the enemy position, the Commandos started to drive the German defenders in the trenches to ground but the pillbox withstood all attempts to neutralise it; PIAT anti-tank rounds had absolutely no effect on it. With little progress the Germans started to leave their positions in the first of several brave counter-attacks on the Commandos. Lofi committed his reserve to his right flank and at the cost of several casualties the enemy were driven off with difficulty, especially as the K-guns became unreliable as carbon residue started to build up in the guns' workings.

So the situation remained. Even though the bombardment had been generally effective, the heavy concrete casemates and troop shelters had survived and proved to be beyond the capability of a lightly armed Commando troop, which had already suffered significant losses on the beach and approach march. Eventually, elements of 2 E Yorks took over masking the now isolated enemy position, which surrendered shortly afterwards.

Meanwhile, the depleted 1 Troop (French) was now the leading element of No. 4 Commando had continued along the coastal road. About forty minutes after landing, reaching the outskirts of Ouistreham, Kieffer and the Troop turned north up a side street that led to the rear of the Casino strongpoint, while the British element of the Commando continued on into Ouistreham. There was an unforeseen problem, the side road taken by the French was blocked by a seven foot high concrete anti-tank wall some fifty yards from the perimeter of the casino strong point but 'In the middle of the wall there was a gap just wide enough to let a man through'.

*The Casino at Ouistreham, a hive of German machine guns.*

> *The advance on the pavements to left and right took place in the shelter of this wall, and the Germans who were to be eliminated were unable to see their enemy. Once the wall was reached it was enough to make a quick movement through the gap and to disperse down each side as had been planned. Though the strength of Troop had by now been reduced by a third, its fire power had not been, as the automatic weapons of the wounded and dead were now being used by those who previously had only been armed with rifles.*
>
> *The Troop was spread evenly on both sides of the street, with two Bren guns, four Tommy guns and one flame thrower on each side. Everyone had orders to fire on the embrasures of the strongpoint which was now only forty metres away.*

In accordance with the plan, the attack opened with the Troop's PIAT opening fire on a 20mm anti-aircraft position and the bunker. In this case a lucky hit near the embrasure sent splinters into the casemate with a devastating effect on the occupants but the Commando's fire position had been spotted and was

*Men of 4 Commando during a lull in the fighting.*

engaged by a gun firing high explosive from the strongpoint further to the east. The Commandos were forced to abandon their good position as the building started to collapse.

*Marcel Lefevre*

An ageing veteran of the Great War, Marcel Lefevre, joined the Commandos in fighting to liberate his country and was promptly armed with a rifle. He told Kieffer's men where some German telephone cables were buried. They were duly cut with 8 kilos of plastic explosive. It is widely acknowledged that this simple act alone did much to undermine the enemy's will to fight by effectively isolating them from their chain of command and its urgings to fight on, as well as, denying them calls for artillery support.

With a stalemate similar to that at *WN 18* developing, Kieffer was contemplating the dreadful prospect of an expensive direct assault on his objective, when his British radio operator reported that he had heard on the 8 Brigade radio net that he was monitoring, that the surviving amphibious DD tanks were now off the beach. Kieffer, with his batman, immediately retraced his steps to the minefield breaches at the rear of Queen Red and eventually persuaded a squadron of 13/18 Hussars to lend him the services of one of their tanks. Riding on the engine decks he returned to the Casino in a style that few Commandos ever enjoyed. It was now 0925 hours. Philippe Kieffer recalled:

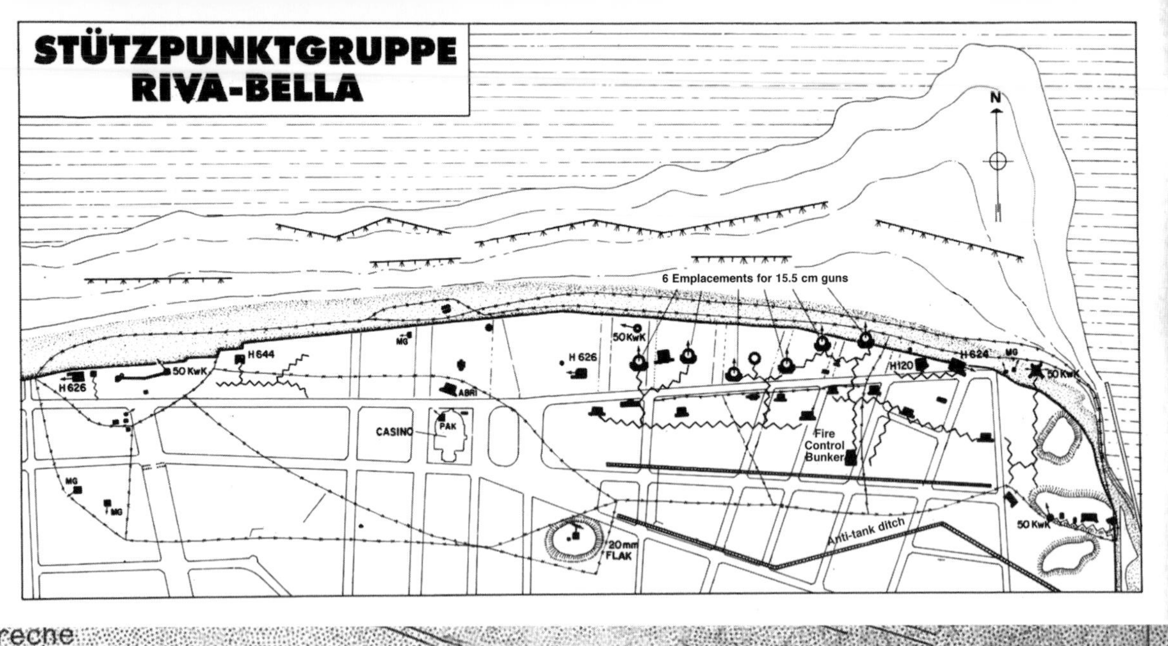


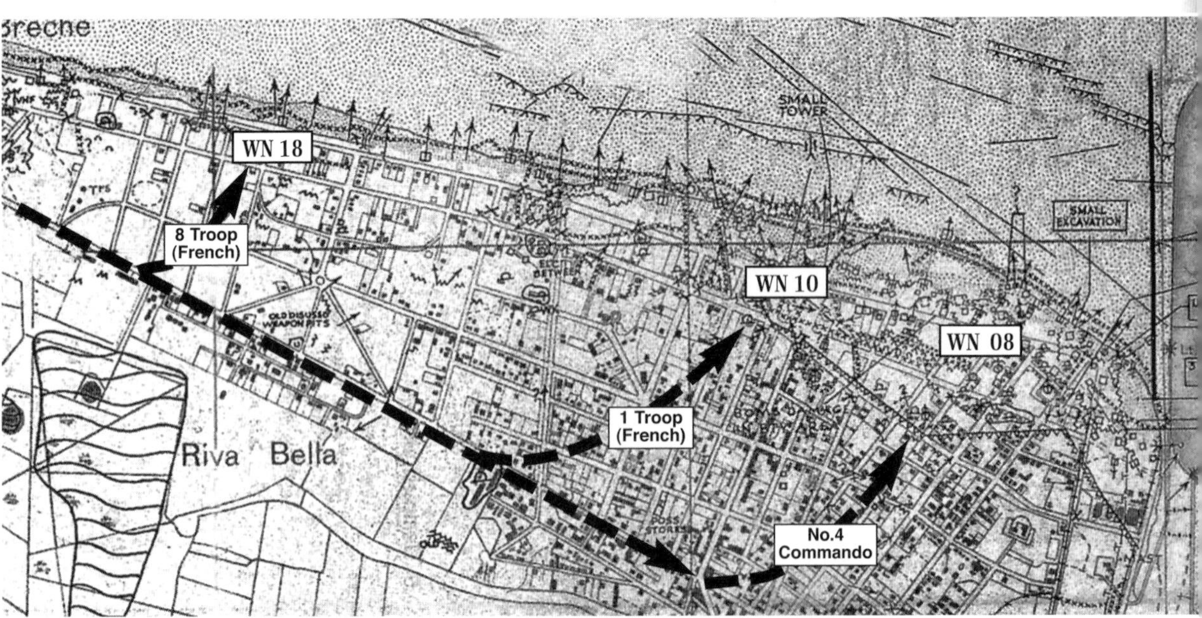


*I decided to keep the wall as a protection and went with the tank through an adjacent courtyard where we set up in front of the Casino and commenced firing under my directions. The first two shells went straight into the Casino, which stopped two of its guns from firing. At that moment I was once more lightly wounded in the right arm by a rifle bullet, and I came down from the tank and went forward five metres behind a wall to continue directing the tank's fire by hand signals. I ordered the tank to fire into all the German positions, and the fire from the machine guns stopped.*

By 0955 hours, Kieffer, with the enemy's fire much reduced by the tank's suppressive fire ordered forward a 'sections to both the left and right flanks.'

> *Resistance seemed to be most intense on the right-hand side in the direction taken by Lardennois and his section. It came from the water tower which was firing on our right flank. After bandaging my arm we got back on the tank and got it to turn and face the water tower, so that we went no more than 100 metres from it. With four shells it was silenced. The section on the right now moved forward an cleared up the area, and Lanternier brought back the first eleven prisoners of whom three or four were Poles. While they were being brought back one of them threw a grenade which slightly wounded two of my men. At once we fire and killed three of them.*

Lord Lovat's report summarised the operation:

> *Heavy casualties were inflicted on the enemy, who put up a stiff resistance from strong fortifications and cunningly camouflaged blockhouses. The concrete gun emplacements had withstood the terrific air and naval bombardment extremely well and severe fighting took place before the enemy position finally became untenable and several surrendered. The battery was taken, but casualties on both sides were heavy and after the engagement medical orderlies from opposing sides worked side by side succouring the wounded.*

The landing and capturing of the Ouistreham Casino strongpoint cost 1 Troop all five officers and twenty-three of its men. Fighting with bravery and determination to liberate their homeland was proving an expensive business.

## Ouistreham

The main body of No. 4 Commando headed along the road into the ruins of Ouistreham. The town had been regularly bombed in the run-up to D Day and had most recently been shelled during the preliminary bombardment. The process had, of course, also been complemented by the Germans clearing fields of fire. Consequently, much of the central and seaward part of the town was devastated. The Commando's objective was the defences around the gun pits and casemates covering the mouth of the river and canal.

The order of march along the same coast road taken by the French troops a short while earlier was C Troop followed by D, A, E and F Troops. Lieutenant Knivett Carr's B (Support Troop) brought up the rear or, as in the case of the 3-inch mortars, set up and prepared to support the attacks.

C Troop with the help of another DD tank, made good progress clearing along the road but shell and mortar fire caused casualties along the length of the Commando's column; wounded men were left in the flanking ditches to be collected by the medics who were following up behind. Doc Patterson had established an RAP near the Commando's Assembly Area in the cover of ruins and the piles of dumped bergens. Here he received a steady flow of wounded from across the brigade, who he stabilised and dispatched back across the dunes to the beach for evacuation. The lucky ones were back in the UK port hospitals by that evening. The dead were covered and discreetly left for burial by 101 Beach Group in temporary beachside cemeteries.

As was the case with the French Troops, C and D Troops occupied fire positions in the ruined buildings from where they

*Commandos and a DD tank in the ruins of Ouistreham.*

began a fire fight that would cover the approach of the last three troops. Bill Bidmead recorded:

> *We were soon installed in one of the top rooms of a house. The rest of the Troop were in other nearby houses. What a marvellous view we had of the battery position. But in the midst of it was a 60 ft observation/control tower, which we were told, in our briefing, would be a pile of rubble. It still stands today and is a museum. The Germans were throwing grenades from the top at our men getting in position for the assault. Then all hell was let loose as our K guns opened up.*

This subdued the grenade throwers but, overlooked by the fire control tower, the Commando's first major obstacle was the anti-tank ditch, which of course was protected by barbed wire and covered by machine-gun and mortar fire. Casualties were inevitable and the aluminium ladder that D Troop had planned to use to cross the ditch had been lost during the landing when it and the men carrying it were smashed by an exploding shell. Captain Pat Portéous recalled that he '... needn't have worried as the Germans had left some planks bridging the ditch for their own convenience,' and the fire of the tank and C Troop suppressed the enemy sufficiently long for D Troop to cross.

This was of course as far as the tank could advance but it continued to support the Commando, albeit, in this case, without the personal direction of the commander and at a greater range

With D Troop inside the perimeter of the defended area of Ouistreham they gave covering fire to E and F who crossed into the battery and set about clearing the numerous casemates, bunkers and shelters. In this they were greatly assisted by the earlier shelling by HMS *Frobisher* and other fire support craft who had together taken much of the fight out of most of the German defenders; there were certainly no organised attempts to counter-attack, as there had been at the less heavily engaged French objectives.

A and C Troops having crossed the anti-tank ditch joined the action and when the Commandos reached the dunes, stripped of all vegetation by the bombardments, the damaged gun pits were found to be empty. The 'guns' seen in the latest air photographs

*The Ouistreham anti-tank ditch and a direct hit on the fire control bunker from seaward.*

proved, as at Pointe du Hoc, to be telegraph poles. According to inhabitants of Ouistreham the 155mm guns had been moved to their new casemates at Objective DAIMLER only a matter of days earlier. As the Commando reorganised, the leading Arrmoured Vehicles Royal Engineer (AVREs) were beginning to arrive for their part in the clearance of Ouistreham. Lieutenant Knivett 'Muscles' Carr of 4 Commando Heavy Weapons Troop recalled that having:

> *... captured and cleared the German coastal gun battery and the assaulting troops made their way to our original assembly area. Here I found a two wheeled horse-drawn cart, unfortunately without the horse! We loaded all the three inch mortar bombs and the two mortars onto it and with relays of six men pulling it we set off across country on the road leading to the only road bridge over the Caen Canal and the River Orne just east of the village of Bénouville.*

Taking a more direct route than that taken by the remainder of the Brigade, No. 4 Commando came across plenty of evidence of their passage.

*There were dead Germans everywhere especially in the village* [St-Aubin-d'Arquenay] *but at one place there were both the bodies of Germans and men of No. 6 Commando's Cycle Troop. They had clearly been ambushed and fought it out.*

No.4 Commando reached Pegasus bridge over the Canal de Caen at 1530 hours, where Lieutenant Gilchrist who had been sent on ahead by Major Menday, who was temporarily in command, to 'Get information and be ready to meet us'. Gilchrist explained:

*I was to be the advance party of one... a man nearby had a folding parachute bicycle. We had managed to bring a few of these light-weight machines ashore, just in case – I was the case. I left my bergen rucksack in the care of my batman, McCall, and Menday's batman, Macaulay, volunteered to bring it along, carrying it between them like a baby's portable cot.*

There was a short pause while the Commando regrouped and organised themselves in small groups to rush across the bridges. Lieutenant Knivett Carr recalled his bit in getting his troop across the Bridge:

*The bridge was under intermittent sniper fire so I arranged for a quick smokescreen from one of my mortars to be put down on the bridge and we managed to get our cart and ourselves across without any casualties. We then crossed the bridge over the River Orne without any opposition...*

Another Commando said that the strong afternoon breeze rendered the smokescreen less than fully effective and a number

*The second of the two bridges; the bridge over the River Orne.*

of men were killed and wounded during the crossing, but 1st SS Brigade, complete, were across the Orne and now under the command of 6th Airborne Division.

### Visiting the Battlefield

This short tour starts on the seafront at QUEEN Red Beach at Colleville-Montgomery Plage, nears the statue of Montgomery. A little to the east is a memorial near the **WN 18** casemate, which was attacked by the French Commandos. Take Avenue du 4eme Commando back to the D514 coast road an turn left towards Ouistreham.

In Ouistreham turn onto the Boulevard Winston Churchill and drive down to the beach. Turn right and park between the Casino and the French memorial. This is the scene of Commandant Philippe Kieffer's action to capture the **WN 10** defences. The memorial commemorates the D Day dead by name. There is a museum to No 4 Commando opposite the Casino.

Drive on past the Casino on the D514 Boulevard Maritime. In about 500 yards there is a belt of trees park opposite Rue de Berny. In the centre of the go-kart race area and under the sand dunes to the seaward side of the road are the abandoned gun-pits of **WN 08** and just a short distance inland down the next right turn, Avenue de la Plage, is the fire control tower. This is the Atlantic Wall Museum and is well worth a visit.

Chapter Eleven

# Into the line

Major General Gale.

On crossing the double water obstacle of the Canal de Caen and the River Orne, which were to protect the left flank of the Second Army's beachhead from a flanking counter-attack, 1st Special Service Brigade came under command of Major General Gale's 6th Airborne Division. This division's role was to provide a buffer to the east to keep the Germans well away from the obstacle (canal and river) and off high ground from where they could look deep into the beachhead.

Determining the Brigade's D Day task east of the Orne was not straightforward. Lord Lovat in his memoir explains and is worth quoting at length:

*At one briefing I expressed surprise at the vagueness of my remit. 'You will infest this area!' stated General Gale, placing a large hand upon the map and blotting out a land-mass of sixty square miles of territory, including the coast towns of Cabourg and Franceville Plage, and stretching back inland to cover enclosed wooden country between the Dives and Orne river systems. I welcomed independence, but a suspicion had been growing, and I asked, 'Does that mean my four Commandos are considered expendable, and only required to wander about like the maquis in no-man's-land, harrying unspecified targets, without any fire support or supply system?'...This caused an explosion. It was a tactless question, and I was hurried out by Gale's GS01* [operations staff officer]. *It was clear the general expected blind obedience from subordinates. But I was determined to get the right answer before leaving England...*

*My last opportunity to get a hearing occurred at a final conference at Bulford, with General Browning in the chair, attended by high-ups in 1st Corps and 3rd, 6th* [Airborne] *and*

*50th Divisions or their representatives. Certain officers holding responsibilities on D Day were given a hearing, or asked questions. I raised the matter again. "Sir, Phase 1, from the beach to the bridges, presents no serious problem, but I have misgivings about my Brigade's subsequent tasks, which remain undetermined. With respect, I wish to offer suggestions for consideration. With no specific targets after crossing the River Orne, four highly trained units… are apparently going to be dispersed, in order to wage guerrilla warfare. If my Brigade scatter they will be lost as an effective formation, and bush-whacking, with only a German battery at Cabourg to destroy, seems a waste of key men …"*

*Gale and his planners looked askance; the other generals sat in silence but our corps commander seemed interested. General Browning… encouraged me to go on. "As I see it, the high ground across the river controls the battle, and responsibility must turn immediately to its defence… My priority task is surely to consolidate the length of the ridge between Amfréville-Le Plein-Hauger to the sea coast, dug into positions, penetrating deep and sufficiently far, inflict maximum damage to communications and troop concentrations, always returning to previously prepared positions before first light through standing patrols, to give warning of enemy approach? While the defence line has priority importance, it appears essential to disrupt any advance along approach roads which channel traffic to the Orne bridges. It is here Brigade can expect to be attacked. I see little sense in beating up the area, or pushing Commandos out to Cabourg."*

*Lord Lovat at the Caen Canal Bridge.*

*Gale wangled the inevitable compromise over Cabourg… After the meeting General 'Boy' Browning said, "I have got the message and am in full agreement. The idea of wandering about in the blue will get us nowhere, and I liked that crack 'to dig in, lie low, and don't shoot 'til you see the whites of their eyes'".*

*General 'Boy' Browning*

The area that Lord Lovat was so concerned about was principally between the Amfreville ridge and the inundated Dives River valley. The causeways across which were to have been cut by airborne troops. General Gale believed that enemy left in this area would be cut off, lack heavy support and be easily isolated, neutralised by naval and artillery fire and then destroyed in detail. Extending the Commandos' reach out far beyond the inundations was, however, conceded a being as being beyond practicality. Expeditions to the Gonneville and le Mont batteries south east of Cabourg were quietly dropped.

## Enemy and Plans

The enemy in the area that 1st SS Brigade was to 'infest' were elements of *Generalleutnant* Josef Reichert's *711. Infanteriedivision*. Their major defensive positions were in the dunes flanking the seaside village of Franceville Plage. Of these one was sited to cover the Orne Estuary but further east on a slim isthmus of land between the inundations and the beach was a ribbon of relatively light defences. Inland the major German position was a well defended and protected battery of what were assessed by RAF photo interpreters as being four casemated 155mm guns: the Merville battery. The area occupied by the battery and its outlying positions was in excess of a thousand yards square. To the east of the village of Sallenelles was a large concrete bunker containing a *Luftwaffe/Kriegsmarine* radar control station, as usual protected by barbed wire and machine guns. Inland from Sallenelles, at Hauger/Point 35, a modest position overlooked the village and the coastal road. This was the location of battalion HQ of *642. Ost Bataillon*, who were attached to *711. Infanteriedivision*. A modest position but even modest defences would be a challenge to the lightly armed and equipped Commandos.

**See map on page 249**

The obvious and growing strength of the defences of *711. Infanteriedivision* immediately east of the Orne, argued against any landing on the coast beyond the Orne and the Canal. A short and direct route from beach on this bit of coast to the area of operations was not a practical option. The amount of firepower necessary, a further extension of the frontage of the landing not to mention the likely cost of fighting through the defences in taking the short route, meant that the longer march from SWORD Beach was decided upon.

The tasks that Lord Lovat was eventually given by Major General Gale were as follows:

> 1. *On coming under my command your role will be to mop up and subsequently secure the coastal area FRANCEVILLE PLAGE – CARBOURG 2180 – VARAVILLE – LE PLEIN.*
>
> 2. *It is essential that the LA PLEIN feature should be denied to the enemy. Your plans will therefore envisage the holding of LA PLEIN. You will not lock up your force in the static defence of this feature.*
>
> 3. *Working from the MERVILLE – VARAVILLE areas the remainder of your command will operate offensively in the coastal belt, so infesting the area as to make its retention by the Germans impossible or if this is impractical, hazardous and difficult. Should you be able to dislodge, destroy or capture all German positions in this area, your aim must be so to worry them that they will be incapable of interfering with the beach landings on the front of 3 British Infantry Division. You must be prepared to infest this area over a period of days. Your plan should therefore envisage a series of reliefs for the more actively engaged troops.*
>
> 4. *Such a role as has been allocated cannot be fulfilled by any form of static defence this is indeed is not required of you. As a corollary it is appreciated that German infiltration through your screen may well be possible. This risk I accept. You should however, be able generally to give me information of such movement, and even though you may be unable to stop it, the information is all I require.*

The Brigade's initial presence in this rather large area, still twenty-four square miles, was to be No. 6 Commando followed by No. 3 Commando. 45 RM Commando, at General Gale's insistence, was to take over from Colonel Otway's 9 Para at the Merville battery or complete its capture, should the pre-dawn attack have failed. After this they were to push forward through Franceville Plage towards Cabourg. No. 4 Commando would follow into the area in the early evening, once it had cleared Ouistreham and returned to collect their bergen rucksacks from their Assembly Area back the beach. The plan was in essence, a combination of that advocated by Lord Lovat and General Gale's aspiration to dominate the ground as far to the east of his main defences as possible, in what he hoped would be a vacuum.

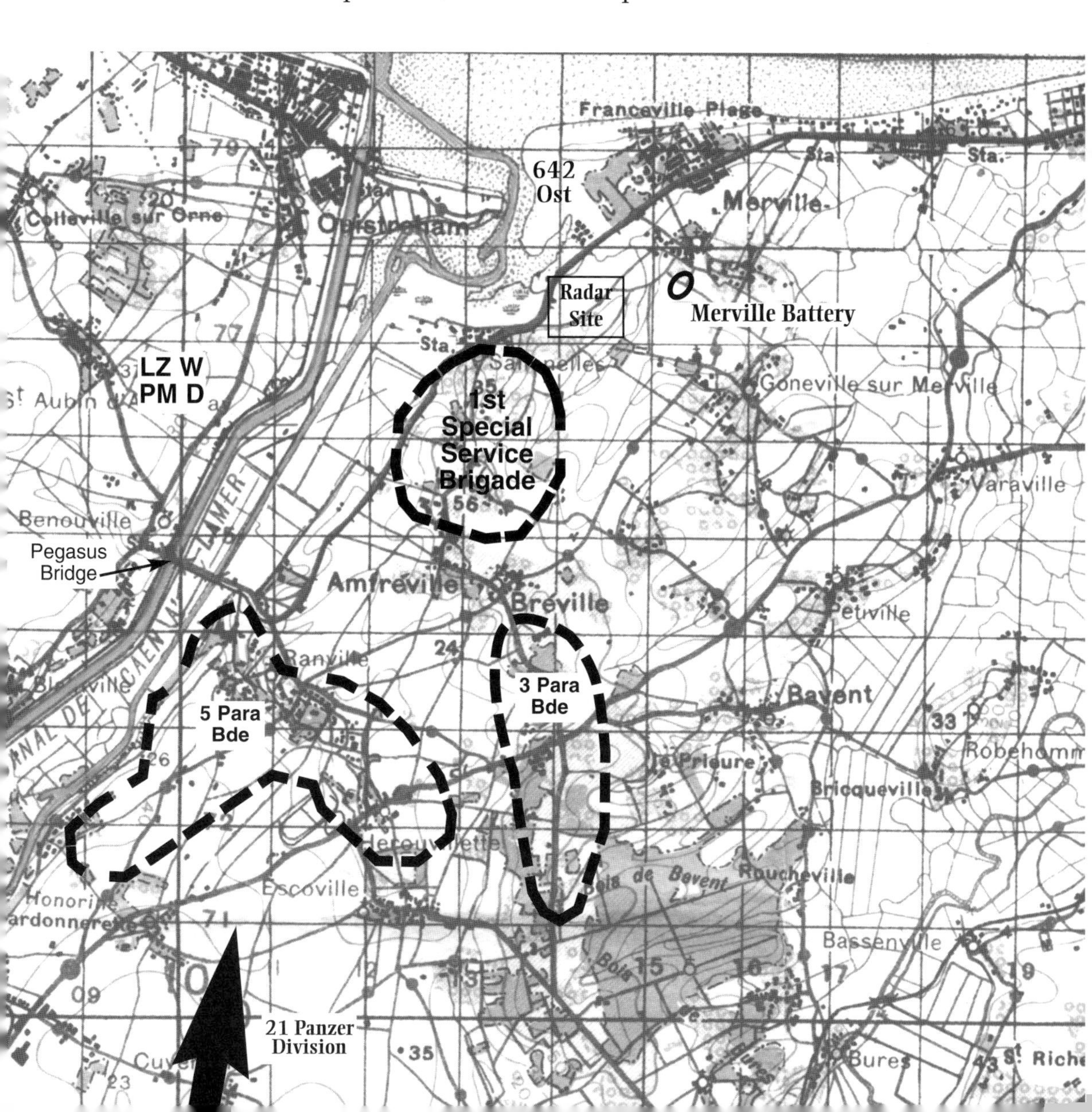

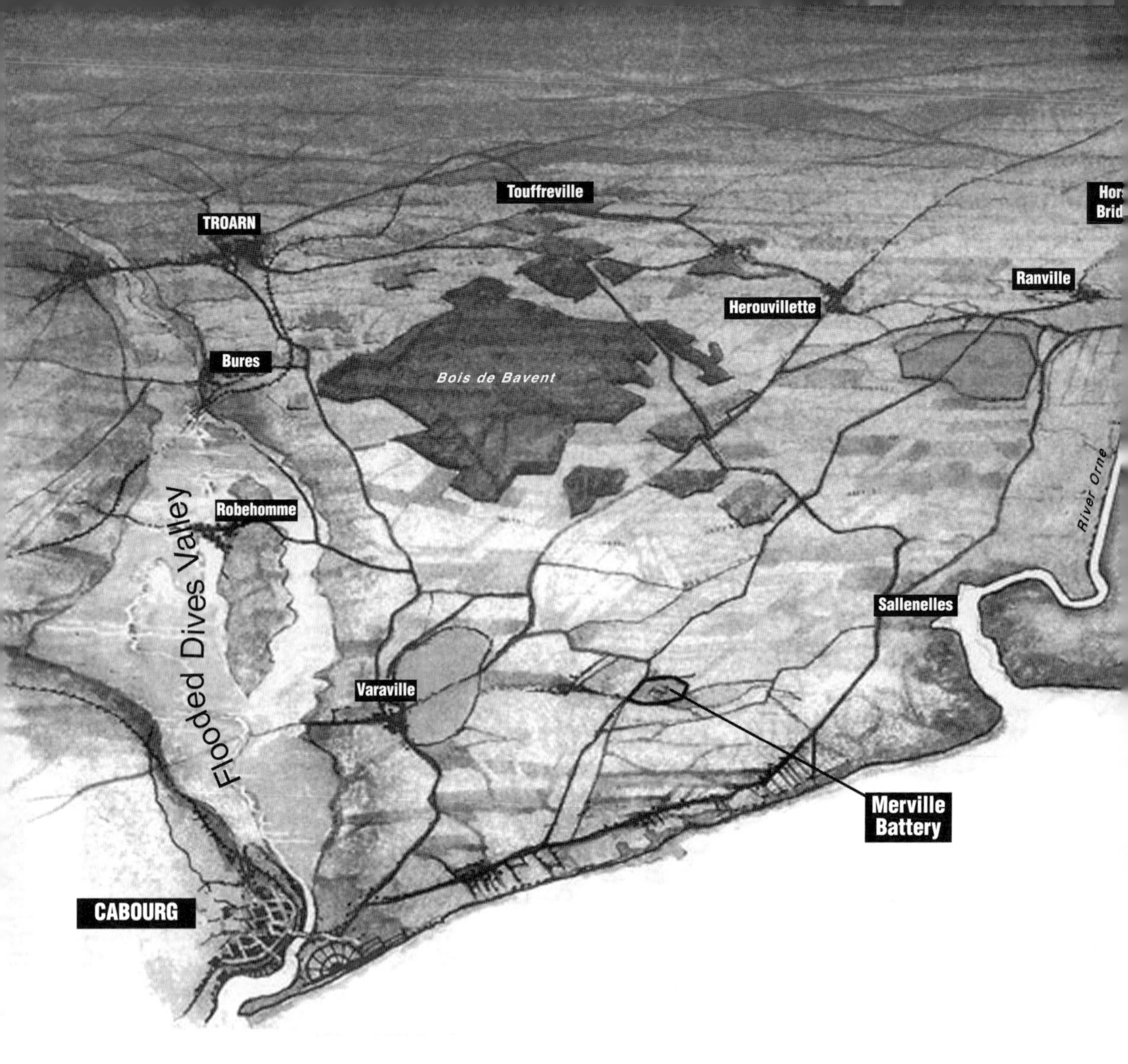


## The Advance from the Bridge

In theory the next leg of the Brigade's march to its allocated area on the very left flank of the Second Army would be across ground held by 6th Airborne Division. Coming up out of the Orne Valley and crossing the edge of the 3 Para Brigade's Drop Zone (November DZ N), however, proved to be only a little less dangerous than their march from the beach to the bridges through enemy held territory.

The cycle troops of No. 6 and 45 Commandos led the brigade off to their objectives but, according to the Brigade report, they were joined by that of 3 Commando who were:

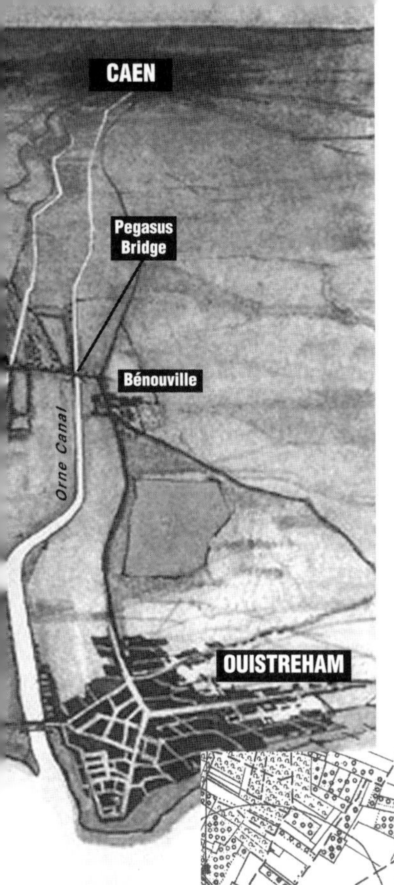


*...held up by heavy shelling and at COLLEVILLE by continuous sniping, sent forward their 3 Troop on cycles which crossed the bridges at 1400 and was ordered to go to the assistance of 9 Para Bn who were holding positions outside the village of LE PLEIN where the enemy were putting up stiff resistance. A combined attack was put in which was at first unsuccessful but a subsequent flank attack by 3 Troop cleared the village during the afternoon.*

It is said that 'no plan ever survives contact with the enemy' and Lord Lovat's was to be no different. While Brigade HQ, Nos 6 and 45 RM Commandos were heading for the high ground, a serious threat to the south of the airborne

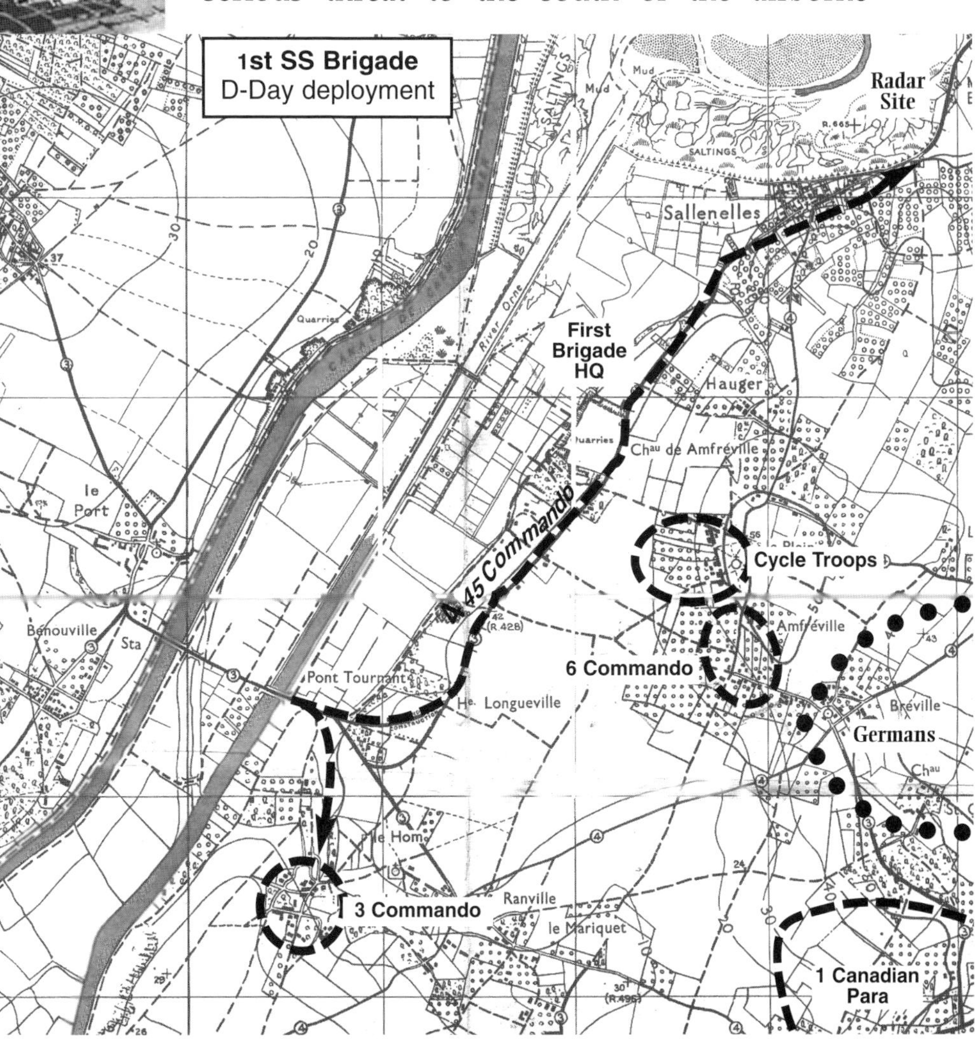

bridgehead was developing in the form of *21. Panzerdivision*. The Brigade report recorded:

> *The main body of 3 Commando arrived at the bridges at about 1530, but on instructions from Airborne Div they were diverted to take up a defensive position near LE BAS de RANVILLE to protect Div HQ. This meant abandoning all hope of carrying out the original plan and the Brigade Commander decided to hold the line of the high ground running from MERVILLE in the NORTH to BREVILLE in the SOUTH. No. 45 (RM) Commando were accordingly ordered not to proceed further than MERVILLE and to dig themselves in there for the night.*
>
> *Brigade Headquarters moved up to the area of ECARDE and set up in a farm, while 6 Commando mopped up the southern end of LE PLEIN and consolidated.*

*Colonel Otway*

Here elements of Colonel Otway's 9 Para were in action, having been reduced to eighty men and it was an easy decision for Lord Lovat to adopt what would have been his preferred plan and hold positions on the Amfreville ridge.

If the enemy held the Amfreville ridge, he would be able to look out over the vast open fields of DZ N that stretched from the foot of the ridge to within a few hundred yards of the River Orne but up on the ridge, the country was more like the bocage. Unlike the US sector where the hedgerow country extended for over thirty miles south of Carentan, in the British sector patches of small embanked and hedge topped fields and orchards were to be found, normally around villages and in valleys. One of the more extensive areas of bocage was to be found on the ridge between the sea at Franceville and the Bois de Bavent to the south. This particular patch of hedgerows encompassed most of the twenty-four square miles that General Gale envisaged the Special Service Brigade being responsible for.

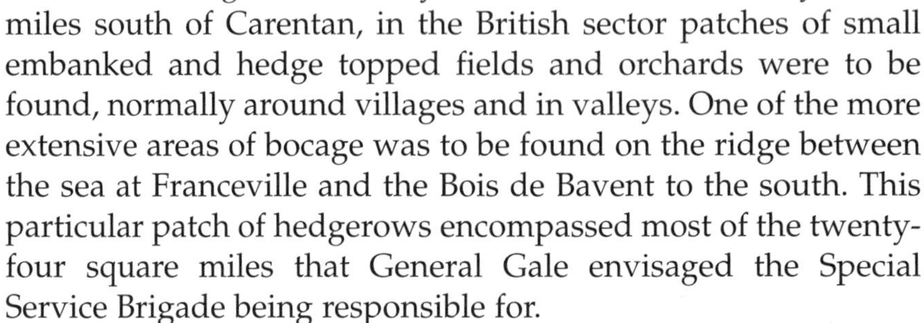

Here fields of fire would be limited to a couple of hundred yards at the most but more often just fifty yards – if the Commandos were lucky but, on the other hand, as the attacking Americans were to find further east, the terrain favoured the defender. With a bit of skill the banks would provide protection from fire and make the Commandos' positions very difficult for the enemy to locate. As elsewhere, the solidly built Norman stone houses and their cellars, provided strong redoubts around which the 'defensive blobs' adopted by the Commando troops, could be formed.

## Number 6 Commando

Lieutenant Colonel Derek Mills-Roberts's Commando crossed the bridges into the airborne bridgehead at 1330 hours. He explained:

> *I planned to approach the village from a cross-country direction, and we took the road near the bank of the River Orne, later turning right up the hill near a quarry. Just below the village we*

*Bréville during the fighting for the village.*

*halted to reorganise, and I sent a reconnaissance patrol forward.*

Needless to say, No. 6 Commando was under pressure to get up and establish itself on to the vital ridge but the return of the recce patrol, with the loss of its commander, confirmed that the enemy were in and around the village of Le Plein. Colonel Mills-Roberts recounted:

*We pressed on until we came out of the gate of a long meadow on to a road which ran through Le Plain. There a soldierly figure, dressed in corduroy trousers and a tweed jacket, greeted us courteously; he quickly explained that he was the owner of the solidly built farm which lay in front of us and that it would make an excellent observation post.*

The implication of this kind offer was made plain to the Frenchman, who answered 'I am an ex-warrant officer of the *Cuirassiers* of the *Garde*' and he passed on plenty of information, armed with which, a fighting patrol was sent into the southern part of the village and further south along the ridge towards the village of Bréville. There was enemy activity on the ridge and Colonel Mills-Roberts's HQ had been spotted.

*I turned back to see that one of our signallers had his hair neatly parted by a bullet. This extraordinary scalp wound had lifted a flap of scalp and hair from his skull, which he cautiously flattened down before getting on with his work.*

Already in action in the northern part of the village was No. 3 Commando's Cycle Troop who had been sent on ahead and joined the other cycle troops reinforcing 9 Para on the ridge. Their first probe into le Plain was beaten off and their commander wounded:

*… Ponsford took command. He ordered the Sergeant-Major to reorganise the Troop, while he made a quick reconnaissance round the right flank and found a covered approach. After clearing some houses which overlooked the village square, Ponsford put one of his sections in position to give covering fire. Here the 2-inch mortar proved invaluable, for its high-explosive bombs, fired at a low angle, did much to demoralise the German garrison.*

*HMS* Ramillies *a formidable gun platform when rendering support with her fifteen-inch guns.*

When the fire fight was won, Lieutenant Ponsford led his men in a charged across the open village square to capture the school, the main centre of resistance in the northern part of the village.

> *Seizing this, the troop then swept through the village, killing six or eight of the enemy and capturing more than twenty others besides several horse-drawn vehicles. In this dashing assault the troop lost not one man. They then took up a position east of the village.*

No. 6 Commando had by now arrived at the southern end of the village and Ponsford, who did not of course know that the rest of No. 3 Commando had been sent to Ranville, placed his men under the orders of Colonel Mills-Roberts.

Arriving in Le Plain, No. 6 Commando, who were little more than what they described as 'a blob on the ridge' were lucky enough to have a surviving Naval Bombardment Officer, who had now they were up on a ridge, established 'coms' with his ships a few miles of shore. From their farmhouse OP the enemy were spotted in the orchards and woods to the north of Bréville and the destroyer HMS *Samaures* was tasked to engage. Mills-Roberts recalled:

> *… the Bombardment Officer … made a rapid calculation and the shell dropped close to our left, in line with us. "That's no good" I said."No" he said, "she's actually steaming at the moment and the target's a difficult one. But I've got two capital ships on call and they are at anchor."*

He explained that 'An anchored ship has a reasonable chance of hitting a shore target. It's a difficult task for vessels on the move.' The fifteen-inch guns of either *Warspite* or *Ramillies* which fired a broadside produced 'a tremendous crash as gigantic shells landed in the wood'. Captain Ponsford, has a colourful addition to the story regarding the initial correction of fire.

*The next shell arrived with a deafening crash about fifteen yards from the group, making a massive crater and tearing branches from the trees above their head. The air was blue with Derek's language.*

Even allowing for difficulties such as these, the support of such ships made even the smallest of Allied units, potentially formidable foes for the Germans.

With the scant remnants of 9 Para on the ridge, No. 6 Commando started to consolidate their position around Amfreville. The fighting patrol that had been ordered south into Bréville, reached the church in the centre of the village but found the Germans around them in strength and occupying Château St-Côme further to the south. Consequently, they were ordered to withdraw and the Commando with artillery support did its best to cover them back from Breville and orchards across 400 yards of open field. There was, however, a problem. The Troop Commander, Captain Pyeman, had been killed and that there were wounded still in the village.

*We sent in another fighting patrol, and taking a Jeep we piled the wounded into it and raced back up to our own position with them. It was getting dark by then, and twilight is always a good time for exploits of this kind – it is the time when no rifleman or light-machine gunner can be sure of his accuracy.*

Colonel Mills-Roberts and his men started to dig-in and to '...fortify our position in the farm area' to create a secure footing on the vital ridge. All this was done behind a screen of patrols to keep the enemy away.

*The Germans were in Bréville and only about four hundred yards separated the outskirts of that place from the farm orchard. The obvious place for us to dig our defensive line was along the extreme border of the orchard facing Bréville, but I decided against this and dug along the line of the hedge some seventy yards back within the orchard. The reason for this was that if you dig in an obvious or suspected place you will inevitably be shelled and mortared. These were our main positions and in front of*

*British casualty in the region of Bois de Bavent.*

*them I ordered standing patrols to be placed which could give us full and accurate information of any enemy advance upon the orchard.*

Carefully avoiding disturbing the natural camouflage of the hedgerow or making obvious tracks in the long grass in front of their positions, the Commandos had dug their two-man slit trenches within two hours. The forward hedgerow was duly shelled, justifying the decision not to defend it; otherwise there was occasional but inaccurate shelling and the odd round or machine gun burst fired at them. The considered opinion was that the Germans were not sure where the Commandos actually were and that this was 'nervous fire' on their part.

Meanwhile, No. 6 Commando's Cycle Troop had, as planned, pressed onto Varaville; the original area where they were supposed to deploy and dominate. On arrival here they took over the defence of the village from Canadian Paras, who had earlier blown a bridge on the causeway across the inundation. However, with 'the German failing to keel over as General Gale had expected' and with the reduced combat power of 6th Airborne Division, due to its dispersion, the result of the night drop in poor conditions, 'holding a position as far forward as Varaville was impractical'. Eventually, the Troop was ordered to exfiltrate back to the much reduced eastern flank of the airborne bridgehead on the Amfreville ridge, where according to the Brigade report they were:

> *... sent to take up position on the SALLENELLES – RANVILLE road covering the left flank of the Brigade line where it was thought that the enemy might attempt infiltration round the low ground near SALLENELLES.*

**45 Royal Marine Commando**

Major Nichol Gray had now taken over command of Four Five from his wounded CO and set off eastwards with C Troop mounted on bicycles acting as his advance guard for the move to Franceville/Merville. Just beyond the village of Sallenelles, however, the cycling Commandos turned off the main road and headed due east, unseen by Commando HQ and the following troops. As a result, Major Gray and E Troop blundered towards the defended radar control station some 250 yards away. The radar site should have been cleared by 9 Para after its capture of the Merville battery. 45 Commando's historian wrote:

> *This was spotted but too late. Both sides opened fire simultaneously and Marine Irvine, of E Troop's leading section, bravely stood his ground in the open and hit a running German at 200 yards range with a rifle shot fired from the standing position – a splendid piece of marksmanship. The enemy defences were well sited and the HQ and part of E Troop were pinned down in the roadside ditch.*

The remainder withdrew back into Sallenelles leaving those who were pinned down to either face a long crawl back down the ditch or to wait until nightfall and then try to find the unit!

Major Gray ordered his mortar section into action to cover his next move. 'This delighted the mortar crews who had been carrying their heavy weapons and bombs ever since landing.' Under the cover of 'thirty rounds fire for effect' on the enemy position the Commando bypassed the radar site to the south and continued on its way to Merville, which the advance guard troop found to have been reoccupied by the enemy.

The battery had been attacked by 9 Para and captured but the guns had only been lightly damaged and, moreover, many of the gunners had survived the attack by hiding in the cartridge case sumps beneath their guns. Periodically the battery had come into action throughout the day, only to be silenced by the naval gunfire of HMS *Arethusa*.

Major Gray was preparing orders to re-capture the battery, when he was told by Brigade HQ to bypass the battery and occupy Merville village for the night and the advance to Franceville Plage was cancelled. This change of plan was a result of the diversion of No. 3 Commando to Ranville, which left 45 Commando isolated from the Brigade's main defences on the Amfreville Ridge, with little prospect of support.

45 Commando's historian described the occupation of the village:

> *The village of Merville was largely in ruins as a result of heavy pre-invasion bombing by the RAF. The civilian population had departed but their place was taken by German snipers who hid amongst the rubble. These had to be carefully winkled out and it wasn't until seven o'clock that evening that the village was finally cleared. Even then the men couldn't relax as the Troops had to be deployed and defences prepared in case of a counter-attack. Commando Headquarters was established in two broken down cottages. Longing eyes were cast at a big undamaged farmhouse nearby, but it was decided to sacrifice comfort for safety – this was a fortunate decision*

*A German Sniper with a K98k rifle and a telescopic sight*

*as the house was demolished later that evening by an enemy self-propelled gun.*

Unlike 6 Commando, 45 had only a few trenches to dig but had instead to barricade and create fire positions in the ruins of the village and, 'as the evening passed relatively quietly', the Commandos were able to use the small Tommy cookers in carefully shielded places to 'make a hot brew' – the first since leaving their LSI twelve hours earlier. The basic food in the two twenty-four hour composite (Compo) ration packs, which each man carried in his bergen, was still a novelty but was one that waned quickly.

On the evening of D Day, most of E Troop were still pinned down in the ditch back at the radar station but were to rejoin the rest of 45 who were withdrawn to positions near Sallenelles in the early hours of 7 June.

**Number 3 Commando**

By 1530 hours Lieutenant Colonel Peter Young's men were largely across the river and canal. His Cycle Troop had, as explained, already gone ahead to join 9 Para.'Ten minutes later the Transport Officer got through with the first of our Jeeps, piled high with reserve ammunition'. These were probably the first vehicles to reach Pegasus Bridge from the beaches. They were followed by a bulldozer driven by a bad tempered Sapper and a lost Royal Army Service Corps truck! 3rd Division's infantry did not reach the bridge until 2000 hours.

To Lord Lovat's annoyance, 6th Airborne Division ordered No. 3 Commando to head south to le Bas de Ranville to bolster the very thin line of airborne troops who had been facing a growing presence of *21. Panzerdivision* since dawn. However, unknown to General Gale, by mid afternoon the majority of the *Panzers* had been directed away from 6th Airborne, around the south of Caen to strike the SWORD and JUNO landings. Nonetheless, the Commando dug-in to protect General Gale's HQ, which was located in the Château. Although, in the event, they were not to become involved in any heavy action during the afternoon and evening of D Day, the Commandos were well sited to see what was going on. The Commanding Officer wrote:

*When we had been in position for less than two hours four German tanks were reported on the rising ground to our south. They were engaged by 3-inch mortars belonging to the Airborne Division, and withdrew. At the same time HMS* Serapis *fired twenty rounds into some German infantry who had been seeing digging in the forward edge of the wood.*

During the late afternoon, HQ 6th Airborne Division asked Lord Lovat over the radio if he could clear the Merville battery, which had again opened fire on SWORD Beach. He replied that he could but he would 'need to have No. 3 Commando back to do it' and, as he said, 'There was no reply'. Clearly the defence of Divisional HQ was more important than a few artillery rounds on SWORD Beach.

With the reduction of the threat from *21. Panzerdivision*, the fly-in of the Horsa gliders of the Airlanding Brigade in the second airborne lift of the day and the subsequent arrival of 1 RUR from their Landing Zones at around 2300 hours, No. 3 Commando was eventually relieved of its task of protecting 6th Airborne Division's HQ. In the darkness, they started to march off across the LZ towards Amfreville ridge.

**Number 4 Commando**

The final element of the Brigade to arrive east of the Orne, at about 2000 hours, was No. 4 Commando. After the successful destruction of the OUISTREHAM Battery, reunited with their bergans, they had made a forced march from the Brigade's original Forming Up Place, of over nine miles under constant sniping and mortar fire to cross the bridges to join with the main body of the Brigade and:

*... were ordered to take up defensive positions in and around the village of HAUGER, just NORTH of LE PLEIN.*

*In spite of heavy casualties and hot fighting over a long period, the Commando was dug in before dawn on D + 1.*

Colonel Dawson's men had marched via Ouistreham further than any other unit who had landed across the beaches.

In summary: for 1st Special Service Brigade, D Day ended with No. 3 Commando still detached, and 4 Commando still digging in. 45 (RM) Commando was isolated at Merville Battery; and there was a substantial gap between the Brigade and the

Airborne Troops. Consequently, the position could hardly be described as secure and the opportunity was taken to 'draw 45 RM Cdo in during the early hours of the morning to positions south of Sallenelles'. As the long line of Royal Marine Commandos was heading through the village the silence was suddenly shattered by the leading troop commander shouting

> *"Come out – I have got you covered!" As he poked his rifle through an open window behind which he has seen something move. Much to his surprise he was greeted by an elderly Madame, looking equally warlike in her curlers, who merely exclaimed "Ah ces Anglais!"*

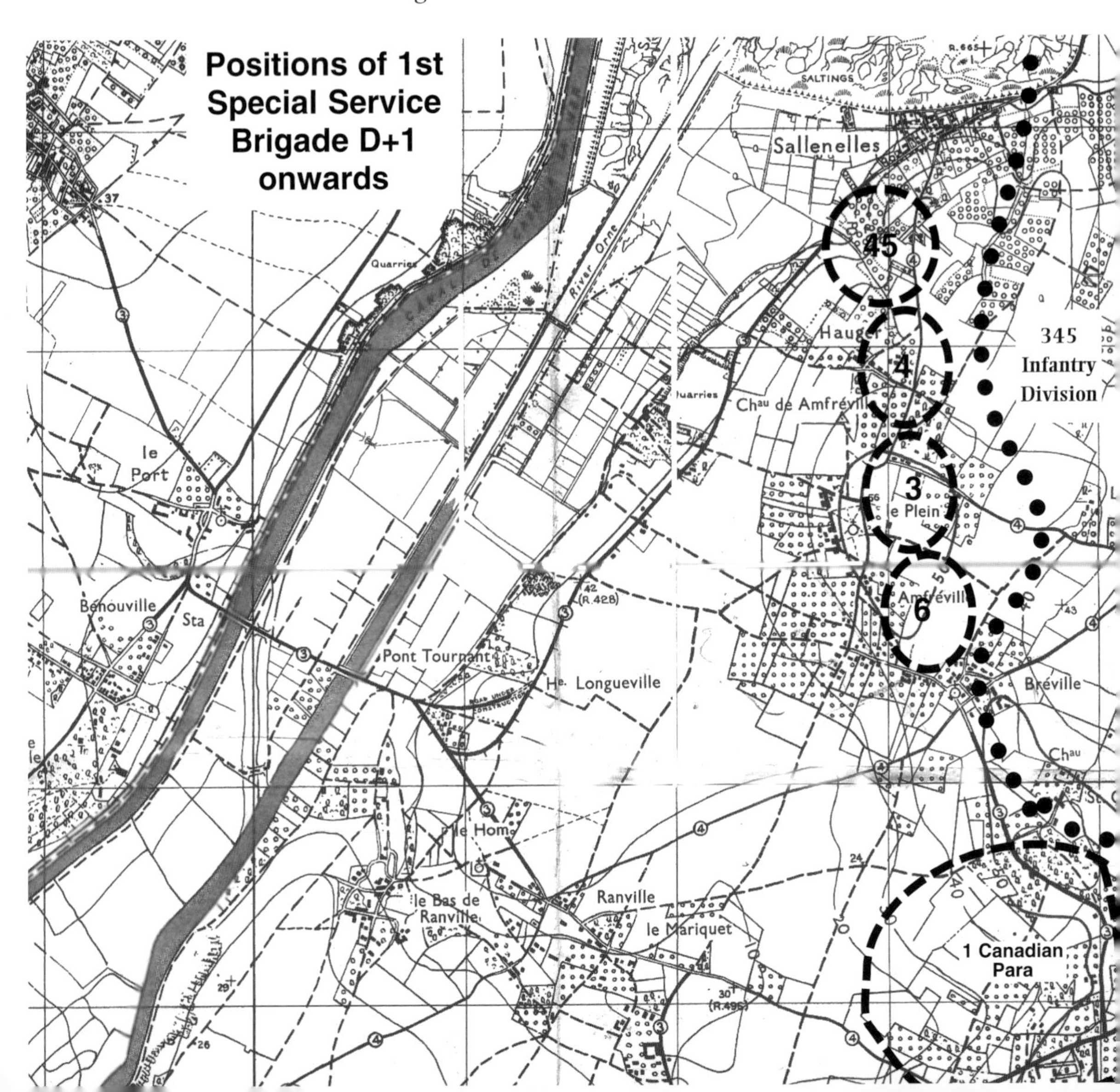

**D-Plus One**

With Nos. 4 and 6 Commandos now dug-in on the Amfreville ridge, at 0300 hours, after a quiet night, 3 Commando came up from Bas de Ranville and took up positions along the Ranville – Sallenelles road South-west of Amfreville. They were in the centre, in effect adding depth the Brigade's positions, with rear elements acting as Lord Lovat's reserve. With 45 Commando establishing themselves on the ridge above Sallenelles, the Special Service Brigade was finally concentrated in the positions that Lord Lovat had advocated.

The Brigade stood-to arms (stand-to) at 0430 hours, fully expecting the enemy to attack. All remained quiet as night gave way to a lightening sky to the east but as the sun rose so did the enemy's artillery fire from the Bréville Wood. Colonel Mills-Roberts recorded:

> *Shortly after dawn the farm and orchard were shelled by field guns and 20mm shells hit the trees above us – the deflected fragments caused casualties. Our positions were slightly damaged and the heaviest concentration fell on the forward edge of the orchard – the obvious place for our defence line, which I had turned down for that reason.*

No. 6 Commando was, however in a position to return the enemy fire:

> *One of the medium batteries was now ashore and their forward observation officer got it on call: we decided to give Bréville Wood a pasting. When the concentration hit the wood a figure was seen running up the road towards our lines; he was a sergeant in the Parachute Regiment and he explained that he had been dropped the night before and landed almost on top of the Germans. The last artillery concentration, he said, had shaken them up and he thought that if we acted quickly we might take advantage of this.*

The opportunity to drive the Germans back and maintain the initiative was seized. Colonel Mills-Roberts decided to counter-attack immediately and started to:

> *...arrange a quick-fire plan. The medium battery would give Bréville a good beat-up, our three-inch mortars trimming the forward edge of the wood; the assault was to attack from the right*

Knocked out British PIAT team.

> *to capture the battery. It was a great success. The troops went through the wood – after the medium battery had clobbered it – like men possessed and captured four field-guns, two 20 mm guns and five machine guns in record time. The only casualty on our side was one man killed. Apart from the guns the raid took fifteen prisoners: we hauled the guns back into our own position by means of two Jeeps.*

With little serious enemy offensive action developing on the Amfreville flank, it was recorded in the Brigade's war diary:

> *During the morning, Major General Gale, Commander 6 Airborne Division visited Brigade HQ and ordered the Brigade Commander to proceed with mopping the up of the coast defence belt at FRANCEVILLE PLAGE, saying that our role of protecting the left flank of the Allied Armies demanded the silencing of FRANCEVILLE at any rate as far EAST as the road running North East from GONNEVILLE.*

This reversion to a scaled-down version of the old plan was a surprise, especially as 45 Commando had recently taken up positions south of Sallenelles. Consequently they were ordered to proceed with their original task and take Franceville Plage.

### 45 RM Commando in Franceville

While Major Gray was at Brigade HQ receiving his orders, 45's Jeeps with their first resupply of ammunition and rations since landing finally arrived. This welcome replenishment enabled the unit to fight a descent battle and for the wounded to be evacuated from the aid post to the field ambulances for treatment.

The resulting Commando orders group in a field near Sallenelles was not without event, as recorded by Lieutenant Colonel Peter Young:

> *Half way through Nicol's orders the Germans began to mortar our group, which was rather large. At first he took no notice but after a few salvos he said lightly: 'The Bad Men are getting more accurate' – to him the Germans were always the Bad Men – and we withdrew to a neighbouring ditch.*

After dawn, at 0505 hours, C Troop led the advanced from the positions that it had just started digging, back towards Franceville Plage. It will be recalled that the seaside village of Franceville was sited between two extensive coastal battery positions, which though damaged were still firmly held by the enemy. Using the cover of hedgerows C Troop reached the houses on southern outskirts of the village and found no enemy present, so 'they swung left to occupy a wood so that it could cover the final assault'. This proved to be an abandoned enemy position with plenty of convenient slit trenches. From here they were able to support A, B and E Troops, whose first task was to capture a German bunker before moving up the main street of Franceville, codenamed PICCADILLY. B and E Troops didn't get far, as the enemy opened a heavy mortar fire when they approached the bunker and these two troops were driven back into cover in houses on the outskirts of the village.

The unit historian recorded the first attempt to overcome the bunker:

*Commando and airborne troops in the bridgehead.*

> *So that Four Five could regain the initiative Captain Beadle moved forward with the E Troop PIAT group, Lance Corporal Davis and Marines Lee and Lowe, in a gallant attempt to fire a bomb through one of the pillbox slits. After one bomb had been fired the group came under heavy attack. Davis was killed and Lowe wounded, but despite this Captain Beadle and Lee dashed back into the open and managed to rescue the wounded man and the weapon.*

Unsure of what was going on ahead of his tactical HQ Major Gray moved forward, as radio communication to his troops had broken down.

Under the eyes of the Commanding Officer the bunker was eventually overcome and the Tac HQ group followed the advance up PICCADILLY. Here a direct hit from an anti-tank gun killed the Regimental Sergeant Major and another HQ Marine. German resistance was becoming stiffer and A and D Troops moved up to take over the lead advancing either side of the main road. 'A Troop were met by heavy fire from houses on the eastern side of the town, where the enemy seemed to be concentrating in strength, and had to fan out clearing each house as they went.' With the radio communications failure, Major Gray was unable to call for supporting artillery fire or as Lord Lovat recorded, 'even report his position to Brigade'.

The war diary states, 'Very stiff opposition was encountered in the village' and Major Gray's DSO citation recorded his part in the battle leading the fight with two troops. He:

> *… with a skeleton HQ personally directed the fierce fighting that took place in both villages. On one occasion the Support Troop was unable to move forward being pinned down by accurate MG34 fire from a well protected position at the top of the main street.*
>
> *Major Gray gathered a few men together and led a bayonet attack against the enemy, shot the gunner with his revolver and put the rest to flight.*

The battle between the thin ranks of the Commandos and the more numerous coastal infantrymen was hard and lasted all day and into the evening, with the enemy being eventually forced back to positions at the end of PICCADILLY, near the beach. 45 Commando had, however, run out of steam after a protracted and unequal fight and needed consolidate their gains. Private Arnold, a German speaker attached from No. 10 (Inter-Allied) Commando, was dispatched forward to the coastal bunkers under a flag of truce 'advising the enemy to surrender as we had three divisions behind us and it was useless to fight on'. Their only reaction to this suggestion was heavy machine gun and

*Coastal infantrymen escorted to the rear during the invasion period.*

mortar fire which sent Arnold racing for cover.

The reason for rejection of this reasonable suggestion was soon apparent for 'At about 2100 hours the enemy put in a strong counter-attack'. This counter-attack aimed not only to regain Franceville but to destroy 45 as well. Coming from a flank to the south of the Commandos, the Germans aimed to drive them north into a pocket in front of the pillboxes that Private Arnold had invited to surrender. The Brigade report summarised the situation:

> *The Commando had suffered heavily in the assault and having lost its heavy weapons was unable to break up the enemy attacks or give support to the troops in FRANCEVILLE. Bitter fighting took place before 45 (RM) Commando withdrew to the area of MERVILLE and took up an all round defensive position.*

Unable to consult Brigade or ask for support from outside the unit, Major Gray took the only viable option; to break out of 'the vice being created by an exceedingly strong force and take up new positions on the south side of Franceville', i.e., Merville.

During 45's withdrawal there was a considerable amount of confused fighting at close quarters, not least because, (as the Commandos recalled) 'as dusk was fast approaching it was often difficult to identify friend from foe'.

The Commanding Officer, along with A Troop, occupied positions on a sandy scrub covered dune on the eastern outskirts of Franceville which overlooked the surrounding area, but the Germans were already working around to the rear and closing in on for an attack. C Troop was still in position in the wood protecting the unit's left flank and they had now restored radio communication with Commando HQ. Colonel Gray, consequently, ordered them to move around to the right and clear the eastern flank of the village. Meanwhile, the troops were extricating themselves from the village with difficulty and making their way to the defended dune. 'Patrols were being sent out to collect the stragglers and wounded left behind after the bitter fighting.' The hour it took to extricate themselves was without a doubt an epic in the history of 45 Commando.

Soon after receiving orders to move around to the eastern flank, C Troop attacked north and after a fifteen minute battle

*German infantrymen during the fighting in the bocage.*

captured a school building from where they could cover the withdrawal of the troops assembling on the dune. The school itself was subject to a vigorous counter-attack from an aggressive enemy. 'The school was held with great courage and 45 was saved from being cut off.'

For a force that had been heavily bombarded and been able to observe the sea 'black with shipping', with men and material disgorging onto the beaches, the German company from *736. Infanterieregiment*, presumably with gunners from the nine coastal guns in the area and *Osttruppen* from *642. Ost Batallon* (Red Army POWs pressed into German service), was truly remarkable. Throughout the day The Royal Marines had, however, been outnumbered, only lightly equipped and isolated from support, a result of a communications failure.

The day's fighting, however, was not yet over. The Commando finally withdrew, at about 2300 hours, to Merville where they surprised some Germans who were in the act of deepening the trenches started the previous evening. The Germans were taken prisoner and under supervision they were encouraged to continue the digging, while the exhausted Commandos looked on. Amongst them was Captain Rushforth who had been wounded whilst leading C Troop's attack to relieve his unit in Franceville and a convenient wheelbarrow was used to wheel him to relative safety in Merville. 45 Commando left some thirty-five dead in Franceville.

## No. 3 Commando at the Merville Battery

As already recorded, Merville battery had been attacked before dawn on D Day by Colonel Otway's 9 Para. The paratroopers had been badly dispersed during their drop but had pressed home their attack with only a quarter of the force that had been planned and with virtually all of their specialists and equipment missing. Against the odds they had succeeded in capturing the battery but amongst those missing were the airborne Sappers and the demolition charges for destroying the guns. 9 Para did their best to render them unserviceable with what they had but were forced to abandon the task, as they were unable to communicate their success to HMS *Arethusa* who was to bombard the battery position at 0550 hours. Consequently, rather than holding the battery position the remaining Paras were forced to withdraw, taking with them all the wounded they could carry.

Once the Paras were gone *Stabsfeldwebel* Buskot and his men appeared from hiding and returned to their casemates, repaired their Skoda 105mm guns and started answering calls for fire from their battery commander *Leutnant* Steiner. He was sited in a concrete observation/command post in the Franceville Plage defences, from where he had a grandstand view of the landings beyond Ouistreham in the SWORD area. Every time, however, he ordered the battery into action, salvos of six-inch naval shells were fired in reply. Being up on a ridge the battery's flashes and smoke were easily spotted by aircraft and the even ships' gunnery directors. After each bombardment, the battery invariably fell silent and a number of calls made by *Stabsfeldwebel* Buskot, the gun position officer, were recorded to Steiner, begging him to stop sending fire missions to him.

However, before dawn on 7 June the Merville battery had come into action again, demonstrating the necessity of destroying it once and for all. With 45 RM Commando clearly going to need all its resources to capture Franceville Plage and the flanking *Widerstandnester* they had no reserves with which to deal with the Merville battery. Consequently, No. 3 Commando, who provided the brigade reserve and who had seen least action so far, were tasked. A message initiated the planning; '2 i/c with two troops to support 45 (RM) Commando in their attack on Franceville Plage'.

Major John Pooley was ordered to silence the Merville guns with Nos 4 and 5 Troops. The Commanding Officer, Lieutenant Colonel Peter Young, recorded:

*Casemate no 4. of the Merville Battery*

*It was obvious that if there was a gun to be demolished they would need some explosives: and as it seemed possible that the Brigade Engineer Troop might be able to produce some, I made my way to Brigade HQ to see what could be done. It was an unprofitable visit. No explosives were forthcoming.*

On the face of it one must question 6th Airborne Division's attention to detail but perhaps

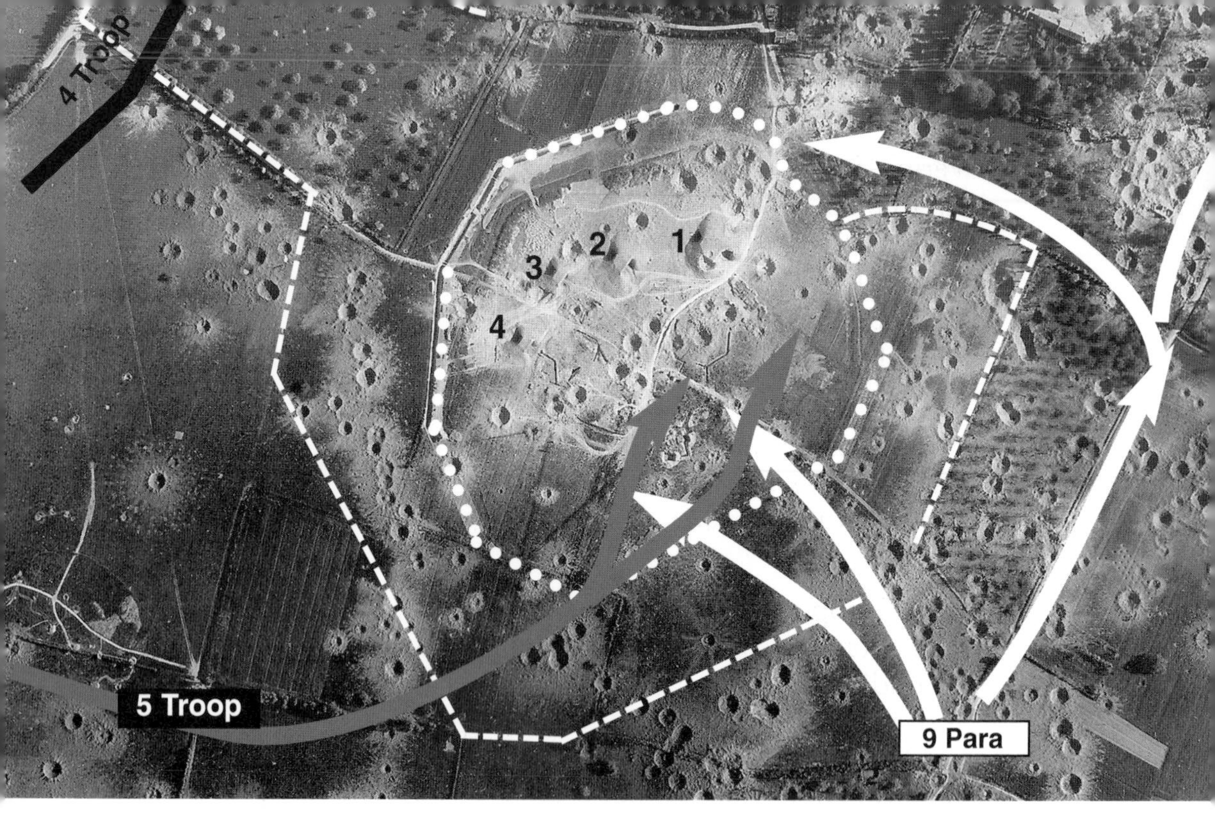


*Attack on the four-gun Merville battery by 9 Para as indicated by the white arrows: diversary feint on the main entrance with the main thrust through the minefield. This was made on D Day. Attack by 4 Commando was made on D + 1.*

General Gale was still hoping to dominate or 'infest' the area as per his original orders rather than simply destroying the guns.

As the Commando was not engaged Colonel Young decided to follow the two troops towards Merville. He wrote,

> *I wanted to get an idea of the country and the route to the battery. From the map it looked as if our detachment was going to be "out on a limb", and so it proved. Accompanied by Ned Moore, Sergeant Spears (the Medical Sergeant), Corporal Christopher and wireless operator, I started out to follow in Pooley's footsteps.*

It is also tempting to think that Colonel Young could have added 'and I was missing out on a good fight'.

Major Pooley and his two troops made their way through Hauger and around the outskirts of Sallenelles, and in the direction of Merville. Casualties were suffered from mortar fire and two of the precious Jeeps, used for carrying ammunition and evacuating casualties, were destroyed. The plan was that No. 4 Troop, at a range of about two hundred yards, would give covering fire across the barbed wire, minefield and anti-tank ditch to fix the enemy's attention, while Major Pooley would go around to the south east corner and attack from that direction, with his old troop, No. 5 Troop. It was during this manoeuvre, in thick hedgerow country that Colonel Young having made his way east along the track 'came rather unexpectedly on the rear of 4 Troop'.

> *No. 4 Troop, who had already had a few casualties, looked far from happy, and did not seem to know the exact position of 5 Troop, but not long after they appeared charging into the battery from the other side.*

With 4 Troop giving covering fire, Major Pooley led 5 Troop, with bayonets fixed into the attack across the open ground surrounding the battery, himself armed with a pistol. The double belt of barbed wire could have been a problem but it had been shredded in several places by the Paras' attack and by the naval bombardment throughout the previous day. However, there was a far more insidious threat:

> *Confronted by the minefield, he had led the men straight through it, a cold-blooded decision to take if ever there was one, but it had paid, for they got through with only three men wounded.*

Colonel Young went forward into the battery:

> *We discovered a narrow path through the minefield, which had obviously been used by the garrison, and through this we threaded our way – not without misgivings. We had just got in when John Pooley ran past – a German stick grenade in his hand.*

According to Colonel Young 'There were not many Germans in the battery', presumably the repeated salvos of naval had made it an unpleasant place for anyone not directly involved in manning the guns to dwell! The Germans who were left in the casemates 'were very resolute and held out for some time'.

Major Pooley directed the mopping-up of the casemates and the reorganisation phase and No. 4 Troop came through the minefield on the same track used by their Commanding Officer and 5 Troop. Captain Brian Butler was directed to 'push on to some houses, which could be seen on the far side of the battery, to clear them and consolidate there'.

Corporal Arthur Chivers was with Major Pooley during the clearance phase and according to Colonel Young 'There had been a few shots, but all serious fighting had seemed to be at an end'. Pooley and Chivers recall that they approached Casemate Number 4 and:

> *We went through the bunker, killed some* [Germans] *and as we went into a trench at the rear entrance, Major Pooley was hit in the head by a bullet fired from the top of the bunker behind us and was killed more or less instantly.*

He had been killed by a surviving *Spandau* gunner in the *Tobrukstand* that was built into the upper surface of the casemate. Having been informed that 'Major Pooley's been killed, sir'. Colonel Young headed towards Casemate Number 4 and:

> *... found Alan Pollock, a small dark young subaltern of 5 Troop, attacking this position on his own, a Gammon bomb in his hand. Angry and distressed, as we all were, at the death of John, he was exposing himself fearlessly. Getting up close to the gun, he hurled in his bomb. Still uncertain whether the defender was dead, some of us got on top of the grass-covered casemate and dropped Mills bombs down the air vent.*

The survivors of the attack reorganised in the lane on the eastern side of the battery, while a patrol was dispatched to reconnoitre Merville to find 45 Commando with whom they were supposed to be operating with but 'There was no sign of 45 Commando...'. They were of course fighting some way off in Franceville and from the number of Germans that the patrol encountered it 'was obviously only a matter of time until 4 and 5 Troops, who had already had a number of casualties, were surrounded and overrun'.

It was clear to Colonel Young that:

> *So far from our own lines, it would be almost impossible to feed them or to replenish their ammunition. There was nothing more they could do to the battery. The best thing I could do was to get them out again, and so, leaving Brian Butler to consolidate, I set off to explain the situation to the Brigadier, whom I found at his Headquarters at Ecarde. He listened to what I had to say and at once agreed that the detachment must be withdrawn.*

With German reinforcements arriving on the scene and pushing westward, Numbers 4 and 5 Troops suffered many more casualties in the withdrawal than in the approach march and the actual attack on the Merville battery. For example, the fighting patrol sent out under Lieutenant Williams to cover the withdrawal, 'ran into trouble, for he was knocked out and Corporal Underwood killed. Sergeant Port and a private were cut off, though they hid for some hours and were eventually captured'.

This was a two-mile, protracted withdrawal in contact with an enemy who were growing in strength and confidence. Each rearward move had to be carefully choreographed, with men positioned to cover with fire the withdrawal of their fellow Commandos, typically to the next hedgerow. Nos 4 and 5 Troops eventually rejoined the remainder of No. 3 Commando at around 2100 hours now just half their established strengths. While the rest of the Commando moved up onto the ridge to reinforce the front 4 and 5 troops, who had been in action for twelve hours were left in reserve to lick their wounds.

**Counter-attacks - D+2**

During 7 June, 6th Airborne Division was under mounting pressure from the south by *21. Panzerdivision*, which was concentrated to the east of Caen now that the *Hitlerjugend* Division had arrived west of the city. The action at Franceville and Merville ensured that the D+1 was quiet on the Amfreville ridge but 8 June, however, saw determined counter-attacks starting to be mounted against Commandos on the eastern flank of the airborne division's lodgement. During the previous days German troops from the *Fifteenth Army* were dispatched west to support *711th Division* and the field grade troops of *346th Division*, who had mainly marched by night, were arriving in significant number and being put immediately into the attack.

It is recorded in the divisional war diary at 1130 hours on 8th June '1 SS Bde report that a hy [heavy] attack is developing on 4 Commando in the area of HAUGER 1275 – SALLENELLES 1376 from the EAST'. If anything, 45 Commando, who had become isolated, as will be detailed, were in an even more unenviable position. Colonel Mills-Roberts described how the attack built up, 'German infantry came searching along the brigade area with fighting patrols, preceded by artillery stonks looking for a soft spot'. Private Bill Bidmead recalled that not all found soft spots but some were just plain unlucky; the morning stand-to had just finished:

> *What a heavenly relief, I wrapped myself up in my blanket and lay by the top of my slit trench. I had not been there long when I heard, "F...ing hell! Germans!" Looking up, coming through the woods, silhouetted in the early morning mist, came hordes of Germans. They must have crept up on us during the night. But they hadn't seen us yet. It was then that 'Taff' Isherwood picked up his K gun and emptied a full magazine into them... The rest of the Troop added their fire power. The screams and cries of the dying and wounded Germans on that June morning were terrible.*

Elsewhere, there was a steady mortaring and when the Germans had identified a target, their artillery joined in as well. In No.3 Commando's area, Lance Sergeant Evans with:

> *...his troop being in an exposed position came under very heavy shelling. Some of the trenches were blown in and became unusable ... with complete disregard for personal safety he left his slit trench to go round his section encouraging the men.*

This shelling was followed by probing attacks that grew in strength as the morning went on. At 0945 hours, the Brigade's units were warned that the enemy were about to launch a battalion attack. The well concealed and sited Commando firepower, supported by artillery and naval gunfire, however, halted all such attacks before they came closely engaged. No. 3 Commando were attacked from the direction of Bréville and by 1045 hours information was coming into Colonel Young's HQ from 6 Troop that '... enemy infantry were advancing astride the Longuemare road and John Alderson ... asked for artillery support'.

> *A Bombardment Officer, with HMS* Hunter *at his disposition, had already joined 6 Troop. We now sent up a Vickers machine-*

A Bombardment Officer puts his party in the picture.

*gun, and also a sergeant to observe for the 3-inch mortar section, though we had not enough mortars to do much damage. Five minutes later one of our own field regiments was ranging on the area in front of 6 Troop's position.*

The Commandos, however, could not just rely on firepower alone to keep the Germans at bay. Partly to convince the Germans that they were stronger than they were and partly because enemy who worked into favourable positions, the Commandos had to remove Germans by force, often from the opposite hedgerow. Lance Corporal Hodgson, as recorded in his Military Medal citation '… showed great courage when on a recce patrol by exposing himself to enemy fire in order to find their position'. Once located the enemy could be dealt with. Sergeant Leech earned a bar to his Military Medal in one such adventure by No. 6 Troop at the height of the morning battle:

*During the counter-attacks on Le Plein Wood … he led a section with great determination, and he himself killed several of the enemy, and his section took numerous prisoners. Although wounded he continued to lead his section until the operation was successfully completed.*

Colonel Young described the final phase of the counter-attack:

*Everyone was enjoying the battle; advances, short pauses to put down a withering fire, including of the 2-inch mortar used point-blank with its base plate rested against a tree – probably just as dangerous to our own side as the enemy, but the effect on the Germans' morale made it worth the risk.*

While 6 Troop were driving the enemy back another troop went

'... down a track, so as to get in rear of the enemy' but they had gone too far and came under fire from a house and were in trouble.

> *An officer of lesser calibre than George Herbert might well have remained pinned down. But in that commanding way of his he yelled out 'Come on we'll go in! Armed with a Bren and flanked by Forsyth and another man, he charged through the gate, firing bursts from the hip.*

The Germans had been beaten by firepower and not least the audacious offensive spirit of the Commandos. The enemy determination ebbed away during the course of the afternoon.

While the situation on the Amfreville ridge may have been stabilised, 45 Commando were under increasing pressure in the village of Merville to which they had withdrawn the previous evening.

### Withdrawal of 45 RM Commando

The Royal Marines' day had begun quietly but was spoilt by warnings of an imminent attack and orders that they were 'to hold on at all costs,' ammunition and food was, however, short. The pattern of enemy activity was similar to that described on the Amfreville ridge. Except to conserve ammunition Four-Five's snipers took a leading role in keeping German probing attacks away from C and E Troops, gaining 'a healthy bag in the process!'

The first serious attack came from the direction of the Merville battery during the late morning but was also driven off 'after some close quarter fighting', with A and C Troops bearing the brunt of the encounter.

The problem of evacuating the eight stretcher cases that resulted from the first attack was solved when two German ambulances mistakenly drove into the Commando's positions. With the casualties loaded, a process that had been respected by the enemy, German-speaker Lance Corporal Saunders of No, 10 (Inter Allied) Commando attempted to bluff his way through but was taken prisoner with his cargo. He later escaped to report that the wounded were being well cared for.

A second attack followed, again from the direction of the

battery, but with a second echelon coming in quietly from the east. This time naval gunfire was instrumental in driving the enemy back. This was, however, not before leading elements of the enemy attack reached the Merville village defences.

Major Gray's charmed life almost ended when going to visit a troop position he stumbled upon a German *Spandau* team. With what he confessed was an equal measure of surprise on both sides, Major Gray shot one of the enemy with his rifle but in his haste to reload it jammed but he just managed to get a shot off at the second with his .45 pistol before the German. Returning to Commando HQ he discovered that the Adjutant had liberated a bottle of Champagne and was sharing it with the HQ troop Commandos. Demanding his share of the loot, Major Gray complained about its poor quality. The Adjutant put this lack of 'generous spirit (given the circumstances)' down the his CO's recent experience!

The afternoon was again spent successfully keeping German probing attacks or patrols away, all the while being mortared; 'a wearing experience,' said one Marine. Gradually though the tempo of enemy activity increased and at 1700 hours, Major Gray received a message from Lord Lovat that 'attempts to relieve 45 Commando had failed'. This is less than accurate, as it was impractical to launch any attempt from the Amfreville ridge position to reach the Merville village with any meaningful force let alone with supplies; surely it was only a matter of time before the isolated 45 Commando would be destroyed in detail.

Whatever the niceties of the brigade's situation, Major Gray was ordered to withdraw to Amfreville once it was dark – in five hours time the effective PIAT and 2-inch mortar ammunition was exhausted. Inevitably the expected attack came, this time with the support of armour. A troop of *Sturmgeschütze* stood off and progressively demolished the houses of Merville around the Commandos, setting those on the eastern outskirts on fire. It was clear to Major Gray that he could not wait until last light to slip away out of contact with the enemy and that he would have to make a fighting withdrawal starting forthwith.

At about 1800 hours, E Troop left its positions to lead the Commando back to Amfreville. Meanwhile, an attempt to help 45 break clean was quickly organised. The naval FOB arranged a destroyer to fire a broadside, timed to strike the village just minutes after C Troop, the last to pull back, had left its positions. This worked and enabled the Commando to withdraw for about a mile unmolested by the enemy. Their luck did not last, as they eventually tangled with the enemy when they approached the Amfreville Ridge and attempted to slip through the German lines and across No Man's Land.

Their direct route was blocked. To the right were minefields and to the left were further enemy positions; Major Gray faced an unenviable decision. In the end he elected to take his unit to the left on a more covered route, with E Troop remaining where it was to hold the attention of the enemy to their front. During this period Marine Green earned an MM:

> *... being in charge of an LMG he was ordered to take up a position on the right hand side of a hedge and to engage the enemy. This he found he was unable to do due to low hanging branches and long grass. Mne Green therefore abandoned all cover and running into the open under intensive and accurate fire during which time a bullet lodged in the magazine of his gun, open fire with such effect into the enemy position that it was silenced.*

Spare magazines were reloaded and thrown to Marine Green who continued to deluge the enemy opposite with long bursts from his Bren gun.

Having successfully engaged an enemy position fifty yards away with No. 68 anti-tank rifle grenades, Sergeant Brown also came out of cover to fire at two further enemy positions. These shaped charge high explosive grenades though not designed as an anti-personnel weapon were none the less effective when bursting in hedgerows or banks and 'the two remaining positions were neutralised'. He too earned the Military Medal for this action.

Such was the dominance that E Troop gained over the enemy that they were able to audaciously attack them and drove them from their position, capturing a pair of 80mm mortars, two machine guns and a motorcycle and sidecar.

Captain Beadle was instrumental in driving back the enemy. His Military Cross citation reads:

> *... on 8th June 1944, Captain Beadle's Troop was surrounded and repeatedly attacked by the enemy. He selected the enemy*

*position that was causing the most casualties and personally led a counter-attack. Due to his quick appreciation and to the great dash and gallantry with which the assault was led, the counter-attack was completely successful, destroying the enemy's positions and inflicting heavy casualties. The action restored a critical situation…*

The Troop had through its amazing efforts cut through the enemy positions in front of them, which was just as well as the Major Gray and the remainder of the unit were in difficulty. By creating this escape route out of what would almost certainly have been a fatal trap for the entire unit, even the phrase 'critical situation' seems somewhat of an understatement.

45 Commando reached the 1st Special Service Brigade's lines between 2000 and 2100 hours and came in through No. 4 Commando, where they were met by Lord Lovat who was in absolutely no doubt about the supreme challenge they had faced during the previous forty-eight hours since the landing. They had fought their way from SWORD Beach and had been the main player in no less than three separate battles. The whole exhausted Commando was fed and bedded down in the area of the La Plein church with the Brigade HQ men providing sentries.

Meanwhile, attacks on the main Commando position were mounting again as night drew in. The enemy's tactics in this renewed attack were based on infiltration and heavy mortar and artillery fire. This time the German's main effort fell on No. 4 Commando on the left flank. An extract from Lieutenant William James's MC citation summed up the attack at Hauger:

*The enemy had broken through the position covering the Commando left flank and were advancing up a valley straight towards Commando HQ which was being held by only a few men. Lieut James realised the danger of the situation and immediately called a few men and started a counter-attack. Although the enemy strength was estimated at one platoon he advanced with his small force and held the enemy's thrust. He personally accounted for many of the enemy by first firing a bren gun until the ammunition for that gun was expended. He then continued to fire with a rifle until all the ammunition for that weapon was gone and finally he picked up a Garrand rifle continued to fire and succeeded-in holding the enemy until a force arrived to assist his small party to drive the enemy back. By his prompt and brave action he undoubtedly prevented the enemy overrunning the position and by containing them formed the base for the counter-attack which restored the position.*

## Holding the Line

Following the withdrawal of 45 Commando and the successful holding of the Amfreville ridge position, according to the Brigade report:

> *... it was agreed by Commander 6 Airborne Division that the role of holding the line River ORNE and the CAEN Canal protecting the left flank of the main landings could now best be carried out by denying to the enemy the ridge of high ground running from HAUGER in the NORTH to BREVILLE in the SOUTH overlooking river and canal. Without this high ground no observed fire could be brought to bear on the beaches near OUISTREHAM or the country between CAEN and the sea and the Brigade was ordered to hold the ridge at all costs.*

The heavy pressure on the Commandos and airborne troops on the Amfreville Ridge, however, continued for a further four days as further elements of *346th Division* arrived at the front. An attack by 12 Para and a company of glider infantry from 12 Devons on the evening of 12 June finally cleared the Germans from their toehold and position of observation on the forward edge of the ridge at Bréville.

With the threat reduced, the front on the Second Army's left flank, however, remained persistently static. The 'number of days' that General Gale required 1st Special Service Brigade, and subsequently 4 SS Brigade as well, to 'infest' dragged into weeks and then months. It wasn't until the breakout and the advance east was well under way that the Commandos could be withdrawn to the UK to rest and refit. As with the airborne and indeed the ordinary infantry, casualty replacements were short. Not only were there the wounded from D Day and its immediate aftermath to replace but also those casualties, principally from mortars, suffered during the routine of defence on a relatively static front.

Defence in the hedgerow country at close proximity to the enemy was an expensive matter. Add the aggressive patrolling tactics of the Commandos, which were necessary to keep the enemy at a safe distance, and a steady stream of casualties resulted.

The Commandos and Rangers all had significant tasks to perform on D Day; tasks which could only be successfully achieved by very special and highly trained troops. Indeed in some cases, such as at Pointe du Hoc and the cross-country march to Pegasus Bridge, tasks many thought to be plain impossible. Even though those landing behind the first assault wave found the beaches and their Forming Up Points under fire and/or un-cleared, they were able to regroup and often seriously depleted, give an excellent account of themselves.

**Visiting the Battlefield**

The route from Pegasus Bridge taken by the Commandos on the afternoon of D Day to their positions on the Amfreville ridge avoided the open DZ. Most took the route along the foot of the escarpment past the quarry. Cross Pegasus and Horsa Bridges and follow the D514 up a bending road from the Ranville roundabout. To the right are the open fields of DZ N and to the left is the cover of the escarpment. After a thousand yards stop at the Ecarde crossroads. The buildings in this area were the initial location of Lord Lovat's Brigade HQ and the Brigade support units. As enemy pressure mounted on their thin defensive line, eventually they moved up into le Plain and became more a part of the defensive scheme – highly unusual for a brigade HQ!

Turn right off the D514 and follow the road up towards Amfreville and le Plain. Park where safe on the eastern side of the large village green. The church where Four Five rested after its Franceville/Merville battles is little changed. Towards the southern end of the green is a small memorial to No. 6 Commando, opposite Bernard Saulnier's farm that was the key to their defences. It was near the entrance to the farm that Lord Lovat was severely wounded on 12 June 1944.

By taking a short walk down the adjacent lane it is possible to appreciate the dense country, hedgerows and orchards, where the Commandos dug in and fought. Several hundred yards further one can look out over what was in effect no-man's-land towards Bréville. This was the scene of many of the 8 June defensive battles.

Returning to the village, drive north on the D37b towards Sallenelles, passing the 1st SS Brigade Memorial and on the right No. 3 Commando's position, the second site of Brigade HQ and No. 4 Commando's position. Leaving the village the ground drops away to the left of the road; the Germans attacked No. 4 Commando on the evening of 8 June up this valley. As the ground starts to drop away into Sallenelles one enters the area where the tactical HQ of *642. Ost Batallon* was dug in overlooking the estuary, dunes and marshes between Ouistreham and Franceville. In Sallenelles turn right onto the D514 and at the end of the Village on the right is the Mairie and a memorial to the Belgian Armoured Brigade who started their breakout to the east from this area in August. Nearby is a memorial to 45 Commando.

A little bit further is a turning to the right taken by the leading elements of 45 Commando on D Day. Drive on past this junction and a short distance around the bend are the bunkers of the radar control station, which at the time of writing is a disco: 'le Bunker'.

Return to the junction and take the Chemin des Banques. This was the route that was repeatedly used by Four Five and No. 4 Commando to bypass the radar station's fire. As one approaches the village of Merville, a track to the right marks the spot from which No. 4 Troop of 4 Commando supported No. 5 Troop's attack on the battery on 7 June. A walk down this track takes the visitor into the centre of the battery for a free but restricted visit, though entry via the village to the displays in the casemates is highly recommended.

From the battery drive past the Merville village church towards Franceville. The lack of old buildings in this area is a testimony to the severity of the fighting here during the period 6-8 June.

Entering Franceville thread your way through the elaborate traffic calming between the Mairie and the Sports Centre and park. There is a small memorial to 45 Commando amongst the group memorials by the flagpoles. The buildings this side of the roundabout and D514 are where the attack on Franceville started. The first pillbox and C Troop's position were in the wooded gardens opposite. Going straight over the roundabout into Franceville, one is driving up PICCADILLY (Avenue de Paris), the Marines' axis for their attack into the town. Most remnants of the battle are buried under the seafront car park.

# Index